D1601170

International Political Economy Series

General Editor: **Timothy M. Shaw**, Professor of Commonwealth Governance and Development, and Director of the Institute of Commonwealth Studies, School of Advanced Study, University of London

Titles include:

Hans Abrahamsson
UNDERSTANDING WORLD ORDER AND STRUCTURAL CHANGE
Poverty, Conflict and the Global Arena

Preet S. Aulakh and Michael G. Schechter (*editors*)
RETHINKING GLOBALIZATION(S)
From Corporate Transnationalism to Local Interventions

Sandra Braman (*editor*)
THE EMERGENT GLOBAL INFORMATION POLICY REGIME

James Busumtwi-Sam and Laurent Dobuzinskis
TURBULENCE AND NEW DIRECTION IN GLOBAL POLITICAL ECONOMY

Elizabeth De Boer-Ashworth
THE GLOBAL POLITICAL ECONOMY AND POST-1989 CHANGE
The Place of the Central European Transition

Myron J. Frankman
WORLD DEMOCRATIC FEDERALISM
Peace and Justice Indivisible

Helen A. Garten
US FINANCIAL REGULATION AND THE LEVEL PLAYING FIELD

Randall D. Germain (*editor*)
GLOBALIZATION AND ITS CRITICS
Perspectives from Political Economy

Barry K. Gills (*editor*)
GLOBALIZATION AND THE POLITICS OF RESISTANCE

Richard Grant and John Rennie Short (*editors*)
GLOBALIZATION AND THE MARGINS

Axel Hülsemeyer (*editor*)
GLOBALIZATION IN THE TWENTY-FIRST CENTURY
Convergence or Divergence?

Helge Hveem and Kristen Nordhaug (*editors*)
PUBLIC POLICY IN THE AGE OF GLOBALIZATION
Responses to Environmental and Economic Crises

Takashi Inoguchi
GLOBAL CHANGE
A Japanese Perspective

Jomo K.S. and Shyamala Nagaraj (*editors*)
GLOBALIZATION VERSUS DEVELOPMENT

Craig N. Murphy (*editor*)
EGALITARIAN POLITICS IN THE AGE OF GLOBALIZATION

Michael Niemann
A SPATIAL APPROACH TO REGIONALISM IN THE GLOBAL ECONOMY

Morten Ougaard
THE GLOBALIZATION OF POLITICS
Power, Social Forces and Governance

Markus Perkmann and Ngai-Ling Sum
GLOBALIZATION, REGIONALIZATION AND CROSS-BORDER REGIONS

Leonard Seabrooke
US POWER IN INTERNATIONAL FINANCE
The Victory of Dividends

Timothy J. Sinclair and Kenneth P. Thomas (*editors*)
STRUCTURE AND AGENCY IN INTERNATIONAL CAPITAL MOBILITY

Fredrik Söderbaum and Timothy M. Shaw (*editors*)
THEORIES OF NEW REGIONALISM
A Palgrave Reader

Kendall Stiles (*editor*)
GLOBAL INSTITUTIONS AND LOCAL EMPOWERMENT
Competing Theoretical Perspectives

Christien van den Anker (*editor*)
THE POLITICAL ECONOMY OF NEW SLAVERY

Amy Verdun
EUROPEAN RESPONSES TO GLOBALIZATION AND FINANCIAL MARKET INTEGRATION
Perceptions of Economic and Monetary Union in Britain, France and Germany

---

International Political Economy Series
Series Standing Order ISBN 0–333–71708–2 hardcover
Series Standing Order ISBN 0–333–71110–6 paperback
(*outside North America only*)

World Democratic Federalism

Peace and Justice Indivisible

Myron J. Frankman

McGill University
Canada

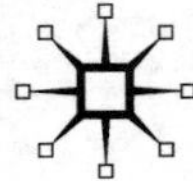

First published 2004 by
PALGRAVE MACMILLAN
Houndmills, Basingstoke, Hampshire RG21 6XS and
175 Fifth Avenue, New York, N.Y. 10010
Companies and representatives throughout the world

PALGRAVE MACMILLAN is the global academic imprint of the Palgrave Macmillan division of St. Martin's Press, LLC and of Palgrave Macmillan Ltd. Macmillan® is a registered trademark in the United States, United Kingdom and other countries. Palgrave is a registered trademark in the European Union and other countries.

ISBN 1–4039–3492–4

This book is printed on paper suitable for recycling and made from fully managed and sustained forest sources.

A catalogue record for this book is available from the British Library.

Library of Congress Cataloging-in-Publication Data
Frankman, Myron J.
World democratic federalism: peace and justice indivisible / Myron J. Frankman.
p. cm. — (International political economy series)
Includes bibliographical references and index.
ISBN 1–4039–3492–4 (cloth)
1. International organization. 2. International economic relations. 3. Globalization—Economic aspects. I. Title. II. International political economy series (Palgrave Macmillan (Firm))
JZ5566.F727 2004
337—dc22 2003064662

10 9 8 7 6 5 4 3 2 1
13 12 11 10 09 08 07 06 05 04

Printed and bound in Great Britain by
Antony Rowe Ltd, Chippenham and Eastbourne

Before I built a wall I'd ask to know
What I was walling in or walling out,
And to whom I was like to give offence.
Something there is that doesn't love a wall,
That wants it down.

—Robert Frost (1914)

I must say to people of good will, to the workers, to the poets, that the entire future was expressed in that phrase of Rimbaud: an ardent patience will suffice to conquer the splendid city that will give light, justice and dignity to everyone.

Thus poetry will not have been composed in vain.

—Pablo Neruda (1971)

Contents

List of Tables

Preface

I consider myself to be a highly privileged beneficiary of the global process of civilization. In countless ways my life has been enriched by the institutional and technological inventiveness of humanity. I do work that I enjoy in a context that is congenial. I am exceptionally free to express my opinion and I can take advantage of a range of publicly and privately provided amenities. I believe myself to have been one of those fortunate enough to have derived clear net gain from the process of globalization. Chance and human design have not been so generous to all. My firm belief that a broader sharing of the benefits of our world can make gainers of us all, in part through its effect in minimizing violent confrontations, whether individual or collective, has provoked this undertaking.

This work represents a statement of a worldview, in two senses of the word: not merely a paradigm, but one that insists that our world must be re-viewed and reconceptualized as an integrated whole which is affected both by our actions and inactions. One's perspective is never really one's own, hence gratitude must be expressed to all who have 'crossed my path,' whether through their physical presence or through their ideas. As in any human endeavor, intellectual or otherwise, the influences that have shaped my perceptions no doubt far surpass my conscious awareness, which is at best only the tip of the iceberg. Some of the thinkers to whom I feel a significant debt are David Hume, John Stuart Mill, Thorstein Veblen, Albert Hirschman, Gunnar Myrdal, Jane Jacobs, and Riane Eisler. There are undoubtedly many more.

Not only are the ideas here not original with me, but the informed reader may have run into them with increasing frequency in the past five or ten years. This should come as no surprise. Charles Darwin and Alfred Wallace both came up with formulations of evolution through natural selection at the same time. The similar analyses of a problem reflect the parameters of the relevant universe, which today are under scrutiny by many thousands of astute observers. It is logical that those currently concerned with the management of the world economy should look for precedents in the operation of nations, particularly federal ones. During the writing of this book I happened to come across many accounts where points that I convey also appear. And yet approaches differ, emphases differ and in an age of information overload, the audience for one book may be completely different from those who read a strikingly similar work. Moreover, a major institutional change of the sort being discussed here and elsewhere requires an almost revolutionary change in perceptions. That does not happen in one day or one year or with one book, no matter how influential. Each observation becomes yet another piece in the puzzle—many, many pieces are necessary before an image is discernible to enough people to alter behavior patterns. How many books have been written sounding the ecological alarm, going back at least to Fairfield Osborn's *Our Plundered Planet* (1948) or Rachel Carson's *Silent Spring* (1962)? Our situation is even more precarious now than it was decades ago, yet environmental concerns still take a back seat to economics in many aspects of human activity.

Enormous gratitude is due to my professors and to my graduate student associates at the University of Texas, Austin, where many of the seeds that have since taken root were first sown forty years ago. It is hard to gauge the influence of Wendell Gordon with his persistent refrain 'it may be so, but then again it may not,' of Walter Neale who patiently urged us to struggle with the ideas at hand and of Clarence Ayres, who shared with us the wisdom of a rich lifetime. It took me a long time to fully appreciate his booming denunciation in the early 1960s of the specter of periodic breakfast-time electronic referenda: 'Democracy is not about voting, it is about discussion!'

Thanks are in order to the following people who read and commented on all or part of the manuscript in its many successive manifestations: Nicole Baerg, Guy Bentham, Mauricio Ernesto Granillo, Anastassia Khouri, Duncan McPherson, Ruben Mendez, Joshua Walker, and Hyder Yasufzai. Words fail to express my appreciation to Keith Hart who provided valuable counsel and encouragement when it was most needed. Particular thanks are due to Robert Sampson for his painstaking editorial efforts prior to the submission of the manuscript. The customary caveat about all blame being mine applies. Whatever praise may accrue, I will gladly share.

While people can be singled out, the thanks are to institutions that gave me the space to think and to exchange ideas. First on the list is McGill University, where I came to practice and to revere Ayres' message about the importance of discussion for democracy. My thanks go as well to the École des Hautes Études Commerciales in Montreal which welcomed me during my 1988–89 sabbatical, to the Department of Economics in the Faculty of Economics and Administration of the Universidad de Chile in Santiago where I truly felt that I had a second home during my 1995–96 sabbatical leave from McGill, and to the

Chaire Hoover d'éthique économique et sociale at the Université Catholique de Louvain where the final draft was completed in spring 2003. Special thanks go to Philippe Van Parijs, the Director of the Chaire Hoover and to the Chair's residents and visitors for providing a congenial environment during the academic year 2002–2003 in which I was able to bring this work to fruition.

The personal *is* political. My evolving sense of the world was strongly shaped by my parents, Sam and Rae Frankman—my father was the first to draw my attention in the 1940s to the connections between oil and foreign policy when I was still too young to appreciate the implications, while my mother never missed an opportunity to draw my attention to rainbows; by my late wife, Patricia Ottolenghi, who challenged my faith in mainstream developmentalism; and by my companion of the last thirteen years, Anastassia Khouri, who has patiently, constructively, and lovingly served as a sounding board for the ideas that are incorporated in the pages which follow.

In a world in which monetary considerations tend to permeate everywhere and everything, the kindness of institutional strangers is one important expression of what is best in human society. To extend the words of Le Petit Prince, what is most valuable is not only invisible, but not subject to measurement. We need to deconstruct the myths that currently support the formation of a world where everything is metered and the fruits of human inventiveness are available only to those who can pay. If this book contributes in some small measure by adding to the force of complementary voices in altering the course of human action, I shall consider myself to have honored the debt that I owe, along with all my contemporaries and those of every generation, to those who have gone before us.

—MYRON J. FRANKMAN

Abbreviations

BWS	Bretton Woods System
DAC	Development Assistance Committee (of the OECD)
EC	European Community
EU	European Union
FDR	Franklin Delano Roosevelt
G-8	Group of Eight (Industrialized Countries)
GATT	General Agreement on Tariffs and Trade
GDP	Gross Domestic Product
GNP	Gross National Product
HDR	Human Development Report
IBRD	International Bank for Reconstruction and Development
ICA	International Commodity Agreement
ICU	International Currency Union
ILO	International Labour Organization
IMF	International Monetary Fund
ITO	International Trade Organization
LDC	Less developed country
NGO	Non-governmental organization
NICs	Newly Industrialized Countries
NIEO	New International Economic Order
ODA	Office Development Assistance
OECD	Organization for Economic Cooperation and Development
OPEC	Organization of Petroleum Exporting Countries
PCI	Per capita income
PWCI	Planet-Wide Citizen's Income
SDR	Special Drawing Right
UN	United Nations
UNCTAD	United Nations Conference on Trade and Development
UNDP	United Nations Development Programme
US	United States of America
WDR	World Development Report
WTO	World Trade Organization

1
Our World

> [T]he point of a nation is not to draw a line in the sand and keep its members behind it, but to create world citizens who are secure enough to treat others equally.
>
> —Gloria Steinem, *Revolution from Within: A Book of Self-Esteem*

> We are in danger of losing the idea that a future is created, bit by bit, out of our political desires and choices. That's why we need positive visions to balance the fashionably cynical ones, need them now more than ever.
>
> —Mark Kingwell, *The World We Want: Virtue, Vice and the Good Citizen*

This book is about agency, yours and mine: our ability to effect changes; change in ourselves and in our environment, at whatever level we choose from local to global. Choice is key, we must choose to be active and we must choose the issues that we wish to be the focus of our direct action and of our varying degrees of support through voice, loyalty, and contributions in cash and/or kind, including that scarcest of resources, our time. We must also choose the means that we wish to employ, what combination of words and deeds, what form of expression, whether 'merely' staying informed and maintaining a questioning attitude; writing letters to the editor, scholarly works, op-ed pieces, poetry, or plays; engaging in direct political engagement, participating in campaigns; or any one of countless other modes.

The focus is on agency because we live in a time of interconnectedness, rapid change, and peril to all forms of life on this planet. Some of these perils are manifest every day, some are unknowable surprises lying in wait at some undetermined point in the future linked to processes of which we are reasonably well aware—like climate change, ozone layer destruction, habitat destruction and degradation, and water shortages—but choose to ignore.

One of the most insightful concepts that has come to us in the computer age is that of default settings. Our default settings are like path markers that keep us on the sidewalk and off the grass. Narrow path markers simplify our daily trajectory by keeping a range of issues off our agenda; we do not need to worry our 'pretty little heads' about them. Default settings make life more comfortable, as they help us make our way through the world without being distracted by a sense of responsibility. In many computer programs changing certain default settings is possible, but not transparent. Agency resides in recognizing undesirable practices as default settings that are subject to change through our individual action and/or collective engagement.

Globalization is a word on everyone's lips today. It is necessarily neither a curse nor a blessing, but rather a process that poses pressing challenges for the human journey. Our trial and error adventure, which constitutes the essence of our existence as a species, confronts us in each new epoch with the task of reconstructing our ideas and our institutions. We are today conscious, as we never have been previously, of living together in an interrelated manner on a single small planet. Our guidance mechanisms have been crafted over the centuries into curious contrivances that, while more or less appropriate for their respective times, are hardly suited to the unique dilemmas that presently perplex us.

Planetary guidance is the task I have set for us in these pages. In this respect, I would appear to be yet one more social scientist that has fallen into the trap of grand synthesis. Yet, is that not part of our raison d'être? There are probably few unique ideas contained in this book. What I believe I have to offer the reader is the particular juxtaposition of a series of notions that have come to prominence over the past decades. The original concern of my work was to outline a set of institutional arrangements for global *economic* governance. This work was prompted by a firm belief that an integrated world economy needs appropriate public institutions with world-level responsibilities to perform some of the functions one has long encountered at the national level: namely, those of taming the economy and providing various kinds of compensation for the adverse consequences of market activity.

Listen carefully when the problems associated with globalization are discussed. Frequently the diagnosis will be impeccable and will lead ineluctably to a threshold. The analyst will pull back from crossing the threshold because of habits of thought, fear of the unknown, the comfort of living with present instability or an 'I'm all right Jack' lack of empathy for those who are victims of our current limits. What I am suggesting here is that we need to consider the next giant step in our thinking and in our institutional design.

We need to put giant steps on the agenda as a serious possibility. Until we change the discourse, we are powerless to do anything other than muddle through. The signs suggest that urgency and bold steps are needed. We have lost precious years by the timidity of our thought, often in the grip of words that have shaped our perceptions.

Words matter

> Language . . . is not neutral. It is never simply denotative. It is not limited to naming things. It is loaded with interpretation. It offers us a completely value-laden map of the world. Thus, language is our first initial dogma.
>
> —Estanislao Zuleta[1]

As my writing on responding to the challenge of globalization proceeded, my views on a range of related topics changed markedly. I have come to watch my words, discarding some and trying to reclaim the best meaning of others, which have been appropriated to serve narrow interests. Democratic government has emerged as a key thread running through the discussion. I have chosen to speak of government rather than governance, as I have come to regard the latter term as often being a cloak used by those who wish to replace 'inefficient' democratic processes with expert solutions. When I speak of democracy, I mean it in the sense of an open society in which equity and equal opportunity are operative guiding premises and not merely rhetoric relating to an always-remote future. Another element in this work is that of the centrality of shaping a set of consistent and humane organizational principles from the local to the global.

To be conscious of the tyranny of words requires a major awakening. I have tried to bring to the study of world government the same kind of critical sensitivity to keywords that feminist scholars have provided us in highlighting the predisposition created by supposedly gender-neutral words. I doubt that I have been fully successful, but I invite you to join me in this endeavor. Among the words that have provoked me are sovereignty and nation-state. I mention these first as they are particularly conflict-provoking words that bedevil the modern world. They carry a universe of confrontational connotations that often lead the young into battle to die for the short-sightedness of their elders, the weak to sacrifice on behalf of the powerful, and neighbors to rise against the 'other.' The phrase 'nation-state' may once have merely served to distinguish a geographically extensive political unit from a city-state, but is often associated with the presumption of a state being appropriately and optimally comprised of a single ethnically defined group. Reification of the phrase has served as a device for denying rights to minorities living within a state's borders and even as justification for genocide.

In today's world the word 'sovereign' is a mischievous relic however it may be used in the context of both nations and individuals. The much-heralded sovereignty of the consumer and the citizen conveniently masks the realities of concentrated power and a saturation of broadcast images that limit the real and perceived economic and political options of individuals. What Edward Herman and Noam Chomsky refer to as *Manufacturing Consent* shapes perceptions by withholding or distorting information available to the public.

Words and phrases moved from a specialized context into daily discussion serve to cloud discussion. I have even tried to be cautious in the use of the word 'economy,' to try not to fall into the trap of conveying the impression that this is an independent domain which is or should be immune from limits imposed by society or the even more threatening possibility that societal needs must take a back seat to that which is construed as an 'economic imperative,' which is said to trump other human considerations.

Words can serve to lock in a course of action (or inaction) and to silence dissent. To oppose an innovation that bears the label modern or developmental or progress can be virtually traitorous. Ivan Illich refers to stop words: words that so powerfully condition a discourse, that one is almost unable to conceive of an alternative perspective. Such words discredit opponents and can serve as a substitute for thought and for analysis. George Orwell discusses the use of charged words to preclude the necessity for thought in his classic essay on 'Politics and the English Language.'[2] To label an adversary (be it 'reactionary,' 'communist,' or 'terrorist') is a convenient alternative to thought. In the extreme, it denies the humanity of opponents and justifies their execution. Tarring all opponents with a single brush and a single label has been a very convenient tactic in discounting the message of those protesting at various economic summits dating at least from the 1999 Seattle meeting of the World Trade Organization (WTO).

Certain cherished concepts have been appropriated to serve interests. It is time to either replace or redeem those words. Governance is a term that I have chosen to avoid in this work because it is one of these compromised concepts. In the past decade 'good governance' has come to be a code word for decision by experts, often associated with the Bretton Woods institutions, that is, the International Monetary Fund (IMF) and the World Bank. Good government is not something to be defined away and replaced by 'good governance' by economists at the World Bank and the IMF, but rather it is the product of open political processes which allow people to influence policies by exercising their informed judgment. Good government is not something to be measured by a ratio of government expenditure or government debt to gross product, but changes with the temper of the people. Governance, on the other hand, tends to be distinctly antithetical to open, deliberative democratic processes. Moreover, 'good governance' has come to imply the implementation of a set of neoliberal policies and practices. For lack of a better phrase, the term 'anti-politics' has been used to refer to the external imposition of such blueprints. In fact, this is more properly referred to as 'anti-democratic,' as the misnomer 'anti-politics' reflects a particular kind of political process which is closed to public scrutiny.

'Democracy' is a most elastic word, which, like 'capitalism,' is applied to vastly different political configurations that may share little more than periodic elections. At one end of the spectrum we have what Barry K. Gills and William I. Robinson refer to as 'low intensity democracy,'[3] at the other end we have what Chantal Mouffe and others have called 'radical democracy,'[4] where questions of equity are taken seriously. Functional democracy may be a first step, but we must not lose sight of the goal of substantive democracy.

On the subject of equity, we find that the concepts of 'entitlement' and 'income redistribution' have fallen on hard times. Provision of any 'largesse,' however minimal, is said to dampen the incentives, the integrity, and the initiative of recipients. This is the most ironic of objections and, indeed, is truly a smoke screen. In the last 40 years we have witnessed worldwide (regressive) redistribution of income of monumental proportions. Apparently it is only progressive redistribution that is anathema. Similarly, the entitlements of the rich and powerful are secure and expanding daily. Nobel Prize winner Amartya Sen made an important contribution in validating the centrality of entitlements for the avoidance of malnutrition and even starvation,[5] but until the entitlements of the wealthy are subjected to evasion—and avoidance—proof progressive income (and profit) taxation, efforts to transform Sen's insight into practice will likely remain a cruel deception.

Social fractals

The more I have searched for the will for expanded global action, the more I have come to the conclusion that we must have a unified view of the social order from the immediate family to the global family and that institutional arrangements must mirror that viewpoint. That unified view must condition interpersonal relations in virtually all social settings. It is the idea of a unified view that accounts for my invocation of the notion of fractals, a central concept of chaos theory, which I understand to be irregular, complex patterns which are repeated at all scales of magnification from the microscopic to the macroscopic. This physical concept, like many others, can be regarded as having a social analog. One representation of this is found in André Gunder Frank's 1967 analysis of the chain of surplus expropriation/appropriation running from the sub-subtenant in distant agricultural regions of Latin America to the firms occupying the commanding heights of global capitalism.[6]

An alternative perspective consistent with the concept of social fractals is found in Riane Eisler's analysis of what she terms the dominator and the partnership models of human interaction. For Eisler, the ideal societal norm that we should be striving to develop is that of the partnership model where 'social relations are primarily based on the principle of *linking* rather than ranking... [and] diversity is not equated with either inferiority or superiority.'[7] In the still very prevalent dominator model, in contrast, the emphasis is clearly on obedience, deference to authority, and a rigid hierarchical ordering of society, 'backed up by force or threat of force.'[8]

In spite of considerable evidence to the contrary, I contend that the unified view necessary for expanded world organization and survival is, in fact, emerging. The complexity of social life often blinds us to changes that are occurring all around us, especially when we may still have to behave differently in each of the numerous social sets of which we form part (nuclear family, school association, neighborhood association, work, car pool, to name but a few). The transition from order to disorder and then to a new order, which is clearly discernible in retrospect to a historian poring over archival materials, is rarely so apparent to those who are living the experience, as I firmly believe is our case today. Our transitional task is a difficult one of envisioning the possibilities of the new order so that we may assist, by our daily behavior, in hastening its arrival. A cautionary note is in order, however, as 'context is all.' A focus on the individual and on the local initiative can be and is increasingly used as a strategy for denying causal connections between levels and as a means of enhancing inequality-generating structures of wealth and power.

The last two decades or so have seen the blossoming of a new vocabulary: everywhere that we turn, north and south, we hear about empowerment, participation, non-governmental organizations (NGOs), local control, democratization, grass-roots initiatives, human rights, and freedom. While the old paradigms are still around, animated discussion and action have been set in motion by this succession of phrases which reflect a new viewpoint and an emergent reality. Indeed, to the extent that free markets lead to the flourishing of individual initiative and are a complement to, not a substitute for, collective action, then they too can be thought of as part of the transition to a new order. The 'directive power' in the new order comes from the individual and finds its expression at all the many different levels of society at which the individual interacts.

Perhaps the 'lack of directive power' of the emerging keywords can be related to the geometry of the social fractals of the slowly waning old order. In the view of Riane Eisler, central to the configuration of our social order is the 'dominator model.'[9] The dominator model can best be illustrated by a small sample from the countless popular sayings and admonitions associated with its lengthy reign over the social order. For example: 'Children should be seen and not heard'; 'If I want your opinion, I'll ask for it'; 'You can't fight City Hall'; 'Ours is not to reason why, ours is but to do or die'; 'My country, right or wrong.'

The list could be multiplied—I'm sure some painful examples can be supplied from your own experience, but the idea is a simple one: the emphasis is clearly on passive acceptance and active defense of the status quo. The dominator model exerted a powerful, but not fully exclusive, influence on the fractal geometry which tended to characterize the family, the workplace, the school, the community, the congregation, and the polity.

Eisler argues that in antiquity the dominator model had largely displaced the 'partnership model.' She urges us to make the effort both as individuals and as unashamedly normative social scientists to help speed the return of the partnership model.[10] The nature of the dominator model virtually requires an adversary. In a world of nation-states, loyalties tend to stop at boundaries that have been drawn on maps, carefully staked out with control points and barriers and reinforced by a multiplicity of conditioning rules.[11] Over the past century a variety of social safety nets were laboriously crafted in the industrialized countries. Citizens of a jurisdiction tended to be entitled to the full set of the available benefits, with distinctions often applied to resident aliens. While *charity* may extend beyond national boundaries, solidarity as expressed in existing social programs begins and ends within one's home jurisdiction. Under the sway of free-market dogma and preoccupation with government deficits, even the scope of national solidarity has now withered substantially.

These conventional limits to our vision of the social order are both anachronistic and dangerous in a context in which human activities are increasingly globalized. Yet blinders and habits of mind persist. As Gloria Steinem observes: 'Even those of us most skeptical of nationalism have drifted into considering it a necessary evil.'[12] Acceptance of the logic of the partnership model implies that our loyalties extend beyond the heretofore customary limits and that we see ourselves as not only having allegiance to a particular nation and a nested set of its subnational jurisdictions, but ultimately to all the peoples of the Earth.

In fact, the dominator and partnership models have always coexisted in varying combinations. Partnership tends to be the strongest in the groups with which one has affinity by proximity or conditioning—family, village, co-workers, ethnic group, co-religionists, co-nationals—and weakest in dealing with 'outsiders.' Recent thinking not only rejects social Darwinism with its suggested necessity for a dominator model, but the very notion of an outsider is beginning to lose force. To use the phrase of recent security strategists, mutually assured destruction (MAD) is a likely outcome of even identifying 'others' in a world with an abundance of nuclear weapons. It makes sense in every respect to cultivate the partnership model and to limit the scope of the dominator model. It is not only safer and less costly to cooperate, but more fun as well. In short, it appears to be a win–win strategy for all except the manufacturers and the dealers of armaments.

The key notion of fractals as patterns repeating at each level of magnification can be a powerful device for re-envisioning the world around us. Certain practices are condemned and given deprecatory labels when they occur at one level, while the parallel practice at a different level is regarded as perfectly acceptable. South Africa was an international pariah for almost one-quarter century for its apartheid policies. And yet we live in a world where passports, visas, and immigration laws impose apartheid on the globe. The black South African, who now is free to move within his country, is restricted in a myriad of ways from moving internationally. Curiously, while South Africa's domestic apartheid galvanized opposition, the continuing accretion of restrictive national immigration laws and practices proceeds with little effective protest.

Similarly, due process which is a central value in societies governed by the rule of law is almost universally denied to individuals denied entry to a country by border guards. Even the rights of citizens to participate in discussion leading to democratic decision-making were flaunted in those European Union (EU) countries that adopted in secret the Schengen Convention in 1990 tightening conditions for entry of foreigners. All these 'exceptions' cast a cloud over the smug pretenses of countries which are otherwise regarded as defenders of human rights.

I am suspicious of all-encompassing logical systems of explanation superimposed on human activities. Yet, cautiously applied, analogies can be remarkably insightful. In approaching questions of world order, including world public finance and world democracy, a number of overlapping concepts are useful: subsidiarity, federalism (including fiscal federalism), and fractals. All imply multi-leveled relationships. When considering the social fractals of government and taxation, we would expect to encounter broadly homologous features at each level of jurisdiction. Details, of course, vary, but consistencies tend to predominate. This parallelism has yet to be achieved at supranational levels and least of all at the world level.

Culture contact

We live in a bountiful world. There is plenty to go round if we organize to do so. The comfort that some of us have and the discomfort of so many others are by-products of the world that we have shaped. Our practices open the door for some and deliberately close the door for others. Buckminster Fuller spoke about making the world work for 100 percent of its people[13] and the post-World War II rhetoric of economic development expressed that same objective. Yet progress toward that cherished end has been mixed. Institutional developments have instead brought us to our present global mix of security and insecurity.

We are starstruck about 'Prometheus Unbound'—the technological advances that represent expressions of human creativity. But human creativity has also bound us together and enriched us collectively by lifting our spirits and by lightening our travails in non-material ways. Ivan Illich spoke of 'Tools of Conviviality.' Others speak of solidarity, camaraderie, and even love. What are these expressions—humor, caring, giving, appreciation, love, song, dance, sports, storytelling, oral history, myths, the written word—if not means to meet what Abraham Maslow termed the 'higher needs'? Our forms of camaraderie represent a balancing and an interplay of the individual and the life of the group. Globalization in its most positive manifestations is the extending and making permeable of group boundaries, the celebration of diversity, the recognition of common values, and the quest for peace on a global scale. While celebrations of technological change are legion, insufficient attention is given to human characteristics that drive that change. Our history is a record of the tensions between the collective and the individual, the free and the directed, and rules and unlimited horizons. The playing out of competing visions of how widely and how best to spread the benefits of being human have produced both desired and perverse outcomes.

Karl Polanyi spoke of various kinds of 'exchange' mechanisms[14] or ways of social provisioning: markets, redistribution, and reciprocity. Marcel Mauss spoke of the gift,[15] a 'transaction' in which neither the quid pro quo nor the eventual compensation is evident. Within the Mauss framework, a gift can be intragroup, intergroup, or intergenerational. Gifts from the old to the young are acts of passing the torch to the next generation. This is the kind of gift given within a family to the young, within a school to the learner, within a team by a coach, and within a craft to the apprentice. In his irreverent essay on 'Salesmanship and the Church,' Thorstein Veblen spoke of 'vendible imponderables.'[16] In a like manner, to the extent that we seek to leave an earthly legacy, we are likewise dealing with an imponderable that the economist's calculus of benefits and costs is hard-pressed to accommodate. Building a society, whether local or global, is a matter of responding to both material needs and inner needs of individuals and groups. The eclipsing of redistribution- and reciprocity-based exchange by market-based transactions in recent times has imperiled the place of inner needs—needs which cannot readily be reckoned in monetary terms.

Globalization is as old as the earth itself. Agents of this relentless isolation-destroying process have been microorganisms, the flora and fauna (including humans and their inventions), wind, water and fire, and an array of natural phenomena. John E. Lovelock in his work on the Gaia hypothesis describes a natural process of global change that generated the atmosphere that coevolves, supports, and is interconnected with all life on the planet.[17] The global impact of 'local' processes, with or without human intervention is nothing new. The eruption of Krakatoa in Indonesia in the latter part of the 19th century may well have been the first natural local event which was *perceived* to have global impact and a temporally extended one at that time.[18] Even today when plate tectonics is the well-established paradigm in geology, we commonly hear it said that an earthquake in one part of the world has no connection with temporally proximate temblors in other parts of the world, both near and far.

Our awareness of global interconnections in the physical realm grows daily. As late as the 1950s, El Niño, associated with periodic shifts in the northern reach of the Peru Current off the Pacific Coast of South America, was thought to have only local consequences. We now are well aware that the effects of the phenomena are quite far-flung. During the 1997–98 occurrence of El Niño, almost every weather disturbance around the globe was blamed, rightly or wrongly, on the phenomenon.

Although humans have been latecomers to our planetary home, we have been active agents in uniting the globe. Paradoxically, worldwide influences have spread even when humans have acted in the name of local interests. The roots of human globalization can be traced back (conceptually, if not in evidence) to the first occasion when the paths of two groups crossed. When defined and variously differentiated groups meet and interact it can be as friends or as enemies, as subjects or as objects. Relations between and within peoples are a changing mix of amity and enmity, of cooperation and domination. This mix is not new and has no doubt represented two sides of the process of globalization throughout the millennia of human habitation on earth. The fragmentary records at our disposal of these culture contacts attest to our primordial wanderings. When peoples have been 'conquered' militarily or symbolically, their productive activities have often been harnessed for a distant formal or informal imperial center. This was as true in early empires as it is today when what is characterized as 'free trade' governs the world.

What is new about globalization today is not the destruction of species, the disappearance of cultures, and the replacement of diversified local agricultural production by monoculture, but rather our growing (but by no means pervasive) collective consciousness of our either being near or having already crossed thresholds that threaten our continued survival on earth. We live in an age of limits, when terrestrial frontiers have disappeared. The common phrase 'to throw something away' has been replaced by the precautionary 'there is no away.'

We live in a networked, interconnected world in which our text, voice, and/or image can reach someone halfway around the globe almost instantaneously at little or no direct financial cost to either sender or receiver. The wonders of communications have become so commonplace with us that we do not even bat an eyelash in response to a report that one-third of the world's six-billion people watched the final match of a Football World Cup.

In the human realm we know that globalization touches each of us profoundly, but few sense that we might be able to make a collective response to alter the nature of that process. Lacking a *sense* of the possibility of action, the kind of initiatives that might be undertaken represents a moot point. And yet the human possibility is implicit in our every waking moment and in our every thought and deed. We are among both the effects and the causes of our common planetary evolution.

We tend to periodize human history in numerous ways, including with respect to perceived changes in the scale of human activities. Globalization is a label usually reserved for the most recent events in the drawing together of the world's people, particularly by instantaneous communication. We speak today of an age of 'virtuality,' but we started down that path with the advent of the first telegraph signals in 1837 when transmission of messages transcended the limits of distance over which the loudest sound, the brightest light, or a projectile can travel and the limits of overland speed for carrying tangible objects. While 'virtuality' has quickened the pace markedly, the global 'project' truly can be said to date from prehistory.[19]

The role of human agency in the formation of one world has been a lengthy process. It did not start yesterday, but began with simple roaming (at one's peril), exploration and long-distance trade and the resulting contact of cultures and our role in the spread of flora and fauna around the world by accident and design. With the contact of cultures came 'rules' of engagement: an instrumental vocabulary, guidelines for frequency of meeting, place of meeting, and protocols governing gift-giving and exchanges.

Societal globalization has largely been an anarchic process, not part of a grand design, although there have been periods of organization and elaborate planning. The formation of large overseas empires, the vast human migrations (forced and 'voluntary'), the growth of trade have all played their part, together with technological changes, in creating a shrinking world and a world in which the inhabitants of different parts of our globe are able to communicate in the language of various colonizers and proselytizers—Arabic, English, French, Portuguese, Russian, and Spanish, to mention but a few—and where a common ethic and set of social expectations has spread to many parts of the world.

In looking at the organization of business firms, analysts point to advantages that may be had by incorporating into an enterprise services previously obtained through contracts with external sources. In a like manner, the spread of one's language, religion, and values can have beneficial effects in terms of the ease of executing a range of transactions, whether commercial or personal.

The spread of Islam and Christianity, and the mutual encounters of spatially separated peoples, not least of which were those of Europeans with the peoples of Asia, Africa, and the 'New World' of the Americas have all been part of that process of globalization. The effects have been mixed, especially where circumstances involved armed conflict and conquest. The world system experienced major expansion from the mid-15th century through to the beginning of World War I. Products previously unknown in Europe—potatoes, tobacco, chocolate, coffee, and tea among them—had a significant cultural impact on the region. Remarkably, several of these products came to be associated with the importing countries where they were processed and commercialized and not the areas of production, such as Dutch chocolate and British tea. These Europeanized goods then found their way to the remainder of the world. Consistent with the counsel of 17th-and 18th-century Mercantilist writers, goods were brought from one part of the world by merchants, then processed and transshipped to other parts. South Asian tea re-exported by British merchants became part of the way of life in many parts of the world.[20]

Exploration and trade brought the spread of foods, clothes, diseases, and social customs. We have a written chronicle of this spread for the last millennium or two; earlier episodes would likely have varied only in detail. Each new invention brought the world closer together in its wake. Colonial empires sped the process and also contributed gradually to the mixing of genetic stock that diminished to varying extents the significant visual distinctions associated with notions of diversity, as eventually incorporated in the concept of 'race.' The prior relative isolation of human populations began to disappear. The resulting cultural, visual, and genetic continuum forged by a mixing of people meant that unambiguous fine-line distinctions between defined groups could no longer be easily made. Where local practice maintained the separation of peoples into discrete groupings, classification was either based on genealogy, legal definition, and/or an invented pseudo-scientific standard. The contact of cultures has been part of a gradual movement toward the shaping of a planetary humanity, which the social constructions of race, nation, class, and religion have been unable to constrain fully.

Arthur Koestler spoke of an eternal dialectic between integration and self-assertion.[21] This same dynamic tension can also be observed at the level of societal units, including especially the nation. This ever-changing process is a simple, but powerful idea to keep in mind when examining the process of globalization, which has entailed shifting boundaries for the process of integration. The terms of integration—what an individual or a group may perceive to be at risk—need not lead to violence, however, that has too often been the case.

Our world has evolved, at times gradually, at times precipitously, at times peacefully and cooperatively, and at times violently, through technological development, individual efforts, volition, imposition, legal creations, and institution building. As human numbers have grown, we have moved from 'merely' pressing against the carrying capacity of localities to the limits of the earth itself.

The growth and subsequent suppression of the international slave trade is an episode of norms being defined and later redefined. The British were a key player in both the creation and the suppression of the transatlantic slave trade. Curiously, at the same time the British were patrolling the high seas to enforce the ban on slavery, large numbers of Chinese, whose condition unequivocally was one of bondage, were being brought to the west coast of the Americas to work principally in railroad construction.[22] Each of these elements is part of the unification of the world and the eventual formation of a global civil society.

One of the major acts of global standardization which revolutionized the daily life of peoples around the world was the creation of 24 time zones, a product of the need for transcontinental railroads in North America to be able to coordinate their scheduling. It is hard for us to imagine a world in which seconds, minutes, and hours are not 'ticking' by relentlessly, yet prior to the 1870s, in many parts of the world the 60 minute hour was unknown. There were places where hours existed only between sunrise and sunset (and varied in length with the season) and there was no agreement across cultures when the day should be regarded as commencing—among the variations were days which started at sunset, sunrise and noon. The creation and spread of a system of uniform time is surely one of the least chronicled of the major episodes of global standardization.[23] The needs of the railroads may have led to standardized time, but the coming of the telegraph, the telephone, and the radio essentially conquered time and space. With the instant transmission of messages, our globe shrunk exponentially and the age of virtuality was upon us.

The electronic age

The electronic age and the Pax Americana are the keys to understanding the quickening pace of global integration since 1945. The objective of American foreign economic policy was to build world capitalism through the freeing of foreign trade and payments and ideally foreign investment as well, although the latter was not incorporated explicitly into the institutional infrastructure that was created in the 1940s. The American project, subscribed to by most of the other nations of the non-communist world, succeeded so thoroughly that American jobs and well-being are said by some to be threatened by the very success of their project and a failure to anticipate the possible consequences of that success. As early as the mid-1970s Richard J. Barnet and Ronald E. Müller were speaking of the 'Latin Americanization of the United States' as jobs and the tax base migrated offshore.[24] From their perspective, the allegiance of American multinational corporations was increasingly to earning profits and not to any particular country, not even their putative home. Increasingly, it makes little sense to speak of the nationality of a company. In the extreme, the only tangible meaning of a company's 'home' is to identify which government is appealed to for subsidies, bailouts, and other forms of support.

The spread of a consumption-intensive civilization in a context of rapid population growth has brought problems of environmental degradation, social alienation, and exclusion. In a variation of the myth of the hydra, for each ostensibly positive outcome there have been associated negative effects that in the long run threaten the gains achieved. The capability of the earth to accommodate our assaults is the greatest question mark confronting us. Our hubris still inclines many to sweep aside mentally these concerns as being eventually amenable to timely intervention. Thornton Wilder's play *The Skin of our Teeth* describes our fortuitous escapes from precarious situations in past human history.[25] Tomorrow we may not be that fortunate. We have set in motion chains of events, like climate change, which have lengthy gestation periods where our ability to reverse processes in motion, which we do not fully understand,[26] may be negligible. Like Nevil Shute's chilling account, in his novel *On the Beach*, of the last humans playing out their remaining hours before the certain arrival of nuclear clouds,[27] we may yet witness a human population crash that disrupts our technologically intensive lifelines—a latter-day equivalent of the Black Death in Europe in the 14th century or the nameless 16th-century native holocaust in the Americas as diseases previously unknown in the Western Hemisphere spread like wildfire.[28]

The advantage of the United States of America (US) in having a unified market where scale economies in production could be realized gave impetus to the movement for economic integration in Europe and subsequently elsewhere in the world. Producers in other countries, lacking the domestic market, were nonetheless able to realize scale advantages by concentrating on exporting to the unified markets in the US and Europe. Improvements in transportation and communications simplified greatly the task of keeping tabs on trends in distant major markets. In a like manner, domestic firms began to globalize their production and distribution. Turning to external markets has often meant a policy of the devil take the hindmost at home and abroad, individually and collectively.

Over 150 years elapsed between the introduction of the smallpox vaccine in 1794 by Edward Jenner and the eventual declaration that the disease had been eradicated globally. Today we take for granted that innovations will find their way around the world in weeks or months, as in the case of the World Wide Web, rather than decades. By way of contrast we still carry many mindsets, values, default settings, and prejudices whose origins span centuries. While we have now reached the point where the global reach of human activities is well known, many of our guiding principles are still those appropriate to less complex times.

During the continuing Pax Americana the world has been reshaped into a single emerging composite, with still quite distinguishable local expressions. As always, cultural contact rarely involves unidirectional adaptations. No culture is static and that of the US is no exception. Americans have absorbed and transformed influences from the many cultures represented by successive waves of immigration and by the foreign travel, study, residence, and investment of its citizens and even by the search by grandchildren and great-grandchildren of immigrants to rediscover and/or reinvent their long-lost roots—a response to perceived cultural homogenization. Even supposedly, homogenous cultures differentiate daily.

The Third World debt crisis of the 1980s, the collapse of the Soviet Union, the fall of the Berlin Wall in 1989, and the opening of coastal China to production for foreign firms have been among the elements that have quickened the pace of global cultural integration in the past two decades. These developments opened the way to the worldwide expansion of financial capital, which has been associated with a self-serving agenda whose central neoliberal tenet is that the government that governs least, governs best. The Bretton Woods institutions have been among the key agents spreading that particular gospel. Like missionaries before them (and still) spreading the true word, the IMF and the World Bank are major players in a network spreading a uniform approach to economic policy management and societal organization.

Neoliberalism is yet another crusade in a long series intended to bring salvation either in the after-life or the current one.[29]

As the computer revolution is still very likely in its infancy, so, too, is its worldwide cultural incidence. The major changes that many of us have already experienced in the way we work and in our social relations are likely to be but a modest beginning. Consider, for example, the current coexistence in different parts of the world of marriages arranged by parents between eventual mates who may still be infants and the 'meeting' by others of their future mates in internet chat rooms. We are surely no more able to accurately predict the eventual impact of the electronic revolution than were 15th-century Europeans able to foretell the consequences of the introduction by Gutenberg of movable type. Nonetheless, we can try to imagine. The democratization of information that has already been produced by the ongoing internet-based communications revolution offers the prospect of a re-formation even more sweeping than that which followed the dissemination of printed books.

Yet analyses by social scientists tend to fixate on the nation-state. Economics in particular with little attention paid to hierarchical structures in the reigning paradigm, directs attention to the autonomous individual, firm, industry, and/or nation. We are blinkered by our analytical frameworks and try to force solutions into them. We are blinkered as well by our upbringing, by our schooling, by stereotypical representations of others. And we are blinkered most grievously by our inability to see the complex interactions of wholes and parts, but only spatial fragments: nation, province, and city—each affirming its 'sovereignty.'

A sketch of the way in which the context facing national policy-makers and economic actors has changed is useful. We live in a world of international rivalry between firms for the access to resources, for the use of capital, for the services of labor, and for the sale of their offerings. That intense competition translates into pressures on nations, firms, unions, and economic agents in general. Associated with these pressures are rapid changes in some places and fairly limited changes elsewhere. The 1974 United Nations (UN) General Assembly resolution on the New International Economic Order (NIEO) called specifically for the advanced countries to take steps to facilitate global economic restructuring. This was a recommendation in the clear long-term economic interest of the industrialized countries. The response instead was to restrict markets through voluntary export restrictions and cartel-like arrangements (the multi-fiber arrangement).

The interplay of technology and institutions was a recurring theme for Thorstein Veblen. In *Imperial Germany and the Industrial Revolution*[30] he sketched the effect on a society of the incorporation of new technologies developed elsewhere. He emphasized that in the society where these originated there had been cultural change to gradually accommodate the new machines, while in latecomers adaptation was more likely to lead to socio-political disruption. In *The Theory of Business Enterprise*[31] Veblen devoted one chapter to the cultural incidence of the machine process. For Veblen, our preoccupation with measurement in almost all aspects of human endeavors is an outgrowth of the logic of the machine process.

Although globalization has become a household word, there continues to be an insistence on speaking of the international, whether it is the realm of politics, economy, or society, and not of the world. It is surely time to begin speaking of the world. If we are to construct appropriate institutions for the circumstances in which we now find ourselves, we need to start with words that do not distort the discourse by limiting our terms of reference. Local solutions, which may be called for in many instances, are not sufficient to deal with problems that have a global reach. Indeed, changes which are occurring daily involve the shifting of the locus of decision-making from its historic location: some problems require action at a lower level, some at a higher level. Where higher and lower jurisdictions are missing, it is the task of our times to create institutions at those levels. In terms of the cultural incidence of the electronic process, we must be ever attentive and critical to assure that we embrace those ennobling opportunities that the new technology has to offer.

Limits and liberation

Today, everyone talks about globalization, but it seems that many have adopted what the political scientists call the realist model. One author after another explores the limits of policy measures either in the industrial countries, the transitional countries, or the developing countries and either confidently proclaims that market processes will solve all ills or is unable to go beyond handwringing about these being particularly difficult times. For example, in an article about the growth of the working poor in the US after observing that 'most of us are only a restructuring, a re-engineering, a firing, a major illness, or a divorce away from joining them,'[32] the author concluded despairingly: 'what we have here, in short, is a circular, self-generating crisis for which it is hard to come up with convincingly efficacious solutions.'[33]

In the North, where the play of democratic interests has prevented a full implementation of economic liberalism, its consequences have nonetheless been substantial. This same set of policies applied in many a Third World setting has been a recipe for disruption and not for the successful launch of a (re)birth of civil society. There may be no viable national solution for many of the problems countries confront today.

H.G. Wells is often quoted as suggesting that humankind is engaged in a race between education and catastrophe. As with so many words out of context, this barely begins to convey the thrust of Wells' message. In fact, Wells' full original quote addresses the evils of nationalism and of education distorted by those who choose to use nationalism for personal advantage.[34] Most of us are products of an educational system that has done its best through passive learning to neutralize knowledge and to create a society with an anti-political bent. We still live in a world in which education is harnessed to the nation and in which saber rattling is still celebrated. Barren islands, pieces of desert, outlets to the sea, and the invocation of previous losses are all used to incite people who one would expect to be more sensitive than to value the prospect of the national honor triumphing at the cost of the lives of the young. Indeed in a world of surplus labor, the loss of young lives in war may be one grotesque way to deal with the lack of jobs. If there were ever a testimony to the lack of social imagination, that would indeed be it.

How do we expand our range of allegiances to truly embrace the humanity of 'others'? How do we shape an allegiance to all the world's humanity, if not all its creatures, that supplements and alters the nature of our attachment to the nation which we call home? Feeling Canadian or Kenyan should not set us against others, but should be but one among our loyalties. Recognition that we are subject to the same global processes and that we form but one human race, may be the first steps.

The task which I have set for myself in the remainder of this work is to convince the reader, if she/he is not already so convinced of the following basic points:

1. We live in one interconnected world.
2. We are still burdened by default settings, many of which are residual symbols from a world of warring tribes. These 'givens,' of which we are scarcely aware, are scripts which celebrate the primacy of the local or the national and of the difference between us and them. They are dangerous constructs in urgent need of replacement by precepts more appropriate to our epoch. Proclaiming our uniqueness has its time, place, and limits. Where, however, it entails a zero-sum encounter, it can be a major contributor to inequality, violence, war, and ultimately destruction of life on Earth.

3. We are the beneficiaries of a rich inheritance from the past and from others. A just world requires that we fully accept an obligation to share and a responsibility to others based on a recognition that our good fortune derives from the existence of a social order and a cumulative process of civilization.
4. Open discussion and participatory structures are most suited to steering our structured social universe.

Ways ahead

The common person is not immune from acting internationally, but these modes are still at a limited stage of development. A globalizing economy is but one element in the unification of our planet. The global spread of goods and services has been central to speeding up a number of related processes, most notably the growth of cities, the devastation of natural habitats, and the extinction of countless animal and plant species. One element of current globalization is that some of our national steering and control mechanisms have been weakened and no satisfactory substitutes have yet been fashioned.

Although our lives have already been touched by the global economy in innumerable ways, the full impact of increasingly integrated global markets has scarcely begun. In the meantime, adverse consequences of the globalization process are already beginning to appear in our neighborhoods and our societal responses are, by and large, no different from what they have been for the past few decades, if not, more generally, for the last few centuries: to try to close the nation in one way or another and to the extent possible to external influences. The history of globalization is an account of the changing balance between integration and self-assertion writ large in a context where the 'players' do not meet on an equal footing.

We need a philosophy of human solidarity and of planetary oneness, a symbolism of one and many, of the richness of diversity. We must return a sense of meaning to the peoples of the world. This is part of the constructive response to globalization, a response which takes us off the path leading to internecine wars. This kind of rallying project, which is already going on is what must be generalized. The sense must be instilled in the young (and belatedly in those of us who are older) that we are part of a beautiful world of opportunities and responsibilities.

To shape our guiding principles, we must shake off obsolete perceptions. Development and sustainable development are not distinct local challenges, but rather must be seen as an interconnected project for the extension of social justice and ecological sanity worldwide. If development is not be a code word for destruction and despoilment, deliberative processes must be open and the people must be free to be heard.

The idea of world order and world peace is not new. Immanuel Kant wrote about perpetual peace in the 18th century. William Ladd in the US and James Lorimer in England were among those who offered proposals in the 19th century.[35] Leonard Woolf and John Hobson both addressed questions of world government in the first quarter of the 20th century.[36]

The locus of allegiance and centers of government has changed over time. These shifts in part have been supported by sets of ideas often cast in sophistic terms by interests who stood to profit from the shift in guiding norms. Once the 'level of magnification for government' has been established, then the political process begins to operate to adjust the division of gains in a manner which may not have been intended by those who supported mercantilism, colonial empires, free trade, and other strategies. In a like manner, the debate which has been framed as being of nation vs region or globe, is not one of opposition, but rather of accommodation. Only by abandoning the zero-sum competition of nations for advantage can we shape a humane future world.

One message contained here is quite simply that an integrated world economy, which is what we now have, requires for its smooth functioning world government, without which the hundreds of other forms of interdependence, integration and diversity are endangered. It is no exaggeration to assert that without democratic institutions at the global level the preservation and extension of the freedom and peace that provides the opportunity for the liberation of the human spirit would likely be imperiled.

The continuing daily denial of adverse developments and the logic driving them is not only very costly, but may eventually be actually catastrophic in the fullest sense of the word. Canaries were once used in underground mines to warn, by their silence, of impending danger. Today, we who live on the surface in the full (now dangerous) rays of the sun have countless warning signs that should spur us to act, among which are disappearing species, holes in the ozone layer, falling water tables, rising sea levels, increasing income inequality, periodic financial contagion, and a rise in the incidence of civil wars. If life (as we know it) on earth is to continue throughout the 21st century and beyond, humanity will need to engage in institutional innovation on a major scale.

Organization of the book

The world system is still spoken of as the Westphalian System—a system of nation-states that emerged based on principles contained in the Peace of Westphalia in 1648. The key elements in the Westphalian System are the sovereign equality and the internal inviolability of nations. Many of the nations that existed at the time of the Peace of Westphalia have been absorbed into larger units, despite the intent of the framers of the Treaty to preserve the integrity of principalities. This phenomenon of historical scale shifts is taken up in Chapter 2, with the intent of drawing precedents for the scale changes that surround us today.

In Chapter 3 and elsewhere I review proposals that have been made for governing global economic activity. The experience of the Great Depression of the 1930s generated numerous schemes for planetary management originally intended to head off another major economic downturn. The urgency of this design task was enhanced by the perception that the Depression catalyzed the forces that brought on World War II. I also review the unique experience of economic coordination in the Western Hemisphere during World War II.

Superimposed on the Westphalian System in 1944 was an economic system, the Bretton Woods System (BWS), which committed member countries to the freeing of international trade and payments. The BWS was said to have broken down in 1971. In truth, nothing of the sort happened: only fixed exchange rates disappeared and, at that, principally among the industrialized countries. Indeed, one could argue that the globalization of capital markets in the 1980s represented a triumph of the BWS, or even an achievement far beyond the wildest imaginings of those who gathered to create the System at the opulent Mount Washington Hotel in New Hampshire in mid-1944. In the 1980s and 1990s,[37] an extended set of neoliberal principles, known as the Washington Consensus, was added to the apparatus of the BWS. I will argue that these systems are no longer appropriate, if they ever were, to maintain the peace between the peoples of the world. The scale changes associated with changes in transportation, communications, certain types of production, and human impact on the Earth call out for changes in the scale of institutional arrangements to assure the enjoyment of human security for the world's people. As long as nations do not meet as equals and the voice of the people is ignored, the functional internationalism that characterizes our fragmented approach to global government is no longer sufficient.

The case for world taxation and progressive redistribution is developed in Chapter 4. One of the commonplaces of the age of globalization is that there are limits to the taxing power of national and subnational jurisdictions. If national corporate profits tax rates exceed a certain level, freely mobile investment funds are said to be likely to migrate elsewhere. The corollary to a reduction in taxing power is a reduction in ability to spend. This alone would suffice to diminish social services. But the reality of globalization has been complemented by the careful promotion of an opportunistic mythology of the state as necessarily inefficient and parasitic. If tax bases migrate, then the locus of taxing authority must shift as well (to a higher level) if the means to finance the provision of the public good is to be preserved and promoted locally and globally.

The system of national exchange rates is examined as a major potentially destabilizing element in an increasingly integrated world. I argue in Chapter 5 that the time has long been ripe for vigorous steps to be taken to create a world currency and the institutions that must necessarily go with it. Anything less perpetuates a powerful mechanism for generating income inequality and for forcing some nations to despoil their natural resources and even to sell their sons and daughters into bonded labor or prostitution.

We can have a new system in place. With luck and hard work it will not be born of war, but rather of a realization that our present course is both unsustainable and immoral. If humanity responds imaginatively, the Pax, of which we are living the transitional and *highly* imperfect early years, will not bear the name of a country whose might preserves the peace, as did the Pax Britannica and the Pax Americana, but rather will be known as the Pax Humana. Essential to that peace is the introduction of a democratically controlled global public sector with both the power to raise revenues and to reduce what are already untenable levels of inequality of access, opportunity, income, and wealth in our evermore unified global society. Chapter 6 complements the discussion of a single currency by addressing questions of global-income disparities. The discussion relating to equitable distribution is brought back squarely to the realm of social imagination and collective will with my espousal of a planet-wide citizen's income (PWCI).

I believe that institution building and innovation, particularly, but not only, at the world level, is essential for all of humanity to prosper and indeed to even survive. The quest for sustainability and social justice will as surely require establishing systems of entitlement worldwide as national harmony was once believed almost axiomatically to require a functioning welfare state.

Even more essential than a specific set of technical measures is the process through which institutional measures are shaped. A Pax Humana which privileges our common humanity would not be the work of one conquering party; there would be no glorious planting of the flag,[38] no hegemon that imposes its way. It will be the work of near-anonymous individuals, you among them, who will have labored selflessly and tirelessly in diverse ways, formal and informal, to shape the guidelines necessary for the continuing process of supporting planetary social order. It will be an outcome which (in the words of Jane Jacobs) will do honor not only to the multitude of participants, but also to civilization.[39] It will be the expression of individuals and groups joined in a common cause across the globe. Unlike previous systems of government, this will be one in which half of humanity (women) and far more than half of humanity by another way of reckoning (the peoples of the developing countries) will have had a major input.

Gunnar Myrdal was a great believer in making his values explicit. I try to follow his example. I have tried throughout this work to exorcize the mystical potency of economic forces. People are behind economic processes and policies. Market forces may appear to impose limits, but our hands are not tied. Laws that are the product of human agreement can be altered by human agreement. In the words of Matthew Arnold:

> all rights are created by law and are based on expediency, and are alterable as the public advantage may require . . . Legal society creates, for the common good, the right of property, and for the common good that right is by legal society limitable.[40]

The Chilean biologist Humberto Maturana insists that our human achievements, including triumphs of engineering like the Pyramids, the Taj Mahal, and the Great Wall of China, can be understood as products of a network of conversations.[41] Quite simply put, to change our world requires changing our discourse.

As I make clear in the conclusion (see Chapter 7), I believe in democracy not as a slogan, but as a guiding principle to enshrine in human endeavors at all levels. Democracy carries with it various corollaries: among them the centrality of discussion, of access to information on which to base that discussion, and respect for and protection of minority rights and diversity. As a goal, I believe in struggling to narrow the gap between words and deeds, and between the letter of the law and the reality—to translate de jure rights and privileges into de facto rights and privileges. Some of my learned colleagues derive great amusement from my naive conception that the 'government should be us.' Perhaps with a narrowing of the gap between formal and substantive democracy, the government will be us. In this regard, when I speak of action by governments and policy-makers, I specifically wish to convey that this action derives from the advice and consent of the governed.

'The answer to the question either/or is always both/and.' This brief paraphrase of a passage by Joan Robinson has been a great source of inspiration since I first read it well over three decades ago.[42] I had for years thought of it merely as a central critique of the economist's method of equilibrium thinking. Our habit of mind was always fashioning tradeoffs, such as guns vs butter, consumption vs investment, full employment vs inflation, a steel mill vs a fertilizer factory, and so on. All these necessary hard choices flowed from the customary assumption in economic theory of full utilization of resources. That indeed was the context in which Robinson intended the thought. But in preparing this book, I have seen her observation to be far more powerful than that. Order and disorder, for example, can be seen as complements and not as mutually exclusive. These are elements that must always coexist in an everchanging tension. Hierarchy and anarchy, as well, are not dialectical opposites, but complements. To think only in either/or terms is to straightjacket action and to precipitate often-pathological results.

A basic message that I shall make here is that both the state and the market are societal creations and that there is a dynamic inter-relation between state, market, society, and technology. We see this globally today. As people become freer and freer in every aspect of their beings, the myriad old social rigidities and limitations are crumbling everywhere.[43] Simultaneously, governments, at whatever level, need to reshape the nature and the areas of their involvement, adding new initiatives as appropriate. The balance is not always 'right,' but if the steering process remains open, then the succession of hands at the helm is indispensable in guiding the spread of freedom.

For the dynamic balance between order and anarchy to work its magic, we must extend the domain of world public order. Its absence is a threat to world peace and a threat to the survival of life on earth. What nobler project for today's supposedly dispirited youth than to join in the collective construction of a democratic global order?

Notes

1. Estanislao Zuleta, *Educación y democracia: un campo de combate* (Bogotá, Fundación Estanislao Zuleta: Corporación Tercer Milenio, 1995).
2. George Orwell, 'Politics and the English Language', *The Collected Essays, Journalism and Letters of George Orwell Volume 4: In Front of Your Nose: 1945–1950* (New York: Penguin Books, 1970), pp. 156–70.
3. William I. Robinson, *Promoting Polyarchy: Globalization, US Intervention, and Hegemony* (Cambridge: Cambridge University Press, 1996) and Barry K. Gills, 'American Power, Neoliberal Globalization, and Low Intensity Democracy: An Unstable Trinity', in Michael Cox, G. John Ikenberry and Takashi Inoguchi, eds, *American Democracy Promotion: Impulses, Strategies, and Impacts* (New York: Oxford University Press, 2000), pp. 326–44.
4. Chantal Mouffe, ed., *Dimensions of Radical Democracy: Pluralism, Citizenship, Community* (London: Verso, 1992).
5. Amartya Sen, *Poverty and Famines: An Essay on Entitlement and Deprivation* (New York: Oxford University Press, 1981).
6. André Gunder Frank, *Capitalism and Development in Latin America: Historical Studies in Chile and Brazil* (New York: Monthly Review Press, 1967).
7. Riane Eisler, *The Chalice and the Blade: Our History, Our Future* (San Francisco: HarperCollins, 1987).
8. Ibid., p. xvii.
9. Ibid., p. xvii.
10. Ibid., pp. 185–203. See also Riane Eisler and David Loye, 'Chaos and Transformation: Implications of Nonequilibrium Theory for Social Science and Society', *Behavioral Science* 32 (Jan. 1987), pp. 53–65.
11. Here is what Gloria Steinem (1992, pp. 15–16) has to say on our image of nationalism: 'It remains insular and territorial, a dangerous anachronism on this fragile and shrinking planet where neither war nor environmental dangers can be contained by national boundaries anymore.'
12. Ibid., p. 16.
13. This was the objective of the World Game, a simulation exercise developed by R. Buckminster Fuller in which recourse to war automatically occasioned a player to lose the game.
14. Karl Polanyi, *The Great Transformation: The Political and Economic Origins of Our Time* (Boston, Beacon Press, 1957).
15. Marcel Mauss, *The Gift: Forms and Functions of Exchange in Archaic Societies* (New York: Norton, 1967).
16. Thorstein Veblen, 'Salesmanship and the Church', *The Portable Veblen*, Max Lerner, ed. (New York: Viking Press, 1948), pp. 499–506.
17. J.E. Lovelock, *Gaia: A New Look at Life on Earth* (Oxford: Oxford University Press, 1979).
18. Simon Winchester, *Krakatoa: The Day the World Exploded, August 27, 1883* (New York: HarperCollins, 2003).
19. William L. Thomas Jr, *Man's Role in Changing the Face of the Earth* (Chicago: University of Chicago Press, 1956).
20. Pablo Neruda recounts how, when he was a Chilean Senator in the 1940s for the nitrate-producing areas, his constituents asked him to use his influence to assure that shipments of tea reached them regularly. Pablo Neruda, *Confieso que he vivido: memorias* (Barcelona: Editorial Seix Barral, 1974), p. 240.

21. Arthur Koestler, *The Ghost in the Machine* (New York: Macmillan, 1968).
22. Watt Stewart, *Chinese Bondage in Peru* (Durham: Duke University Press, 1971).
23. Daniel J. Boorstin, *The Discoverers* (New York: Random House, 1983), pp. 26–78. Clark Blaise, *Lord of Time* (Toronto: Knopf Canada, 2000).
24. Richard J. Barnet and Ronald E. Müller, *Global Reach: The Power of the Multinational Corporations* (New York: Simon and Schuster, 1974).
25. Thornton Wilder, *The Skin of our Teeth: A Play in Three Acts* (New York: Harper, 1942).
26. William H. Calvin raises the possibility that global warming, rather than being a continuing unidirectional process, may soon lead us to a switch point, which will reverse our course and take us within decades, not centuries, to a new ice age. William H. Calvin, 'The Great Climate Flip-Flop'', *The Atlantic Monthly*, 281 (Jan. 1998), pp. 47–64.
27. Nevil Shute, *On the Beach* (New York: W. Morrow, 1957).
28. Nicholas Sanchez-Albornoz, *The Population of Latin America: A History*, Translated by W.A.R. Richardson (Berkeley: University of California Press, 1974).
29. Harvey Cox, 'The Market As God', *The Atlantic Monthly*, 283 (Mar. 1999), http://www.theatlantic.com/issues/99mar/marketgod.htm.
30. Thorstein Veblen, *Imperial Germany and the Industrial Revolution* (London: Macmillan, 1915).
31. Thorstein Veblen, *The Theory of Business Enterprise* (New York: Scribner's, 1904).
32. Jack Beatty, 'Who Speaks for the Middle Class?', *The Atlantic Monthly* 273 (May 1994), p. 66.
33. Ibid., p. 78.
34. 'This search for the methods of a world pax is essentially an intellectual matter, a psychological problem; it is an attempt to save mankind from the insane obsessions of patriotism; it is a race of education to avert another and greater catastrophe.' H.G. Wells, *The Work, Wealth and Happiness of Mankind* (London: William Heinemann, 1932), p. 650.
35. William Ladd, *An Essay on a Congress of Nations for the Adjustment of International Disputes Without Resort to Arms, 1840* (New York: Oxford University Press, 1916). James Lorimer 'Book V. The Ultimate Problem of International Jurisprudence', *The Institutes of the Law of Nations: A Treatise of the Jural Relations of Separate Political Communities*, II (London: William Blackwood and Sons, 1884).
36. Leonard Woolf, *International Government; Two Reports Prepared for the Fabian Research Department, with an Introduction by Bernard Shaw* (London: Allen, 1916) and John Hobson, *Towards International Government* (New York: Macmillan, 1915).
37. John Williamson, 'Democracy and the "Washington Consensus"', *World Development*, 21 (Aug. 1993), pp. 1329–36.
38. E.B. White, *The Wild Flag: Editorials from The New Yorker on Federal World Government and Other Matters* (Boston: Houghton Mifflin, 1946), pp. 20–23.
39. Jane Jacobs, *The Question of Separatism: Quebec and the Struggle over Sovereignty* (New York: Random House, 1980).
40. Matthew Arnold, *Mixed Essays* (London: Murray, 1903), p. 62.

41. Humberto Maturana, *La democracia es una obra de arte* (Bogotá: Cooperativa Editorial Magisterio,1995), pp. 13–14.
42. The exact quote is 'Do not listen to those who say you want this rather than that... You always want both.' Joan Robinson, *Economic Philosophy* (Harmondsworth: Penguin, 1964), p. 116.
43. 'All fixed, fast-frozen relations with their train of ancient and venerable prejudices and opinions are swept away... All that is solid melts into the air...' Karl Marx and Friedrich Engels, *The Manifesto of the Communist Party* (1848), http://csf.colorado.edu/psn/marx/Archive/1848-CM/.

2
Steering and Scale Change

> A map of the world that does not include Utopia is not worth even glancing at, for it leaves out the one country at which Humanity is always landing. And when Humanity lands there, it looks out, and, seeing a better country, sets sail. Progress is the realisation of Utopias.
>
> —Oscar Wilde, 'The Soul of Man under Socialism'

> There is no longer a clear division between what is foreign and what is domestic—the world economy, the world environment, the world AIDS crisis, the world arms race—they affect us all.
>
> —Bill Clinton, 'First Inaugural Address'

Learning has been central to the human experience: learning from errors, successes, others (both near and distant), and the records (in whatever form). The applications gained from systematic observation, science, have been key to the human experience. No people could have survived without such observations forming the basis for individual and group practices. Imitating, reacting, adapting, and combining have been at the heart of the contact between cultures from the very earliest times. Nonetheless, who may learn and what may be learned is commonly subject to societal controls shaped by community goals. When stability is held to be a higher value than change, unfettered curiosity-driven inquiry is regarded as a threat and certain lines of critical scrutiny are discouraged.

Our daily lives are guided and limited by rules, both written and unwritten, by habit, tradition, and custom. Folkways and mores condition our lives and allow us to proceed through our activities with relative security and predictability. These rules become a part of us in many ways. Among them there may also be an extensive array of catchphrases, embodying folk wisdom, that were invoked repeatedly as powerful conditioning devices during child-rearing. Internalized patterns may be complemented by explicit signs (no parking, one way, buckle up, exact change only, stand behind the yellow line) posted along our trajectory to either inform or reinforce. Each social unit from the small (individual, couple, family, association) to the large (nation) has its complex set of interrelated system maintenance 'rules.' To be effective in imposing a modicum of order on social relations, rules need to be long-lived. These institutional guideposts, which help stabilize a society, tend to change in response to changed circumstances. That they do alter with a considerable lag makes them effective in minimizing societal turbulence in the face of ephemeral events and fads.

Rules, however, can outlive their usefulness. Too much ballast can prevent us from setting sail to reach new accommodations. We live today in such a period of rapid transition, guided still by many rules grounded in understandings appropriate to earlier times. Many system maintenance rules were developed in the era of nation-building; others have longer roots, no doubt even extending back to antiquity. The underlying perceived national interest of many of our guiding principles are presently steering the world on a perilously unsustainable course, which serves neither the national parts nor the global whole. In this chapter, I examine prior instances of scale change for the insights they offer as we try to shape a peaceful future for ourselves. I argue, among other things, that the generalization and strengthening of democratic structures, principles, and practices may be our best insurance against the possibility of war, whether local or global.

Steering is not an issue at times when established mechanisms, whatever their nature, are perceived to be performing acceptably in guiding a society. One may be scarcely conscious of the rules implicit in our daily behavior patterns. If we do not perceive limits to what we wish to do, then the match between the rules, our social conditioning, and the environment may be ideal for us. Changes in that perception may arise as a result of contact with other societies because of technological changes that alter the parameters within which a society functions or a new idea about the realm of the possible taking hold in a society. Or more simply, change can simply be a generational matter, with the young embracing new possibilities inconsistent with established practice.

At one point in its history, a society may endure stoically an infant mortality rate of 250 per 1000, while at some later moment massive efforts may be directed to reduce the rate from 25 to 15 per 1000 within a relatively short-time horizon. Where there is no knowledge of alternative courses of action, resignation may be an appropriate response. When a society is aware of the possibility, even the ease, of change, passivity is no longer a tolerable attitude.

Steering can be of various sorts. Top-down steering has been a common form: an easy option, but one that pays little attention to process and favors outcome. Process may be seen as threatening because of its disorderly, unpredictable nature and its often leisurely pace.[1] The shaping of a workable relation between top-down and bottom-up decisional processes is a never-ending process. With changing technology and social organizations, what made sense yesterday no longer makes sense today. Markets, democracy, and distinct social orders are sets of steering frameworks, but the content of each and the interplay between them is subject to a myriad of variations. As the scale of human activity is now palpably global, yesterday's arrangements, many of which are still rooted in local autonomy and defense against outsiders with their supporting symbolisms and mythologies, are no longer suited for our increasingly interconnected world.

We currently are experiencing multiple mismatches. The cumulative daily changes in the technology and institutions that condition our existence reflect actions which have global impact not matched by competent institutions at levels above that of the nation-state. International cooperation has come a long way, but it is not yet equal to the ever larger tasks at hand.

Interested steering: persistence of paradigms

Free inquiry can be a destabilizing influence, hence there may be good reason to create taboos against knowing, building walls which direct inquiry into accepted channels. The intent may be to foster the work of a scientific 'discipline' which endeavors to fit its practitioners from the acolyte stage with blinders. Although Thomas Kuhn's classic book *The Structure of Scientific Revolutions* deals at length with revolution, it celebrates normal science as the condition of scientific progress. Normal science, focused as it is on problem-solving, precisely requires that practitioners adhere to a particular viewpoint.[2] In the words of Thorstein Veblen, it 'visibly furthers the accredited work which the science has at hand.'[3] Good sense is often not a match for obstinacy as we learned from Kuhn: an impeccable and even devastating critique of an entrenched paradigm or a hegemonic discourse is rarely sufficient to dislodge it. Indeed, as in Kuhn's retelling of an experiment with a playing card bearing the wrong color, some never perceive the mismatch between expectations and reality.[4] In effect, believing is seeing, rather than the contrary.

Limits to free inquiry may be intended to protect the identity of the peoples of a country, a religion, or an ethnic group. Rules which had one purpose may grow in importance, well beyond their original intent and become badges that identify the group members. This badge is a system maintenance device to build solidarity of the group and indeed may provoke the wrath of outsiders, which then strengthens group solidarity.

Economics was born in the early days of the industrial revolution. Mechanical breakthroughs overwhelmed society and the mechanical analogy took root in economics. That analogy was so powerful that a focus on evolutionary processes was ignored by most economists for almost one century. Alfred Marshall in his *Principles of Economics* urged economists to turn to biology for inspiration and insisted that he had said the final word on economic mechanics and that the 'Mecca of the economist lies in economic biology rather than in economic dynamics.'[5]

Marshall's plea fell on deaf ears as his followers embraced the mechanical approach. Evolution was, at best, on the fringes of the economics discipline. Veblen, a contemporary of Marshall, had already asked in 1898, 'Why Is Economics Not an Evolutionary Science?' Evolution is by no means the only scientific paradigm that has come to prominence since the middle of the 19th century. Each had many promising perspectives to offer to economics. Some found their way into the canon, but, remarkably, in the last quarter of the 20th century the neoclassical market model, the roots of which are in the late 19th century, has had an unprecedented resurgence and took a firm grip on the general orientation of policy in many countries.

Consider the limitations of the basic elements of economics for dealing with the global economy. Countries are the unit of analysis and more often than not the approach is conditioned by the closed economy model, that is, an economy with no foreign transactions. To illustrate this point it is sufficient to observe that it was only in 1980 that Rudiger Dornbusch felt it appropriate to entitle a treatise *Open Economy Macroeconomics* to communicate that a nation's economic links with the rest of the world were to be integrated into the analysis from the outset.[6] Until that time textbooks had simply tucked away the influence of foreign trade and payments in the last two chapters as a special case, a deviation from the self-sufficient closed national economy.

If the closed economy model is relevant at all, it is at the level of the world. Even then, the approach is flawed insofar as our principal energy source is, in fact, sunlight. The model reflects not an approximation to reality, but rather the fact that economics ceased to be a science when it closed itself to developments in other realms of scientific discourse. Even more fundamentally, the essential theoretical model ignores the physical environment. There are neoclassical agricultural production functions, for example, that take no account of temperature, rainfall, and sunlight. There are firms that produce goods without using raw materials and without generating wastes. The central proposition in the basic theory of the firm still has only homogeneous labor and capital (machinery) as the necessary and sufficient elements. Remarkably, for one century, students of microeconomics have devoted their energies to mastering models of a firm's production choices in which the use of two productive factors is be optimized and have largely failed to notice that products materialize without any reference to raw materials being used.

The economists are no more to blame than any other blinkered set of professionals. In understanding our predicament, one must not underestimate the extent to which the steering process is corrupted by those who seek gain through obfuscation. Patricia Marchak details the substantial funding provided by large corporations to establish neoliberal think-tanks, to fund professors, to 'educate' students, teachers, politicians, journalists, and ultimately the public into the merits of free markets.[7] She describes how evermore sophisticated marketing techniques are used in creating public opinion. Sophistry run rampant has taken national and global steering well off course. This single-minded project has been most skillful in twisting information to particular ends and in shaping the direction of inquiry. Others who have commented in detail about the self-interested misshaping of societal values include Edward S. Herman, Noam Chomsky, and Robert W. McChesney.[8] David Korten in particular points to the creation by corporations of non-governmental organizations (NGOs) with seductively 'right-sounding' names, so that one has difficulty in distinguishing who is, say, the real friend of the forest and who is the clear-cutter.[9]

Among the willing instruments of this elaborate campaign have been economists, blinded to their own maxim that there is no free lunch. Each paid lunch and each paid trip brings substantial dividends to their benefactors. Economists, who have been trained to see markets as the path to be privileged, are delighted to be in such hale company which asks little more of them than that they continue to look through market-tinted lenses. If trained incapacity blinds one to the limitations of one's rhetoric, one can hardly be accused of lacking intellectual integrity, can one? If the market paradigm has so many friends, who are either moneyed and/or in high places, what incentive is there to challenge a venerable worldview which one has labored long to internalize?

Deirdre N. McCloskey has been one of those engaged in the battle, to little avail, to arouse economists to their rhetorical tricks, going so far as to question their integrity.[10] There is, as well, an Association of Heterodox Economics[11] and a movement that began in France in the late 1990s to create a Post-Autistic Economics.[12] Nonetheless, we find the sophistry continues. Economists go from elaborate, but restrictive ahistorical, timeless models to suggest that the resulting analyses provide highly reliable guides to a national policy of free trade, free capital flows, reduction in the role of the state, and flexible labor markets. In doing so they either simply suggest that the model and reality match well or they invoke popular mythology—they invoke the superstitions of the ancestors to convince the unwary. The familiar ring of the underlying analogies when combined with hourly repetition on the radio and television news are highly effective in shaping and setting limits to the discourse of most concerned observers, even those who stand in opposition. Milton Friedman's suggestion that the experience of the tiny politically dependent city-state of Hong Kong can serve as a reasonable model for the rest of the world to adopt free trade[13] is by no means the most extreme example. The instances can be multiplied.

One of the remarkable transgressions that economists commit relates to their violation of one of the basic tenets of their discipline: that one cannot make interpersonal comparisons of utility. This is an idea, together with the notion of scarcity, that all those who have ever studied economics probably learned in their very first week of class. Once the disclaimers are made, the caveat is cast aside and one plunges headlong into the world of interpersonal comparisons, which lie at the heart of both national income accounting, used as a key referent for growth and economic well-being, and cost–benefit analysis, an analytical technique which is central to evaluation of major public investments. For a limited set of individual or corporate decisions with little bearing on outsiders, a cost–benefit comparison may be a useful analytical device. It is, for example, a reasonable way to compare the choice between buying and renting a vehicle. For projects where there are distinct groups of gainers and losers and outcomes without market value, this requires the practitioner to treat the tally of the estimated monetary projections of all future gains and losses as commensurable and equally reliable. The analyst's projection that my likely loss of nine dollars is more than offset by the corresponding estimate of your ten dollars of gain is all there is to the matter, unless the losers are offered some compensation. Here we clearly enter the realm of pseudo-science as subterfuge, of political decisions masquerading as objective analysis.

As economists colonized our everyday language, many words lost their common sense connotations and have taken on the unique technical meanings that economists assign to them. Reality does not exist independent of the observer. One set of observers is now trying to convince us that their technical reality is equivalent to what we should also be observing. To put it another way, some economists have convinced themselves of a perfect congruence between their abstract models of the world and the world itself in all its complexity. The word 'real,' for example, is used by economists to refer to a monetary or price measure that has been adjusted for price changes. To call it real is a fiction: few of us are likely to consume the average basket of goods (either in the composition or the proportions) that is used as the basis for the calculation.

'Free' markets: persistence of myth

Markets are a powerful anarchic device for interchange. Markets offer an array of benefits that are often underestimated, but we also can be led (and are) at our peril to overestimate benefits of markets as they operate in the real world. The Canadian economic historian Harold Innis spoke of the penetrative powers of the market (which he preferred to speak of as the 'price system').[14] These penetrative powers have expanded over time with the increase in scale of enterprises. Those market powers have had different implications in different epochs. The scale of those impacts is now global and the pace of the spread is vertiginous. For critics of globalization from above, 'markets' have come to have a bad name, as they are invoked to describe in benign non-controversial language as a 'market economy' a system characterized by vast imbalances of economic and political power which bears no relation to the Panglossian textbook world of perfect competition between atomistic economic agents. In the world in which we live, it is wholly appropriate to speak, as *Le Monde Diplomatique* does, of 'les Maîtres du Monde' and of the urgent task of belling the cat of corporate control. Let us not be misled by those bent on misrepresenting situations of concentrated economic power with the circumstances of the small and medium producers who must rely on their ingenuity rather than a steady stream of cost-plus contracts.

Markets always exist within a social setting and as such are governed to the extent that it is possible for sovereign authorities to control markets. Karl Marx also recognized subversive powers of markets in their free-trade embodiment as a mixed blessing, impoverishing the poor, but undermining the established order as well. As Marx observed:

> the protective system of our day is conservative, while the free trade system is destructive. It breaks up the old nationalities and pushes the antagonism of the proletariat and the bourgeoisie to the extreme point. In a word, the free trade system hastens the social revolution.[15]

For all its blessings, an unfettered market was likely to be a curse, as Karl Polanyi observed in *The Great Transformation* in 1944:

> a self-adjusting market . . . could not exist for any length of time without annihilating the human and natural substance of society; it would have physically destroyed man and transformed his surroundings into a wilderness.[16]

The shifting role of state and market is a recurrent theme in human affairs. At times governing powers search for a balance between these two ideal types. At other times, one alternative or the other is seen to represent a utopian solution to human ills. Polanyi provided a historical chronicle of this changing balance. Today we are in the midst of witnessing a process that Polanyi described as follows: 'A nation may be handicapped in its struggle for survival by the fact that its institutions, or some of them, belong to a type that happens to be on the down grade . . .'[17] He spoke of 'groups [which] are pushing that which is falling . . . and may even be perverting the trend to make it serve their aims.'[18] Many of the measures taken by societies to protect themselves have been and continue to be swept aside. Once again the possibility of annihilation of the 'human and natural substance of society' confronts us.

In the continuously transforming world in which we live today, the solutions implemented in an earlier age no longer seem viable. Our societal defenses are being singled out as being in opposition to our economic competitiveness. Polanyi spoke of 19th-century society as being constricted by economics[19] and referred to 'the pernicious nineteenth century dogma of the necessary uniformity of domestic regimes within the orbit of world economy.'[20] It would appear that we returned to the situation of uniform prescriptions at the end of the 20th century. The gold standard may have vanished, but we remain with the 'necessity' to deflate prices, devalue the currency, and despoil the social sector in the often-vain hope of being able to compete in a world where between low-cost mass production, the dismantling of most anti-trust enforcement, and the attendant ascendancy of merger and acquisition activity, many industries have come to be dominated by a few large firms.

As complexity increases, simple steering techniques no longer are equal to the task at hand. The answer is neither only the market nor only the state. The Hungarian planner and mathematical economist Janos Kornai already remarked in 1970 on the near impossibility of detailed central economic planning in a context where the prices and quantities of thousands of products enter into play.[21] Political and economic Brownian motion from which pattern emerges out of chaos may appear to be an efficient and necessary approach, but it is hardly sufficient. 'Uncontrolled' markets are not our salvation. Arguments for eliminating regulation by government, which in principle is in the public interest, are often a smoke screen for the establishment of concentrated private control. Individuals are not particles, but rather active participants in multiple, often non-overlapping, social settings. Complementing disorder with regulation and public action to limit and correct imbalances through mechanisms of adjustment would appear to offer the opportunity for greatest long-term stability.

The Bretton Woods institutions and the General Agreement on Tariffs and Trade (GATT) were established to assure the growth of free trade, the restoration of which was a prime concern of the Americans who had the dominant hand in shaping the post-war institutions. American hegemony was expressed in the underlying open borders agenda of these institutions, which played a critical role in transforming the post-war world by relentlessly reducing barriers to trade and payments. As the world economy has changed over the last half century, these institutions have altered their steering to give increased importance first to foreign direct investment and subsequently to free financial flows, neither of which were part of the original Bretton Woods design. The shocks associated with the resulting permeability of borders to goods and societal values can be seen as being at the heart of the globalization debate. While both the Bank and the Fund are beholden to the US for a portion of their finances, they too have become increasingly accountable to private financial markets. He who pays the piper calls the tune to which the Fund, the Bank, and all of us, for that matter, are dancing, and not very joyfully.[22]

The adverse effects of continuous global market expansion may finally be tipping the balance away from movements supportive of the prevalent trend and in favor of effective counter-movements that check the 'expansion in definite directions'[23] that Polanyi spoke about in his discussion on the 'Self-Protection of Society.' A constructive counter-movement must have on its agenda for serious early consideration the building of democratic institutions at the world level as well as building and strengthening systems at lower levels.

Competitiveness

Consistent with the Westphalian focus, all—industrial, developing, and transitional countries—are committed to the pursuit of national competitiveness. Some countries have come on board of their own volition; others have had to be coaxed. Although the ubiquity of 'competitiveness' is relatively recent, the notion is akin to that which guided 17th- and 18th-century mercantilist thought. The implications for the common person are little different today from what they were when Thomas Mun provided a list of appropriate policies for national dominance in the early 17th century.[24] The people were to be frugal in their food and clothing lest they reduce the exportable surplus and were certainly supposed to avoid the unnecessary consumption of imports. Edgar S. Furniss spelled out very forcefully in his *The Position of the Laborer in a System of Nationalism* (1920) what national strength meant for the common person in 18th-century England. His chapter on 'The Doctrine of the Utility of Poverty,' contains the following passage from a volume written in 1771 by Arthur Young:

> Every one but an idiot knows that the lower classes must be kept poor or they will never be industrious; I do not mean, that the poor of England are to be kept like the poor of France, but the state of the country considered, they must (like all mankind) be in poverty or they will not work.[25]

Today the language is slightly different. The key phrase is 'flexible labor markets.' The association of such flexibility with poverty and unemployment tends to be swept under the rug, as markets are supposed to be self-equilibrating.

Paul Krugman described competitiveness as a dangerous obsession, which distorts policy on a wide range of issues, many with little direct bearing on international trade.[26] As Krugman put it:

> if an economic doctrine is flatly, completely and demonstrably wrong, the insistence that discussion adhere to that doctrine inevitably blurs the focus and diminishes the quality of policy discussion across a broad range of issues.[27]

It is wrong, in part, because a nation is not a corporation with a clearly identifiable bottom line. A nation is as much a psychological construct as it is a legal once. A more general criticism of why such an approach is wrong is that made by Ursula Franklin in her description of what she calls the production model:

> Production models are perceived and constructed without links into a larger context. This allows the use of a particular model in a variety of situations. At the same time such an approach discounts and disregards all effects arising from the impact of the production activity on its surroundings. Such *externalities* are considered irrelevant to the activity itself and are therefore the business of someone else... production models now become almost the only pattern of guidance for public and private thought and action.[28]

Of course, the fact that an approach is demonstrably wrong may not be evident to many observers. And those who raise their voices in opposition may at best succeed in doing little more than preaching to the convinced. In an environment hostile to dissent, however, untoward consequences may ensue.

As Krugman observed, policies aimed at national competitiveness are essentially confrontational, an unsuitable approach to the conduct of affairs in a rapidly globalizing society. The focus on competitiveness carries with it a we–they approach to the world. In times of economic strife, 'they'—the adversaries—are the ones who are robbing our jobs. 'They' are not only foreign countries, but also minorities or even majorities (women, to identify an obvious majority) in our midst. Violence toward the 'other' is not uncommon in circumstances in which jobs disappear and real incomes shrink. The doctrine of national competitiveness may manifest itself in either a free market format—an even more dangerous obsession in its pure, unmitigated form—or an industrial policy format or an admixture of the two: subsidies to capital and flexible markets for labor.

In the early 1960s Albert O. Hirschman identified balance-of-payments difficulties as being the privileged problem for policy-makers in the Third World.[29] Today, the external balance seems to be the privileged problem throughout the world. Every country seems to be striving to run a trade surplus, a balance of payments surplus or both. Clearly, though, not every country can be a net earner of foreign exchange. Is the universal quest for a payments surplus not at the heart of many of our problems in today's world of increasingly integrated global markets with largely uncoordinated national decision-making? Does this not pose a greater danger today than it did during the Great Depression of the 1930s? And are not some of the same destructive manifestations becoming visible?

Where does the 'development' of the southern countries fit into this framework? As competitiveness and the downsizing of the public sector is the name of the game in both the north and the south, most governments are today bent on policies which are intended to permit them to pay their own way internationally. Indeed they have no choice but to do so. As simultaneous payments surpluses in all countries are a logical impossibility, many must of necessity fail and those who 'win' do so at a cost. But nations do not 'win'—some people within them win and some lose. To speak of a nation winning requires, as previously discussed, that the nature of distributional gains and losses be swept under the rug. And even the monetary gainers may perceive that their personal security has diminished. In reality, gainers who perceive such threats may clamor for the state to take a hard line against those who dissent about the outcome of the process. National strategies in an integrated world tend to generate an excess of monetary losers over winners in both the winning and the losing countries. The temper of the moment is one in which the few winners are neither disposed to share with the community, be it local, national, or global, nor are compelled to do so to any appreciable extent.

Unable as we seem to be to shift the focus of our analyses, we either persist in using models that are 'completely and demonstrably wrong' (to use Krugman's words again) or we offer ad hoc counsel at variance with both the theory and what we should have learned from historical experience, had we paused long enough to consider the historical record.[30] The counsel we offer to the South is a variation of that which we inflict on ourselves: the state is to be downsized, markets are to be freed, including the import market, and labor markets are to be made flexible.

As a graduate student in the 1960s, I never once imagined that Keynesianism, both baby and bath water, would be unceremoniously thrown out, yet that is what has happened. Progressive taxation has been severely comprised, social safety nets are shrinking, and in a reversal of what Karl Polanyi saw as desirable, society (or what is left of it) has come to be *embedded* in the economy.[31] Henry J. Aaron offered the following comment on today's economic-policy advisors:

> The stubborn unwillingness of so much behavior to fit our models leads to the wry characterization of economists as people who, upon

discovering that reality and theory conflict, conclude that the evidence is mixed.[32]

The committed free marketeer would confidently predict that reality will continue to give ground. And indeed reality is being reshaped.

The small country case

When economists speak about the small country case, which they do with increasing frequency these days, they have in mind a country, which like an individual, cannot influence the terms and conditions of market transaction engaged in. The small country has little, if any, ability to influence the price it pays for its imports, the price it receives for it exports, the average remuneration of its different categories of workers, nor the rate of interest in world markets. Many northern countries for which this category was irrelevant in the 1950s are surprised to discover that they now find themselves in the same boat as, say, El Salvador or Malawi.

The small country case with respect to policy-making is increasingly the rule. When countries break up into smaller units, without the benefit of regional groupings, they are even more at the mercy of larger market forces and have even less economic sovereignty. Moreover, to the extent that boundaries are redrawn along ethnic lines, a prescription for intolerance comes with it. If the intent was to protect jobs and jobs continue to disappear and the tax base continues to shrink, then necessary trade-offs may increasingly pit one group against another. Sovereignty in this case amounts to the freedom to violate rights and to hide behind the shield of national self-determination. Fingers may be wagged in shame, but as long as a government is in control, the inviolability of borders is likely to be respected as in the case of Russian actions in Chechnya.

The small country, without voice, like the firm in the economist's model of perfect competition has to adjust to a range of global circumstances and pay the adverse consequences which result whether it resists or accommodates. The chief form of economic adjustment in a state-centric world is market liberalization. The need to compete brings a plea for flexible labor markets and with it the erasing of institutional arrangements forged by societies over generations, leaving little protection in their place. The exit option is open for skilled individuals, while those unable or unwilling to migrate see their economic position erode. With it has come the slow disappearance of the middle class.

As noted above, Karl Marx spoke of the power of free trade to destroy parochialism and local despotism. The sway of local interests cannot withstand the pressures of the open access associated with the process of globalization. While we can applaud the disappearance of arbitrary action, we are not likely to be as sanguine if diversity vanishes as well. Yet others maintain, such as Samuel Huntingdon in his clash of civilizations hypothesis, that it is still reasonable to continue speaking about distinct human civilizations in more than a vestigial or symbolic sense.[33] Our proclamation of the uniqueness of our 'civilization' poses no particular threat to our neighbor as long as it is no more than a ceremonial manifestation. As our differences are human creations, they are equally amenable to being reinforced (our first inculcated response) or eroded. Even when sharp lines are drawn they are unlikely to keep some from fraternizing and eventually marrying across 'civilizational' lines, anymore than taboos in the recent past have prevented marriage across lines of class, color, ethnicity, or religion.

One response to the downsizing of national governments has been the search for the protection of local authorities, which, at least in principle, are expected to be more responsive than distant centers of political powers. This may, however, be an exercise in self-delusion. Appreciating the true nature of our circumstances may be essential to altering our collective destiny. Local governments are even less likely to have adequate tax revenues to draw on than national governments. Our only effective defense may be the construction of a global 'umbrella' if we wish to save what we truly hold dear locally.

From principalities to nations

By the middle of the 17th century, the redefinition of power relations in Europe led to the creation of an essentially self-assertive backward looking set of guidelines: the Westphalian System. This framework embodied in the Peace of Westphalia (1648) asserts the sovereign equality of states and the right of each state to manage its internal affairs. The creation of the Westphalian System can be seen as an act of resistance by hundreds of European principalities to the growing power of the Hapsburgs. The Westphalian self-assertion was like a finger in the dike to hold back the tides of scale change. Most of the realms that sought protection under the Westphalian System have long since vanished. Yet the world is still in the thrall of a system of nation-states, a system that pre-dates the industrial revolution. Many of today's states were not formed until later and new states, pretending to sovereign equality, are still being added to the list. The state-system predates the steamship, the automobile, the airplane, telephone and telegraph, radio, television, computers, and the internet. It has with some adaptation accommodated these changes. It is doubtful, however, that it can weather the changes that have already been sparked by the electronic revolution. The information age represent a major challenge to the state system and its outmoded operational conventions.

History may not be a reliable guide to what lies ahead, but it is nonetheless instructive in drawing our attention to lessons that may be inherent in past transitions. I will limit myself here to looking at the formation of the Zollverein, the early experience of the Thirteen North American Colonies following their break with England and the experience of the EU. The upward shift in the locus of government may carry with it the threat of loss of identity, loss of language, loss of privilege and power, and loss of 'sovereignty.' When the upward shift is voluntary, it is a response to a series of changes which suggest to those participating that the losses resulting from the shift are likely to be offset by gains or at a minimum may be necessary to defend the units in question from external threat.

One explanation of scale change is offered by Douglass C. North and Robert Paul Thomas who see the period following the European encounter with the Americas as one of substantial market expansion in Europe—a commercial revolution that preceded the Industrial Revolution. For them the growing market was a key element which led to the emergence of territorial-states:

> Existing political administrative units were increasingly inadequate to meet the needs of expanding trade which required a wider scope of fiscal policies, policing protection, and information; consequently, larger political units grew up or consolidated to keep pace with the growing market size.[34]

From the Articles of Confederation to the Constitution

In the early years of American independence, the Confederation Congress had no power to tax, but rather resorted to imposing requisitions on the states. As the states only contributed one-quarter of the levied sums between 1783 and 1789—providing but a fraction of the amount required to meet the interest due on the central government's debt—the US began its existence with a debt crisis. Repeated requests from the Congress in 1781, 1783, and 1785 to be allowed to impose a uniform five-percent tariff on imports failed for lack of unanimous consent by the states.[35] As Samuel Eliot Morison relates, 'Congress was given all the powers connected with war and peace, except the important one of taxation to support a war.'[36] The only taxing power the federal government had was to charge postage. The clearly apparent limits on the abilities of the US central authority led the British to ask whether John Adams, America's first ambassador to London, represented one nation or thirteen.[37]

Morison relates that John Adams, Thomas Jefferson, and James Wilson had tried, without success, to suggest a federal constitution for the British Empire. With the coming of American independence, all the old problems of distribution of sovereign powers were transferred to the states.[38] The difficulties that arose during the years of the Articles of Confederation shifted the balance of opinion in favor of the migration of functions to the central government. Morison refers to the Constitution of 1787 as having set up a 'sovereign union of sovereign states,'[39] but the sovereignty of the states under the Constitution was markedly redefined from what it had been under the Articles of Confederation. Gone were the separate import duties that the states had so jealously maintained; gone as well was their ability to coin money and issue bills of credit.[40] The central authority now had at its disposition 'own resources' previously denied it: the right to collect taxes, duties, and excises. If the 13 Colonies had obstinately dug in their heels and prevented the granting of substantial revenue-raising power to the central government, the US could have been an early example of a failed state.

Nineteenth-century German unification

Let us consider the case of state formation in what is today Germany. There were said to have been more than 1800 customs frontiers in Germany in 1790, levied by more than 300 rulers 'virtually unchecked by any central authority.'[41] The creation of a central authority in the form of a German Confederation in 1815 consisting of 39 sovereign states, when viewed from one perspective, changed matters little as its legislature 'had scarcely any executive authority over the constituent states.'[42] Relationships between states and localities changed considerably, however. The initial migration of fiscal authority went from the localities to the individual states and has been judged to have acted as a stimulant to early German industrialization.[43]

An early substantial revenue migration in terms of the geographic area involved was the elimination of internal tariffs and the creation of a unified external tariff realized by Prussia in 1816–17. Alan S. Milward and S.B. Saul describe this transformation in terms of scale shift:

> The previous local Prussian tariffs had acknowledged the reality of commercial life in a state where each town was a separate local market and the countryside around it was subjected to its commercial domination. The new tariff presupposed the dissolution of these many local markets into one national market.[44]

Others were quick to see the merits of the Prussian example. As early as 1819, some 22 years before the publication of his *National System of Political Economy*, Friedrich List was advocating that the German Confederation follow the Prussian example and create a general tariff for all of Germany.[45] Early in the expansion of the Prussian Zollverein to neighboring territories, an important revenue-sharing arrangement was incorporated: revenue was to be divided on the basis of the population of each of the states, rather than on the value or volume of trade crossing its borders.[46]

Europe: from ruins to union

Already during World War II, there were draft plans for European economic cooperation that would bring countries that were still belligerents together in projects of economic cooperation. After the War, the US conditioned its proposed Marshall Plan assistance on coordinated activities of the Europeans. Among those conditions were provisions that drove the USSR, a wartime ally to whom aid had been offered, away from the negotiating table. The example of the advantages reaped by the US in having a unified market where scale economies in production could be realized gave impetus to the movement for economic integration in Europe as did the profound wish to break the succession of periodic wars in the region.

The key architects of the movement that eventually brought European nations into union were Jean Monnet and Robert Schuman. The vision and efforts of these two men were critical in gaining acceptance for the initial steps that paved the way for the Treaty of Rome in 1957 establishing the European Common Market. Another key actor was Jacques Delors who in the 1980s re-energized European integration with his call for completion of the internal market by 1992 and for recommendations for European Monetary Union by the committee that he chaired.

Jurisdictional jealousy works against the ceding of sovereignty to a higher power. Sovereign rights are devolved to subnational level much more readily than they are allowed to move upward. This is well illustrated in the case of the EU, whose budget grew very modestly from 0.80 percent of the Community's Gross Domestic Product (GDP) in 1980 to 1.09 percent in 1988 and is limited to rise to no more than 1.27 percent until at least 2006, in contrast to an estimate in the 1977 MacDougall Report that no less than 5–7 percent would be required for a Community with a monetary union.[47] The Union's 'own resources' are still limited to a share of revenues collected by member states on imports (including agricultural products) and from the Value Added Tax (VAT), as well as a small Gross National Product (GNP)-related levy on members.[48] This was at the heart of a late 1980's budgetary crisis as the decline in revenues associated with a reduction in proceeds from duties and agricultural levies was not fully offset by a growth of VAT revenues.[49] That which is labeled somewhat inappropriately as 'own resources' remains a share of national taxes earmarked for surrender to the EU. To date, the European countries have not experienced a case where any of its members have withheld the surrender of the earmarked share, but it is as much a possibility with earmarked revenues as it is with a membership quota. Europe's first true community tax levied by the European Coal and Steel Community since its creation in 1952 on coal and steel production within the area is still the only such tax.[50]

A major shift in the rules governing a united Europe came with the passage in 1986 of the Single European Act, which moved the European Council from a rule of unanimity to one of majority on most issues. As unanimity continues to be required on fiscal policy,[51] strict limits on the fiscal resources available to the EU remain in force. Although Jean Monnet and Robert Schuman considered an independent fiscal base to be critical to the success of European integration, that part of their vision has yet to be realized. One compromise in exchange for the surrender of the unanimity-veto allows countries 'under special circumstances, to continue applying national provisions after the adoption of new EC rules.'[52] Differential policies and opting-out were not to be the rule in fiscal matters, however. The unified market was to be pursued, but restraints on fiscal offsets to the effects of market operations were not to be loosened. Nonetheless, the European Council has been exploring EU-based revenue sources including profits from the European Central Bank, corporate taxes, and an energy and carbon tax.[53] As of this writing, no breakthrough has yet occurred in this area.

The sovereign pretensions of the individual states receive strong reinforcement from the conviction of mainstream economics today that markets can be counted on to provide appropriate incentives as long as monetary stability is assured. Implicit in this is the adequacy of a national government's 'own resources' combined where necessary with access to credit markets. Conventional analysis assumes away a changed external environment. European nations, in this view, need only manage periodic external shocks and are not confronting fundamental changed circumstances associated with globalization. Bureau and Champsaur,[54] for example, offer a cautionary view regarding expanded central fiscal activities: 'It is not clear why an evolution toward some kind of fiscal federalism of the type in existing federations would be advisable.' They associate 'robust jurisprudence' with the consistent agreement of European governments 'upon an interpretation that limits severely the scope of externalities open to centralized fiscal correction.'[55] For their part, von Hagen and Eichengreen oppose the Maastricht restrictions on excessive national fiscal deficits as being likely to cause national officials to ask for support from the EU, in turn, 'leading to the transfer to Brussels of power to tax and expanding transfers to member states.' The next step in their logical sequence is increased pressure for bailouts, a reduction of Brussels' capacity to resist, followed by excessive borrowing by the EU, ultimately undermining European monetary stability.[56]

One policy shift of major importance centered on the Common External Tariff (CET) and the abolition of internal tariffs. The EU has for many years spoken with one voice in GATT trade negotiations, a change incorporated in Article 113 of the Treaty of Rome. The CET would appear to have necessitated the transfer of sovereignty over tariff and quota bargaining from the national level to that of the Community. In retrospect, this change seems to have been passed over lightly by chroniclers of the EU, yet commercial policy has been a central area of national sovereign control over the management of economies. In this realm the Community has been said to have been far more effective than in areas where policy coordination has been the rule. Why not one voice in international monetary matters? At present the EU participates at Group of Eight (G-8) summits, but more in evidence are the four discordant European national voices which speak there. Why not one voice for the EU within the G-8, the IMF (see Chapter 5) and elsewhere. Support for a single EU voice is currently strongly held by a number of European Commissioners, including its President Romano Prodi and Pascal Lamy, the Trade Commissioner, but no near term change seems likely.

The 1987 report to the European Commission of the group headed by Tommaso Padoa-Schioppa, deputy director general of the Banca d'Italia, was quite emphatic in its call for action by the EU (then European Community [EC]) on income redistribution:

> Overall, it is the Group's judgment that the Community's present initiatives in the allocation branch do indeed need to be balanced by

> policy developments in the stabilization and distribution branches.... Indeed, if no action is taken in these areas, even the *acquis* in other fields would be at stake.[57]

If a long lead time is necessary for us to accept a major organizational departure, then it is certainly not too early to begin speaking in earnest about international income redistribution. A single fiscal authority would not be necessary, but some central redistributive mechanism would be. Differing fiscal regimes would in all likelihood persist, as they do in federal states at present. This is perfectly consistent with the writings on fiscal federalism, a concept which in the EU has been rendered as the principle of sudsidiarit*y*, that is, functions should reside at the lowest level at which they can be efficiently performed.[58]

An impediment to redistribution within the Community, as elsewhere, is the sense of the 'resourceful' that they have to prop up the 'profligate,' without requiring the less prosperous to look to their own failings.[59] This has always been at the heart of objections to welfare policies. Economists have lent support to this kind of argument by their single-minded espousal of market solutions, with an ostrich-like disregard for the role of imbalances in power and influence in shaping outcomes.

Extending the fractal: from local to global

The rebirth of the local is a reflection of neither technology nor organizational shifts, both of which tend to support greater scale, but rather of the spread of education from the elites to the common people and the spread of societal values promoting empowerment and inclusion. The nature of complexity does in fact require multiple responses, among them local ones. One can indeed argue that the capacity for self-government grows with its exercise and that people are reclaiming their own problems, having previously watched as the locus of decisions migrated to higher levels. Complexity requires government structures at higher levels as well. The challenge is to map problems with jurisdictions at an appropriate level for effective actions. This calls for revitalizing existing jurisdictions and creating new ones at the subnational, supranational, and global levels.

Taxation has always been the prerogative of 'sovereign' governments even when their jurisdictions hardly resembled anything approaching integrated markets. To varying extents, it was expenditures by governments, financed by taxes that contributed to the progressive integration of national markets. Today, in contrast, we have the opposite situation:

a highly integrated world market with barely the semblance of an authority (democratic or otherwise) that can be regarded as sovereign. What we do have, instead, are international bodies relying principally on woefully inadequate voluntary contributions. The annual budget of the UN in 1994 amounted to five-one thousandths of one percent of estimated world GDP. If one compares the UN's resources to world population, we find the 1994 (*annual*) budget was equivalent to 23 US cents per capita, an amount insufficient at the time to buy one daily newspaper in most of the world's major cities. Unless one subscribes to the default setting of UN inefficiency that has been established through relentless assault by many (within the US in particular), one might be inclined to marvel at how much has been accomplished with so little resources.

Those who see the plight of the national welfare state as related in part to the growth of what Robert Gilpin calls the 'non-welfare international capitalist world' regard the maintenance of a tolerable global and local social order to require the urgent establishment of global taxation (subject to democratic control).[60] There is no lack of ideas on the topic of global taxation, a topic discussed in Chapter 4: a rich literature on proposals for taxes to finance global government dates back at least to the work of James Lorimer in 1884.[61]

The impediment to the establishment of global taxation is not a technical one, but rather a political one. Mere technical questions are 'simplicity itself.' The challenge is to change political perceptions that have been influenced and limited by carefully nurtured and often long-standing systems of myths and rationalizations. Building support for a migration of appropriate functions of sovereign authority to a global level will not be easy, but it is of critical importance.

The perception of the appropriateness of shifting taxation to a higher level jurisdiction is likely to be more a question of shifting prejudices than of mustering evidence associated directly with the logic of scale change. We have seen functioning tax systems spread territorially over the Roman Empire and be limited in our time to a sovereign micro-state such as St Kitts and Nevis, a UN member with a 1993 population of 42,000 people and an area of 260 square kilometers. Neither in its time would likely have qualified as an optimum policy area. The one functioned by force of arms, the latter by force of the myths associated with the Westphalia state system, which regards states as black boxes having de jure equality, though scarcely de facto equality, no matter what analytical sleight of hand is performed.

At the current moment, neither state action nor the extension of taxation is particularly fashionable. Many, following the urging of the free-market economists, have lost sight of the formerly commonplace notion advanced by Oliver Wendell Homes that taxation is the price we pay for civilization. National governments are devolving responsibilities to lower level units that neither have nor are given the means to finance these activities. The question Lord Kaldor raised 40 years ago about when the developing countries will learn how to tax[62] can now be rephrased to question when the world as a whole will relearn to tax. The eventual substitution of taxation and revenue sources at the global level for voluntarism is a crucial next step in maintaining a fractal geometry characterized by lower levels of government with the ability to finance tasks best suited to their domains.

The examples considered in this chapter highlighted the migration of revenue raising authority to higher levels. The relative revenue needs at different levels are subject to reconsideration as our perceptions of needs alter and as capabilities at different levels develop or wither. Central to fiscal capability is a revenue base of 'own resources': these provide a jurisdiction with the ability to plan in a relatively reliable manner its revenues and expenditures. When competition arises between jurisdictions, either at the same or different levels, migration of activities can erode the tax base, requiring either an increase of rates (causing more migration), an expansion of the tax base, or a petition for transfers as compensation.

Formula funding may or may not provide adequate resources for an institution. It has been inadequate for the UN and even for the IMF and the World Bank, but for different reasons. As is well known in the case of the UN, no powers are available to assure payment. Payment arrears by the USSR and the US have hobbled the institution at different points in its history. In contrast, the IMF has provisions to suspend the rights and privileges of any member in arrears on its payments. The problem confronting the IMF and the World Bank centers on the link between quota expansion and the high majority (low veto) on special issues (such as revision of Articles of Agreement).

Conclusion

Scale shifts in human history relate to the influences of organization and technology, not exclusively one or the other. There have been extensive empires at a time when messages could be transmitted no faster than by horse or relay runners (as in the Inca Empire). Our reconstructions of the past are at best approximate, but one can provide various measures of scale change: the time required to travel a particular distance or to send a message. One can also consider the size of the world's largest urban areas at different times in human history as a measure of our changing ability to manage increasing complexity.

The locus of decision-making is today changing—migrating up and down to levels that either did not previously exist or which were eclipsed during the ascendancy of national governments. No organizational arrangement is final as each has its rigidities and we lurch along in human history battling against the excesses of rigidity at one moment and the excesses of flexibility at another. At best, the solution of the moment is appropriate for the moment, but equally it may be 'appropriate' only to either a past historical or abstract theoretical moment and not the current one.

A couple of generalizable precedents emerge from my brief, select review that relate more to will than to specific revenue-raising design. The stronger the support for jurisdictional level shift, the better the chances for success in terms of ceding either revenue sources or firmly earmarked revenues. The ceding of important revenue sources is likely to require the highest degree of agreement for jurisdictional shift of functions. In today's context where functions are being reassigned to lower levels with great enthusiasm, there is nonetheless a reluctance to cede revenue raising sources. Function and revenue shift to the supranational and global levels is still barely on the agenda. The grip of the Westphalian System's centrality of the nation-state, still impedes the financing of sub- and (especially) supranational governing authorities.

A key obstacle to the successful level shift of sovereign prerogatives is the granting of a veto to one or more members of a union. Protection must exist for minority rights, but to incorporate veto rights into a union's constitution is to convert its original lofty purposes to mere rhetoric. This is to be seen in case after case: in the American Articles of Confederation, in the UN, in the EU, and in the IMF, to cite but a few examples. If there is a perception that external threat is significant enough, a crisis is deep enough, or purpose important enough, the veto provisions may be abridged, opening the may to upward jurisdictional migration of claims to fiscal sources. Alternatively if common purpose is strong enough, even the possibility of the exercise of a veto can be overcome by deliberation in good faith.

We do not lack for ideas on the financing of world government; rather, we lack a compelling collective consciousness of the need both for such a jurisdictional shift and for that shift to be associated with democratic control. Veblen's 'common man' has still not come to recognize that his/her interests are served well neither by national governments beholden to vested interests nor by adding a layer of government that is beholden to a planetary hegemon, rather than to the people.[63] Humanity must gradually and belatedly opt for peace, which is, as E.B. White suggested, the product of political union and responsible government;[64] responsible, I would add in an even-handed way to all of the world's people. That, most of all, cannot be left to chance and requires major effort on our behalf to try to assure that outcome. That is the objective of this book.

Notes

1. Richard Sennett, *The Uses of Disorder: Personal Identity and City Life* (New York: Knopf, 1970). See also Albert O. Hirschman, *The Strategy of Economic Development* (New Haven: Yale University Press, 1958).
2. Thomas S. Kuhn, *The Structure of Scientific Revolutions* (Chicago: University of Chicago Press, 1962).
3. Thorstein Veblen, 'Why Is Economics Not an Evolutionary Science?', *Quarterly Journal of Economics*, 12 (July 1898), p. 395.
4. Kuhn, pp. 62–65.
5. Alfred Marshall, *Principles of Economics: An Introductory Volume*, 8th edn, 1920 (London: Macmillan, 1949), p. xii.
6. Rudiger Dornbusch, *Open Economy Macroeconomics* (New York: Basic Books, 1980).
7. M. Patricia Marchak, *The Integrated Circus: The New Right and the Restructuring of Global Markets* (Montreal: McGill-Queen's Press, 1991).
8. Edward S. Herman and Noam Chomsky, *Manufacturing Consent: The Political Economy of the Mass Media* (New York: Pantheon Books, 1988). See also Robert W. McChesney, *Rich media, Poor Democracy: Communication Politics in Dubious Times* (Urbana: University of Illinois Press, 1999).
9. David Korten, *When Corporations Rule the World*, 2nd edn (San Francisco: Berrett-Koehler Publishers; Bloomfield, Conn.: Kumarian Press, 2001, co-publishers), pp. 144–46.
10. Deirdre N. McCloskey, *The Vices of Economists, the Virtues of the Bourgeoisie* (Amsterdam: Amsterdam University Press, 1996).
11. http://www.hetecon.com/.
12. http://www.paecon.net.
13. Milton Friedman, *Capitalism and Freedom* (Chicago, University of Chicago Press, 1962).
14. Harold Innis, 'The Penetrative Powers of the Price System', *The Canadian Journal of Economics and Political Science*, 4 (1938), pp. 299–319.
15. Karl Marx, 'On the Question of Free Trade' (1848), http:/csf.Colorado.edu/psn/marx/Archive/1848-FT/.
16. Karl Polanyi, *The Great Transformation: The Political and Economic Origins of Our Time*, 1st edn 1944 (Boston: Beacon Press, 1957), p. 3.
17. Ibid., p. 28.
18. Ibid.
19. Ibid., p. 252.

20. Ibid., p. 253.
21. Janos Kornai, *Anti-Equilibrium: On Economic Systems Theory and the Tasks of Research* (Amsterdam: North-Holland Publishing, 1971).
22. See, for example, Jagdish Bhagwati, 'The Capital Myth: the Difference between Trade in Widgets and Dollars', *Foreign Affairs*, 77 (May/June 1998), pp. 7–12. See also Joseph Stiglitz, *Globalization and Its Discontents* (New York: Norton, 2002).
23. Polanyi, p. 130.
24. Thomas Mun, *England's treasure by forraign trade*, 1st edn 1664 (London: Blackwell, 1965).
25. Cited by Edgar S. Furniss, *The Position of the Laborer in a System of Nationalism: A Study in the Labor Theories of the Later English Mercantilists* (New York: Kelley & Millman, 1957), p. 118.
26. Paul Krugman, 'Competitiveness: A Dangerous Obsession', *Foreign Affairs*, 73 (Mar/Apr 1994), pp. 28–44.
27. Ibid., p. 42.
28. Ursula Franklin, *The Real World of Technology* (Toronto: CBC Enterprises, 1990), p. 27. Emphasis in original.
29. Albert O. Hirschman, *Journeys Towards Progress: Studies of Economic Policy-Making in Latin America* (New York: Greenwood Press, 1968).
30. Ha-Joon Chang, 'Kicking Away the Ladder: An Unofficial History of Capitalism, Especially in Britain and the United States', *Challenge*, 45 (Sept. Oct. 2002), pp. 63–97.
31. Karl Polanyi, *The Great Transformation* (Boston: Beacon Press, 1957).
32. Henry J. Aaron, 'Distinguished Lecture on Economics in Government', *Journal of Economic Perspectives*, 8 (Spring 1994), p. 19.
33. Samuel Huntington, 'The Clash of Civilizations?', *Foreign Affairs*, 72 (Summer 1993), pp. 22–49; Eisuke Sakakibara, 'The End of Progressivism: A Search for New Goals', *Foreign Affairs*, 74 (Sept./Oct. 1995), pp. 13–14.
34. Douglass C. North and Robert Paul Thomas, *The Rise of the Western World: A New Economic History* (Cambridge: Cambridge University Press, 1973), p. 12.
35. Louis Hacker, *The Course of American Growth and Development* (New York: John Wiley & Sons, 1970).
36. Samuel Eliot Morison, *The Oxford History of the American People* (New York: Oxford University Press, 1965).
37. Robert Heilbroner and Aaron Singer, *The Economic Transformation of America: 1600 to the Present*, 2nd edn (San Diego: Harcourt Brace Janovitch, 1984), p. 72.
38. Morison, p. 227.
39. Ibid., p. 311.
40. Hacker, p. 54.
41. William O. Henderson, *The Zollverein* (Cambridge: Cambridge University Press, 1939), p. 20.
42. Alan S. Milward and S.B. Saul, *The Economic Development of Continental Europe, 1780–1870* (London: George Allen & Unwin, 1973), p. 371.
43. D.E. Scremmer, 'Taxation and Public Finance: Britain, France, and Germany', in Peter Mathias and Sidney Pollard, eds, *The Cambridge Economic History of Europe. VIII. The Industrial Economies: The Development of Economic and Social Policies* (Cambridge: Cambridge University Press, 1989), p. 483.
44. Milward and Saul, p. 373.

45. Henderson, p. 26.
46. Milward and Saul, p. 374.
47. John Pinder, *European Community: The Building of a Union*, 2nd edn (Oxford: Oxford University Press, 1995), pp. 184–95.
48. Michael Shackleton, *Financing the European Community* (London: Pinter Publishers, 1990), p. 3. See also Timothy Bainbridge, *The Penguin Companion to European Union*, 3rd edn (London: Penguin, 2002), pp. 411–13.
49. Shackleton, pp. 10–11.
50. Ibid., p. 2.
51. Loukas Tsoukalis, *The New European Economy: The Politics and Economics of Integration*, 2nd edn (Oxford: Oxford University Press, 1993), p. 63.
52. Ibid., p. 62.
53. Pinder, p. 184.
54. Dominique Bureau and Paul Champsaur, 'Fiscal Federalism and European Economic Unification', *American Economic Review Papers and Proceedings*, 82 (May 1992), p. 91.
55. Ibid., p. 92.
56. Jurgen von Hagen and Barry Eichengreen, 'Federalism, Fiscal Restraints, and European Monetary Union', *American Economic Review Papers and Proceedings*, 86 (May 1996), p. 137.
57. Ibid., p. 59.
58. Tommaso Padoa-Schioppa, *Efficiency, Stability, and Equity: A Strategy for the Evolution of the European Community* (Oxford: Oxford University Press, 1987), p. 18.
59. William Wallace, 'Conclusions', in Michael Hodges and William Wallace, eds, *Economic Divergence in the European Community* (London: George Allen & Unwin, 1981), p. 214. This is raised in the context of regional development policies and German industry.
60. Robert Gilpin, *The Political Economy of International Relations* (Princeton: Princeton University Press, 1987), pp. 60–64.
61. Myron J. Frankman, 'International Taxation: The Trajectory of an Idea from Lorimer to Brandt', *World Development*, 24 (1996), pp. 807–20.
62. The answer to Kaldor's question is no different today from that which he gave then: 'the advocacy of fiscal reform is not some magic potion that is capable of altering the balance of political power by stealth.... In a successfully functioning democracy the balance of political power is itself a reflection of a continuous social compromise between the conflicting interests of particular groups and classes, which shift automatically in response to varying pressures.' Nicholas Kaldor, 'Will Underdeveloped Countries Learn to Tax?', *Foreign Affairs*, 41 (Jan. 1963), p. 419.
63. Thorstein Veblen, *The Vested Interests and the Common Man* (New York: B.W. Huebsch, 1919), pp. 182–83.
64. E.B.White, *The Wild Flag: Editorials from The New Yorker on Federal World Government and Other Matters* (Boston: Houghton Mifflin, 1946), pp. 33, 41.

3
The Roads not Taken

> Two roads diverged in a wood, and I—
> I took the one less traveled by,
> And that has made all the difference.
>
> —Robert Frost (1916)

The period extending from the Great Depression through the end of World War II was characterized by an earnest and intense search for formulas that would save humanity first from the economic, political, social, and personal shocks associated with the breakdown of markets and subsequently from the destruction and suffering of global war, seen by many to have been a direct consequence of the absence of a smoothly functioning global order during the 1930s. The hope was that with stronger central mechanisms a renewed outbreak of the beggar-thy-neighbor policies of the 1930s could be prevented and ultimately that peace could be preserved. This period produced dozens of blueprints for a more stable, more secure future, few of them particularly democratic. The lack of concern for democratic form should not surprise us given the then widespread prevalence of rigid hierarchical social and political structures, as well as extensive colonial systems subject to distant control over local conditions.

The world emerged from World War II with institutions largely shaped by the US. More radical plans for ordering the world were swept aside. Among the few that are still mentioned periodically are the International Trade Organization (ITO) and John Maynard Keynes' plans for an International Currency Union (ICU). Even Keynes' plan for a Commodity Control Authority to help stabilize the price of primary commodities had been largely forgotten until the opening of archives brought it to light in the 1970s.[1] The 1948 Havana Charter for the ITO was doomed when the US support for it waned and the ICU was a non-starter as the US already had its plans for the IMF, for which it also offered major financial support.

In addition to reviewing some of the proposals that did not materialize, I shall consider some of the less well-known initiatives that I believe to be instructive for us. During this period four major regional blocs were created: the Commonwealth system at the Ottawa conference of 1932 with its discriminatory imperial trade preferences, the German territorial *liebesraum*, the Japanese co-prosperity sphere, and (Western) Hemispheric Defense. The last of these was already well shaped by an officially neutral US even before war was declared in Europe in 1939, a war which the Americans did not formally join until two years later on 7 December 1941. The endeavors directed by Germany, Japan, and the US all contemplated the integration of economic production over substantial geographic areas. In the case of the US, its state-centered intervention was to be only for the duration of hostilities and was achieved by diplomacy, rather than by conquest. These arrangements in the Western Hemisphere which prevailed in crisis circumstances and which were subsequently abandoned, tell us something about what may be accomplished and how what one day is unthinkable to do becomes unthinkable *not* to do in radically altered circumstances.

The objective of examining these past episodes and ideas is to identify elements that appear to fit the evolving circumstances of our world. The road to international cooperation is strewn with the remains of still-promising proposals that were shunted aside and of collaborative efforts that were abandoned when circumstances altered. Among these are regional trade groupings that either simply fell apart or grew only to limited stature. We have also the case of organizations whose usefulness was limited by the non-participation of a major actor, such as the League of Nations, which was unable to secure the support of the US and the ITO which never got beyond the treaty stage, again owing to lack of US support.

In looking for the ingredients of success, one can point, among other things, to enlightened, inspired leadership; patient, sustained advocacy; and the creation of a sense (if not the reality) of participation in shaping the outcome. One can argue that matters are facilitated if the volume of activity to be benefited is substantial and gain is perceived to be mutual. We have here a variation of Adam Smith's 'the division of labor is limited by the extent of the market.'[2] The demand for cooperation and policy coordination is likely to increase as the interdependencies between countries grow. Regional integration between countries sharing a common border but who previously have not traded with one another is not necessarily doomed to failure, but is not likely to elicit the interest generated by integration between countries where the web of transactions (economic and other) is already relatively dense.

Here one needs to inject an optimistic note. In an article titled 'Obstacles to Development: A Classification and a Quasi-Vanishing Act,'[3] Albert O. Hirschman suggested that it is often when all the reasons have been listed as to why some initiative is doomed to fail, that it defies the naysayers and succeeds (which in retrospect then appears to have been inevitable). Perhaps the key ingredient is enough actors who believe in the possibility of change to invest effort in its success.

The Great Depression and World War II spawned considerable reflection on global organization as a means of spreading economic and political security, and social justice. Building the post-war world engaged the imagination of many, including political thinkers, statesmen, and economists. Their views moved well beyond Woodrow Wilson's 'Fourteen Points' which gave pride of place to ethnic divisions.[4] As I give you a sampler of some of these ideas, you might turn your imagination to what might have been the circumstances of the Third World today if social justice had won the day rather than massive support for security forces that effectively deterred both democracy and development, and still represents a threat to free expression.

The following observation in a chapter entitled 'If We Own the Future' by Max Lerner, from which many would still recoil today—over sixty years later, was part of the discourse of the early 1940s:

> The solution is likely to lie...in a pattern of regional economic collaboration within a larger pattern of world economic control, all this...within some framework of world federation. But this too would involve a qualification of sovereignty....But as for the small nations, how can they be conceived of as losing anything by the partial surrender of what they never had fully? It is somewhat reminiscent of the surrender of the individualism of the worker when he receives a Social Security Card....The truth is that the small states, and large as well, will have to surrender part of the *fiction of sovereignty* in order to get more of the reality of free national action.[5]

Sumner Welles, United States Under-Secretary of State from 1937 to 1943, wrote in *The Time for Decision* in 1944: 'No international organization can conceivably survive unless it is supported by the opinion of free men and women throughout the world. That support will not be forthcoming unless the new international organization assures them all of ... liberty—not an overlordship ...'[6] In fact, we see many international organizations surviving because of the support of both powerful nations and private interests. The support of the 'free men and women' has continued for so long because the impact of these partially captive institutions has not been well understood, much as is the case with our own partially captive national governments.

Building a stable future

Hans W. Singer captured the spirit of the times in his reflections on his wartime and early post-war experience: 'Obviously, a partisan of the social welfare state would be attracted by the thought and possibilities of a global welfare state represented by the United Nations in those hopeful first days of naive utopianism.'[7] Building a peaceful, just world required bold new visions and many were forthcoming.

Discussion of global taxation and income redistribution appeared in the wartime writings of Jan Tinbergen and James Meade, both eventual winners of the Nobel Prize in Economics. Meade was one of the early wartime contributors to the discussion. His *The Economic Basis of a Durable Peace,* which appeared in 1940, bears a dedication dated Christmas 1939. In fact, as Meade made clear on the first page of his introduction, he believed that the 'economic basis' depended, in turn, on a political basis: 'Without some form of International Organization no international regulation of economic affairs is possible.'[8] Success of such an enterprise requires that Member States 'restrict their freedom of action in the economic sphere and grant corresponding powers of economic decision to the appropriate organs of the International Organization.'[9] As the International Organization was to have as an objective the promotion of human welfare and raising the standard of living, it would need adequate financing at its disposal, especially if a wide-range of 'non-economic functions were handed over to the International Authority':

> If the functions of the International Authority are at all extensive, it will need a relatively large revenue; and the raising of this revenue, whether it be effected by means of taxation imposed by the International Authority directly or by means of contributions from the governments of the Member States, will involve the question of assessing the burden as between rich and poor states. The raising of such a revenue will give rise immediately to the possibility of

> reducing the inequalities of income as between the various Member States by a system of progressive taxation or state contributions which imposes the largest per capita burden on the Member States with the highest per capita real income.... In addition to the use of progressive taxes or state contributions to the International Authority as a means of reducing such inequalities, the expenditure of its revenue by the International Authority might be used for the same purpose.[10]

In a later work, Meade provided theoretical support for international taxation by explicitly dropping the customary assumption of economists that interpersonal comparisons of well-being cannot be made. Meade demonstrated that it is possible (theoretically) to *maximize* world welfare through the subsidization of loser nations by the gainers from trade intervention. Meade, in keeping with the extreme brevity of the treatise of economic geometry in which this appears, states in the very last clause of the work: 'we should strive ... to arrange for direct *international* transfers of income from those to whom income means little to those to whom income means much.'[11]

Jan Tinbergen spoke in 1945 of the appropriate level for government action, judging that '... curtailment of national sovereignty with regard to economic policy "is required" if a more stable and prosperous social system is to be realized in the world ...'[12] Tinbergen spoke in 1945 about 'a distribution as just as possible among (1) persons and classes, and (2) nations' as being one of the aims of international economic relations.[13] In what might be termed a 'World Peace through World Economy' approach, Tinbergen observed that the aims of 'as few conflicts as possible, both at home and abroad' and 'as much freedom as possible for the parts' would likely be met to the extent that distribution is just and production as large and as stable as possible.[14]

Tinbergen was but one voice among many calling for a global system far more extensive than the Bretton Woods twins that commanded the support of the US. As Tinbergen's work was published after the 1944 Bretton Woods agreement, he clearly perceived the agreement as having only begun the task of global economic management. Tinbergen later suggested that an international 'agency supervising the main features of public finance, with the power to prescribe their inflationary or deflationary gap would seem the minimum which from the purely economic view-point would be desirable.'[15] By 1959 Tinbergen's notion of a supervisory agency had changed to an International Treasury able to either subsidize or terminate subsidies.[16]

C. Wilfred Jenks, who went on to become the director general of the International Labour Office (1970–73), also addressed during the war years the question of the financing of international institutions. In his detailed discussion, Jenks pointed to the significance of financial relationships between federal authorities and the federated units in all the major federations.[17] He observed that most international lawyers have tended not to address the issue, as they regarded financial matters outside their range of expertise. In Jenks' view it was imperative to prevent a recurrence of the relative penury that prevented international organizations during the interwar period from dealing adequately with economic and social problems. First on his list of suggestions requiring attention from politicians and financial experts is the following:

> The possibility of singling out distinctive sources of revenue which it would be practicable to make independent of national control and to assign to world bodies for the financing of their work. In this connection special consideration should be given to the possibility of an international tax upon any profits accruing from the operations of an international bank, international development corporations, international airways, canals and other means of communication, and internationally controlled monopolies administered as world public services.[18]

Jenks was concerned that the sources of revenue yield a sufficient income that would be assured to increase with the passage of time.[19] In 1946 Theodore A. Sumberg made similar observations:

> Economists could locate the most suitable international revenue sources among the items conventionally included in a nation's balance of payments: merchandise trade, the sales of services (shipping, tourist, and others), investment returns, and immigrant remittances.[20]

It is worth noting that both Jenks and Sumberg focused on the taxation of activities which were dependent on the existence of international order. In effect, those who derive the greatest benefit from the international order should reasonably be expected to contribute to its perpetuation and extension. Also distinctive in the approach of Jenks and Sumberg is that their recommendations appear to call for taxes to be levied by a global authority, rather than depending upon payments being made by national governments. This shift in approach confronts us with the continuing stumbling block of national agreement to grant revenue-raising authority to supranational bodies.

The Washington and London drawing boards

US Secretary of State Cordell Hull relates in his memoirs how Germany's invasion of Poland 'revealed the bankruptcy of all existing methods to preserve the peace' and prompted the start of efforts to build a framework for a new international order.[21] The very day (3 September 1939) that Britain and France declared war on Germany, Franklin Roosevelt, in his address to the American people said:

> It seems to me clear, even at the outbreak of this great war, that the influence of America should be consistent in seeking for humanity a final peace which will eliminate, as far as it is possible to do so, the continued use of force between nations.[22]

The guiding vision for the shaping of a post-war order was embodied in the Atlantic Charter of 14 August 1941 signed by Winston Churchill and Franklin Roosevelt, in which they pledged their governments to eight points, four of which are reproduced below:

> Third, they respect the right of all peoples to choose the form of government under which they will live, and they wish to see sovereign rights and self government restored to those who have been forcibly deprived of them;
>
> Fourth, they will endeavor, with due respect for their existing obligations, to further the enjoyment by all States, great or small, victor or vanquished, of access, on equal terms, to the trade and to the raw materials of the world which are needed for their economic prosperity;
>
> Fifth, they desire to bring about the fullest collaboration between all nations in the economic field with the object of securing, for all, improved labor standards, economic advancement and social security;
>
> Sixth, after the final destruction of the Nazi tyranny, they hope to see established a peace which will afford to all nations the means of dwelling in safety within their own boundaries, and which will afford assurance that all the men in all lands may live out their lives in freedom from fear and want.[23]

Planning for the post-war period began early in both Washington and London. By early 1940 both governments had committees in place whose mandate included post-war arrangements. In Britain, this was the Economic Policy Committee of the War Cabinet and in the US, the Advisory Committee on Problems of Foreign Relations. By mid-1940 a British subcommittee was considering the link between wartime surplus commodities to be denied to the enemy and their use in post-war relief arrangements. In February 1940 the US began diplomatic conversations with 47 governments on 'two basic problems connected with the establishment of a sound foundation for a lasting world peace; namely, the establishment of the bases of a sound international economic system, and the limitation and reduction of armaments.'[24] By November 1942, a Washington-based government committee had even begun discussing a post-war Europe with 'reasonably open trade barriers, reasonably open transport, and reasonably open agricultural and other, similar arrangements.'[25]

The first international conference on the post-war world dealt with food and agriculture and was held in Hot Springs, Virginia in June 1943. The 44 governments represented there committed themselves to founding a permanent organization which was to become the Food and Agriculture Organization (FAO) of the UN. The most well known of the conferences that emerged from the planning of the US and the UK governments were the Bretton Woods Conference in 1944, at which the IMF and the International Bank for Reconstruction and Development (IBRD [World Bank]) were created, the San Francisco Conference at which the UN was founded in 1945 and the Havana Conference in 1948 where an ill-fated treaty was signed to create the ITO. The stories of these three conferences do not require retelling here, as they have been the subject of many accounts. In 1945 President Franklin D. Roosevelt was also supporting plans for a World Conference on Conservation as a Basis for Permanent Peace.[26] Those plans ended with FDR's death in April of that year. The World had to wait for more than one-quarter century for the UN Conference on the Environment in Stockholm in 1972 for 'conservation' to be put on the global agenda.

The Keynes Plans

> His great appeal was that we should treat the whole economic problem as a unity and be prepared to present to the public a total solution which really did present a prospect of a radical solution of the problems of unemployment and of raising standards of living.
>
> —James Meade (on Keynes)[27]

One cannot think of the war years without thinking of the most prolific contributor to the debates and to deliberations on the post-war world economy: John Maynard Keynes. In fact, three volumes of the Collected Writings of Keynes are devoted to the topic of 'Shaping the Post-War World,' with only 40 percent of one of these volumes given over to domestic issues. In Keynes' proposal for an International Clearing Union, one finds a brief reference to international taxes to be levied on balance of payments surpluses, rather than on transactions or national income as is common in many other proposals for global taxation. In his discussion of the use of the Clearing Union for other international purposes, Keynes suggests 'the Union might become the pivot of the future economic government of the world.'[28] He envisioned the Union possibly establishing 'a clearing account in favour of international bodies charged with post-war relief, rehabilitation and reconstruction' which might be financed by a tax on surplus credit balances.[29] Keynes also envisioned a one-time transfer to help jump-start the post-war economy:

> We need an agreed plan for starting off every country after the war with a stock of reserves appropriate to its importance in world commerce, so that without due anxiety it can set its house in order during the transitional period to full peace-time conditions.[30]

Recall that Keynes was a member of Britain's delegation at the Versailles peace conference in 1919. His strenuous objection to vindictive reparations payments led to his withdrawal from the conference. His views found full expression in his *Economic Consequence of the Peace* (1920). The provision in his ICU plan for one-time transfers can also be seen as a reflection of a lesson that he hoped might have been learned from the Versailles experience and its aftermath.

The British Keynes Plan and the plan drafted by Harry Dexter White, the American Secretary of the Treasury, were advanced in the early 1940s for the organization of postwar international monetary arrangements. The extent to which these plan differed is still a matter of heated debate.[31] Whatever similarities may exist, the plans start from different vantage points and make different assumptions about the nature of the postwar world. The US, as the dominant power at the War's end, chose to shape the world according to its conception and was disinclined to seriously entertain sharply competing views. This was clearly the fate of the Keynes Plan, in a context in which the US was to pay the piper. Nonetheless, White's original proposal did undergo many modifications chiefly as a result of regular consultation with the British, most notably

Keynes. Indeed, one British observer regarded the Bretton Woods agreement as 'one of the greatest triumphs of his life' insofar as it embodied 'constructive internationalism.'[32] The contrary view is 'so much did the Americans get their way that in 1946 Keynes doubted the wisdom of recommending the British government to ratify the Bretton Woods agreements.'[33]

My concern here is with elements of Keynes' vision as embodied and clearly enunciated in his plans for an International Clearing Union and for an International Commodity Control authority. One point that strongly runs through Keynes' Plan for an ICU is that the burden of financial adjustment is not to be limited only to countries with external payments deficits. In effect, the ill-fortune of one country is related to the good fortune of another. Countries whose debits or credits with the ICU exceeded a certain percentage of their quota (membership contribution) should be required to pay charges to the ICU. Countries with chronic credits would see those credits used for various international purposes, much as a bank can lend on the basis of deposits that it holds. A chronic creditor would have periodic discussions with the ICU about the 'measures [that] would be appropriate to restore the equilibrium to its international balances,' including reduction of tariff and other barriers to imports and international development loans.[34] On the question of capital controls, Keynes believed these to be desirable under certain circumstances in countries that were experiencing outflows, but he believed that flight capital should not be able to find a willing home. He urged countries to find a way to 'deter inward movements not approved by the countries from which they originate.' He urged the US in particular to follow the British example in this regard.[35]

It is, in fact, the use of the credit balances of the surplus countries that is at the heart of the 'other purposes' that Keynes proposed for the ICU. The counterpart of his observation about the Union becoming the pivot of future economic government of the world is 'without it, other more desirable developments will find themselves impeded and unsupported. With it, they will fall into their place as part of an ordered scheme.'[36] Although he provided no estimates, Keynes saw the ICU provisions as giving rise to substantial funds through the use of overdraft facilities and the use of the chronic international surpluses of creditor countries. In his view these funds could be used for post-war relief, rehabilitation and reconstruction, for supranational policing for the preservation of peace and the maintenance of international order, for international investment, and for stabilization of commodity prices. To put this potential into today's perspective, the end-of-year foreign exchange reserves of Japan's central bank exceeded 50 percent of Japan's annual imports from 1995 through 2001. Its exchange reserves in excess of 50 percent of imports at the end of 2001 amounted to $221 billion. If as a chronic surplus this had been available for global public purposes, it would have amounted to about four times the amount of net official development assistance extended by the countries of the Organization for Economic Cooperation and Development (OECD) Development Assistance Committee (DAC) during the most recent years.

A radical departure in the version of Keynes' proposal for an ICU which was presented to the British Parliament in April 1943 included an internationally created bank-money, called bancor, which was to have been the basis for specifying all exchange rates and would have been the unit of valuation of accounts with the International Clearing Union. Differing annual charges would have applied to the credit and debit balances of countries exceeding one-quarter or one-half of their quota with the ICU. Special Drawing Rights (SDRs) established by IMF members in 1969 bear a close resemblance to Keynes' bancor, but were never conceived to play a key role in central bank operations as Keynes intended for bancor.

The one element of the IMF design that Keynes and the British most adamantly opposed was individual country vetoes. In fact, the US is the only country that ever had a veto in the IMF and continues to have it today. Keynes imagined that he could convince the US that the '80 percent majority rule would limit the power of the US with respect to changes it may desire in an existing status as much as it would increase its power to stop undesired changes.'[37] However, he was not successful in doing so. Moreover, it would appear that over the life of the Fund, the 80 percent (now 85 percent) special majority has not worked in the symmetrical way that Keynes suggested, but rather facilitated the delay of changes that the US was not ready to accept, particularly increases in IMF funding through the upward revision of country quotas.

The commodity control plan proposed by Keynes goes beyond the technical question of regulating the movement of prices. Again Keynes' vision is the key. High cost countries must cease to subsidize and the way must be opened for lower cost countries to gain a position in markets where commodity prices would no longer be volatile. 'Volatile' is about the strongest word that enters the sanguine discourse of economists. Keynes is clearly the exception. In the fourth draft of his commodity proposal, one finds the following examples: 'the extent of the evil to be remedied can scarcely be exaggerated'; 'the violence of individual price fluctuations;' 'frightful price fluctuations' and in the ICU proposal: 'extravagant fluctuations of market conditions.'[38]

Keynes takes pains to argue that low prices should not be at the expense of workers and that labor standards should be enforced. Keynes refers to the 'long-term economic price' as being the target of this proposal. This price, which would eventually force high-cost producers out of the market, would be, in his words, one 'which would yield to producers a standard of living which is in reasonable relation to the general standards of the countries in which the majority of them live.'[39] Keynes insists that a price should not fall below this level and that 'consumers are not entitled to expect that it should.'[40] For Keynes, living standards were at the heart of the efforts to regulate commodity prices, rather than the concern for export earnings of producing countries. Keynes implicitly rejected any dogmatic adherence to the freeing of trade, insisting that 'some "protective" measures must be held in reserve as a proper defence of standards of life for other producers, whether of primary or manufactured commodities.'[41] This led Keynes to accept subsidies to maintain a suitable standard of living for producers in low-income countries and to reject them in high-income countries.[42]

With the displacement of the Keynes Plan with its larger purposes and expansionary bias by the White Plan with its singular focus on stabilization and the freeing of payments on current transactions, Keynes' scheme for commodity price control, which was linked to his proposed ICU, disappeared from the agenda and from public consideration. No new combined approach to commodities was considered until the late 1970s, when the United Nations Conference on Trade and Development (UNCTAD) began discussions of the Common Fund for Commodities, which did not begin operations until 1989.

The International Trade Organization (ITO)

The US and the UK labored hard and long for the creation of the ITO. James Meade, for example, drafted a proposal for an International Commercial Union in July 1942. Considerable joint and separate preparatory work by the American and British governments went into plans for the ITO at the same time that plans were being worked out for the IMF and the IBRD. Between 1943 and 1945 several committees met in Washington under the aegis of the State Department to draft a proposal for the creation of an international body to monitor and assist in the liberalization of world trade. The product of those deliberations were published in late 1945 as *Proposals for the Expansion of World Trade and Employment*.

The first GATT round of tariff reductions took place in Geneva in 1947, a year before the signing of the Havana Charter for the ITO.[43] Accidents of timing favored the survival of GATT, the less comprehensive approach to trade with its focus on reciprocal tariff reductions. By the time ratification of the Havana Treaty was to have been sought in the US, the cold war was well under way. The cold war is said to have made the difference to a recalcitrant Congress when it was considering the Marshall Plan. A.F. Wyn Plumptre in his description of the difficulties that faced the administration of the US President Harry Truman in securing Congressional approval for the Marshall Plan, summed up the critical event that turned the tide in one sentence: 'And then came Czechoslovakia.'[44] In the case of the ITO, then came the 1948 US elections that changed the face of Congress.

The support that was said to back the *Proposals* seems to have vanished soon after the signing of Havana Charter. William Diebold speaks about the perfectionists and the protectionists.[45] Truman, who had his hands full with other matters, certainly did not make ratification of the ITO a priority if one is to judge both from the timing of his initiatives and from his public pronouncements. No doubt Truman had no interest in a policy debacle. Congressional hearings on the ITO did not even commence until 1950 and by the year's end the Truman administration decided to wash its hands of the whole business and withdrew the Treaty from consideration. The fate of the ITO was sealed by delay; once the war ended the spirit of cooperation quickly dissipated in the US.

Diebold suggests that there were too many battles to fight on the trade front for it to have been wise for Truman to insist on the ITO. As the GATT was already functioning, the US did not wish support for it to be compromised by opposition to the ITO. Moreover, since 1934 America had been pursuing trade barrier reductions under the bilateral Reciprocal Trade Agreements program. In a context of growing protectionist sentiment, those who had to endure the heat of the ovens clearly thought it expedient to settle for half a loaf, to mix Truman's metaphor, rather than risking it all. Nonetheless, part of the ITO vision was already embodied in the GATT, which grew and prospered, despite serious doubts about its viability in the early 1950s.

United Nations

One of the crowning achievements of the closing year of World War II was the creation of UN with the signing of its Charter on 26 June 1945 in San Francisco. The first major step for the creation of the UN came less than one month after the US entry into the war, with the signing on 1 January 1942 by 26 governments, including the US and the UK of the 'Declaration by the United Nations.' Over the next three years an additional 21 countries added their signatures. Embodied in the preamble of the Declaration was a statement indicating the acceptance by the signatory nations of the August 1941 Atlantic Charter. The Atlantic Charter was seen in Washington, although not in London, as implying an end to colonial empires, which was one of Roosevelt's visions for the post-war world. This was a consistent point of great contention between Roosevelt and Churchill, especially when the former raised it in connection with India. Not only did Roosevelt's insistence that India be one of the original adherents to the Declaration prevail, but the signer was a native representative, rather than the British Secretary of State for India.[46]

There was criticism of the UN within the US both from isolationists and 'world federalists.' It is the latter source that will occupy me here. The form of the UN came under severe criticism for its democratic shortcomings. E.B. White, the well-known writer of children's story and regular contributor to the influential *The New Yorker* magazine, used the latter platform for his critiques of the UN, and particularly of the Security Council. At his most picturesque, White remarked: 'A security league to keep the peace is a negative project and follows a negative pattern. Peace is not something to be kept, like a pet monkey; peace is the by-product of responsible government.'[47]

In one of his other essays, White made it clear that nothing would suffice to assure world peace short of a UN 'with constitutional authority and a federal structure having popular meaning, popular backing, and an over-all authority greater than the authority of any one member or any combination of members.'[48] I.F. Stone also voiced his strenuous objections to the idea of a Security Council: 'The basic idea at San Francisco is that the big powers must stick together to maintain the peace; this was Metternich's idea in 1815; it is the kindergarten stage in education toward world security.'[49] I.F. Stone decried the lack of vision at San Francisco: 'the conference, for all its glamour, is a meeting of pretty much those same old codgers to whose fumbling we owe World War II. They are still dishing out the same old platitudes and thinking in the same old terms.'[50]

What troubled Stone most was his sense that the American delegation at San Francisco was attempting to build an anti-Soviet world coalition. He expressed concern that too many members of the US delegation held the 'dangerous belief that war between the two remaining great powers of the earth, the USA and the USSR is inevitable'; a belief, in his view, which could make it so.[51] Presciently, he observed: 'There is less forbearance and good will visible since Roosevelt's death.'[52] And yet, for all his criticism, he remained hopeful: the men who lost the last peace 'can give us the first tentative framework of a world order; it is the job of progressive forces to take over from there as soon as possible.'[53] His rallying cry to 'progressives' is as urgent and as valid today as it was in 1945, despite the considerable evolution of the UN in the years since its founding.

United in common cause: the Western Hemisphere at war

> [T]he wartime problem in those countries [Australia, Canada, the UK, and the US], like the development problem, was essentially one of achieving rapid large-scale transformation of the economy, involving rapid and substantial reallocation of resources. Indeed, the reallocation of resources involved was much greater in the fighting of a major war than is required for economic development.
>
> —Benjamin Higgins[54]

My graduate training in economics in the 1960s at the University of Texas (Austin) was a heterodox one in which the ideas of the mainstream and the American Institutionalist School competed for my allegiance. The hallmark of the program was to sow doubt rather than affirm 'Truths.' As my chosen field, economic development, was still in its infancy, there were as yet few if any certainties, few theories and even few textbooks, of which one of my professors, Ben Higgins, was the author of what was one of the earliest and most widely used at the time.

I was intrigued by Higgins' view that, in effect, development was a matter of commitment. As a war baby in the US—a 'scientist in the crib' to use the phrase of Gopnik, Meltzoff, and Kuhl[55]—I lived through resource reallocation. I remember that we flattened all our tin cans and recycled them, remember wartime ration stamps for sugar and coffee, and remember seeing an admonition on a school assignment of one of my older siblings that he should use both sides of each sheet of paper. All of this was in support of the war effort, rather than reflecting any concern about the environment. One of the first things that I discovered as an adult scientist considering reallocation of resources by the US during World War II, was that this was a Western Hemisphere-wide endeavor organized from Washington on a scale and on principles unlike those characteristic of peace-time arrangements. This was a most surprising finding, one that is overflowing with implications if we are truly committed to world peace and development.

As the likelihood of war increased with each passing year in the 1930s, the US changed the label it applied to its relations with Latin America from 'Good Neighbor Policy' to 'Hemispheric Defense.' Well before the formal entry of the US into World War II, the Roosevelt government was making every effort to assist the Allied nations and to frustrate the Axis (Germany, Italy, and Japan). Enlisting the Latin American countries to support this cause was a top US priority. The first regional meeting at which hemispheric security was the explicit focus was proposed by Roosevelt on 30 January 1936 to take place in Buenos Aires in December of that year. In exchange for a unanimous declaration of hemispheric solidarity, the US agreed to a prohibition on intervention in the internal or external affairs of any of the other states. Compliance required that the US abrogate treaty rights authorizing its military intervention and financial supervision in the Caribbean.[56] The next conference that pushed the envelope of continental security and the coordination of defense was held in Lima in December 1938 (Eighth Conference of American States). In Lima-agreement was reached to convene the ministers of foreign affairs of the member states in the event of emergencies that might threaten any one of the assembled states. Two such emergency meetings were convened: in Panama in September–October 1939 and Havana in July 1940. At the latter conference the 21 republics agreed that an act of aggression against any one of them was defined as aggression against them all.[57]

Mobilization of resources required, in the first instance, the denial of supplies to the Axis. Export controls predate America's entry into the war by one and a half years, authority having been given by the Export Control Act of 2 July 1940. That was followed in July 1941 by diplomatic efforts to generalize export licensing throughout the hemisphere in order to exclude sales of strategic goods to the Axis. Implementation required establishing control over direct or indirect transactions with 'persons deemed to be acting for the benefit of Germany or Italy.'[58] More than 1800 names of individuals and business institutions in Latin America were contained in the first 'Proclaimed List of Certain Blocked Nationals' published on 19 July 1941.[59] In that same month the US closed the Panama Canal to Japanese ships.

In the case of strategic materials, exclusive purchasing arrangement for a country's entire exportable surplus was the common pattern. The US was energetic in organizing commodity markets to assure supplies, particularly of strategic raw materials at predictable price levels (and by so doing to cutoff the Axis powers from goods they needed). American initiatives began as early as mid-1940 with the start of negotiations for a long-term purchase agreement for Bolivian tin. The resulting five-year agreement signed on 4 November 1940[60] served as a model for the US Metals Reserve Company's long-term purchasing agreements, *inter alia*, for Bolivian tungsten (May 1941) and lead (Oct. 1941),[61] and for Chilean copper (Jan. 1942).[62] Bilateral contracts for the purchase of most of Latin America's minerals and many of her agricultural exports were negotiated by the US.

Sumner Welles wrote on behalf of Secretary of State Cordell Hull to all the US Chiefs of Mission in Latin America on 1 April 1941 asking each of them to meet with the Minister of Foreign Affairs of the country to which he was accredited to urge the establishment of export controls on strategic materials. Among the items in the extensive list were cobalt, copper, lead, magnesium, manganese, mercury, phosphates, platinum, quartz crystals, quinine, rubber, tin, tungsten, uranium, and zinc.[63] Welles spoke of regulation of the exports in such a way as to give the US 'prior opportunity to acquire them.'[64] On 14 May 1941 Brazil became one of the first Latin American countries to sign such an accord. Brazil agreed to export only to the US a number of products, among which were bauxite, ferro-nickel, manganese, mica, quartz, rubber, and titanium.[65] To assure Brazil's support in the war effort, the US agreed to purchase quantities beyond its own needs of some of Brazil's principal agricultural export crops.[66] While mica and quartz may have been indispensable strategically to the US; coffee, cotton, and cacao, which together accounted for 67 percent of Brazil's exports in 1938, were indispensable financially to Brazil. The US even used its good offices to try to obtain Canadian agreement to commit itself to acquire a portion of Brazilian cotton exports.[67] Similar mineral purchase arrangements were completed with most of the other Latin American countries.

These defense arrangements brought the Latin American countries closer in numerous respects to the US than they had ever been previously. The various Latin American countries found themselves involved with the US in the administration of US export controls, in arrangements for sharing scarce resources such as petroleum, in contracts for the exclusive sale of minerals and other strategic raw materials at fixed prices to the US, in Lend Lease agreements, and a host of other ventures.

As a central element on the (unfilled) agenda of the South for cooperation with the North during much of the last half of the 20th century was the stabilization of either the prices or income from the sales of their raw material exports, a consideration of the unique arrangement during World War II merits attention. Out of the UNCTAD deliberations (as mentioned above), for example, came in the 1970s a proposal for a Common Fund intended to stabilize the prices of ten 'core' commodities. As the Fund did not begin operation until 1989, with limited funding and with the US absent from its membership, Southern countries opted to continue to either work on a product-by-product basis to hammer out international commodity agreements (ICAs) with Northern countries, as they had since the 1930s, or to act through producers' cartels, such as Organization of Petroleum Exporting Countries (OPEC) and CIPEC (copper), to improve their situation. Cooperation from the North has been fairly limited and has consisted principally of periodic participation in ICAs, the EU's Lomé Convention and the IMF Compensatory Finance Fund.

In peacetime the US is one of the foremost proponents of open markets. During World War II, however, the US was most energetic in acting to cut off the Axis powers from goods they needed and of organizing commodity markets to assure itself supplies, particularly of strategic raw materials at fixed prices. Contracts for most of Latin America's minerals and many of her agricultural exports were negotiated by the US. The war years were certainly not a time when 'the metropolis was otherwise occupied' as André Gunder Frank has asserted[68]—the US was more involved with Latin American affairs than it has been before or since. Not only did the US agree to absorb Latin American goods, but it took an active role in encouraging the expansion of production of various commodities, such as rubber, or to allocate output on a hemispheric basis, as with oil.

By many of the conventional measures that we use today to evaluate the external performance of developing countries, the years of World War II were very good ones indeed. Export earnings were growing, trade balances were for the most part favorable, foreign exchange reserves of the various central banks were growing annually and the prices of exported goods were stable. All of this was a reflection of wartime relations with the US and limitations on the ability of the Latin American countries to obtain imports. In a certain sense, one may argue that the Latin American countries, in involuntarily accumulating dollar balances, were making forced loans at substantially negative rates of interest to the US for the war effort. Price stability in and of itself is not a desideratum. The level at which a price is set and the range of permissible variation are key considerations. These have been the subject of lengthy and often unsuccessful bargaining in the various attempts to negotiate international commodity agreements for coffee, tin, cocoa, and other products. In World War II the US set fixed prices with no range of deviations to allow for changes in market conditions. The operation of markets was not deemed to suit the needs of waging a war. Windfall profits were not to accrue to raw material exporting countries as they had in World War I. Both unexpected gain and loss from price fluctuation were excluded by the purchasing arrangements imposed by the US on a largely compliant Latin America (and Canada).[69]

While price control in the US came early in World War II, the fixed price purchase agreements for many of the commodities exported by Latin American often predated the US entry into the war. The determination was firm to avoid allowing out-of-control prices to inflate the cost of armed conflict as had occurred during World War I, when, at its peak the US price of coal was almost seven times its prewar level and for petroleum almost four times. During World War II the prices of coal and petroleum had both increased by war's end by about 25 percent relative to the pre-war level, with the increase for petroleum having come prior to mid-1941. Nelson Rockefeller, Roosevelt's appointee to the position of Coordinator of Inter-American Affairs remarked that the US was paying for Latin American rubber 'about a fifth of what they could have obtained.'[70]

Petroleum

The use of country petroleum committees set up at the suggestion of the US for sharing the economic burden of the war and endeavoring to meet needs as locally perceived dates back to mid-1941, when greatly increased oil shipments from the US to Great Britain raised the specter of acute shortages on the East Coast of the US. A number of leading oil company executives submitted a report to the Office of Production Management calling for a hemisphere-wide approach. In the words of *Time*: 'And if and when the US has to cut fuel and gasoline consumption, the report took it for granted that South America should order "gasless Sundays" too.'[71]

Within two months this became national policy. On 30 August 1941, Hull wrote to the US Ambassadors in Latin America instructing them to obtain the cooperation of each of the various countries in establishing a National Oil Pool Committee.[72] These national committees were to assist in allocating oil on a hemisphere-wide basis by determining imported oil requirements and communicating them to the US-based Petroleum Supply Committee for Latin America.[73] Hull spoke of distributing the reduction in available tanker tonnage 'in such a way as to bring about equality among all the American Republics.'[74] Sumner Welles, the Undersecretary of State, pointing to the early success of the Pool, confidently predicted that not only would the current requirements of each country soon be fully met, but that inventories would be built up as well.[75]

Then came Pearl Harbor, followed shortly thereafter by the wholesale sinking of oil tankers in the Caribbean Sea by German submarines. The resulting shipping capacity shortage was not amenable to feats of reorganization. With much reduced tanker space available, substantial cutbacks in crude petroleum output were necessary in Mexico, Venezuela, and Colombia (19.6, 35.4, and 56.9 percent cuts respectively in 1942 relative to 1941).[76] In these circumstances, 'equality of burden' turned out to be 'equality' among oil importing Latin American countries. Chile's petroleum supplies, which were now coming from Peru rather than California, were sharply reduced by orders from Washington. By mid-1942 Chile was receiving for non-war uses a 'basic allotment' of 40 percent of its 1941 supply. War industries, those producing Chilean copper and nitrates, were to receive up to their full needs.[77] By way of comparison, the current value of US consumer expenditures for gas and oil for user-operated transportation in 1942 was 78.9 percent of its 1941 peak level.[78]

Modern economies and societies run on oil. Without it, activities must be curtailed. By October 1942 Chile had prohibited the use of most private cars and had suppressed the use of more than one-third of the cars used by government agencies and the operation of trucks between Santiago and the port areas of Viña del Mar and Valparaiso was prohibited.[79] As also occurred in Brazil, the Chileans expanded the output of dehydrated alcohol which was mixed with gasoline to cushion somewhat the impact of the shortage.[80] In Brazil despite the machine-shop production of 'gazogene' devices to allow trucks to burn alcohol and charcoal, it became necessary for Brazil to deprive private cars of fuel and to limit, at times, haulage by rail between Rio de Janeiro and Sao Paulo to foodstuffs and wood, the latter being necessary to substitute for coal, imports of which fell in 1942 by over 40 percent of the quantity imported in the preceding year with a marked debilitating effect on the Brazilian economy.[81]

Latin American imports

Common to the preceding paragraphs is the theme of scarcity and the key role of decisions made in Washington on goods to be exported to

Latin America. Those decisions were central to the nature of production, consumption, and investment throughout Latin America during the war years, particularly from 1942. The fact of pervasive scarcity should suggest caution in accepting the hypothesis that significant import substituting industrialization (ISI) occurred in the region during the war years, an idea popularized, but not documented, by André Gunder Frank.[82] The hypothesized occurrence of ISI during World War II is comparable to the anecdote of the desert island economist with a sardine can. Central to both accounts are counterfactual assumptions regarding the means of production. The marooned economist proclaims, 'Let us assume we have a can opener.' Those who allege that major wartime industrialization occurred in various underdeveloped countries take a similar position: they assume the existence of capacity for the production of investment goods in each of the countries in question.

The US played a central role during the war years in providing raw materials, intermediate goods, and capital goods for Latin American industry. The experience of the countries of Latin America during the war cannot be understood without taking account of decisions taken in Washington. A few examples from Mexico should amply serve to illustrate this. For Mexico, the war period is spoken of by many as a period of either export-or demand-led growth. The growth of exports may have stimulated domestic demand, but it was able to contribute little to the needed importation of investment goods. For Mexico, which was still in 1945 dependent on imported capital goods for one-quarter of the value of gross investment,[83] the war was a period characterized principally by industrial expansion through double and triple shifting, rather than major new investments. In some instances, even keeping industry running required deliveries from the US of new electric power plants and equipment for existing ones:

In 1943, for example, the breakdown of electric service in Monterrey caused a temporary suspension of virtually all manufacturing activity in that important industrial area. Even after service was resumed, industry had to operate at a reduced rate for some time.[84] On the matter of new industries in Mexico, Sanford Mosk remarked: 'Uncompleted factories were a striking feature on the Mexican landscape. In some cases, the failure to get one or two pieces of equipment meant that a plant, otherwise complete, could not function.'[85]

There were instances where the US actively tried to support industrial diversification in Mexico to aid in the war effort, but was unable to prevent undue delays in delivery. Discussions which commenced in early 1942 concerning the construction of a high octane aviation fuel refinery in Mexico were at least two years in bringing results despite President Roosevelt's attempts to expedite matters.[86] A US Export–Import Bank loan of $8 million was approved in 1942 to finance the purchase of equipment in the US for the Altos Hornos iron and steel works at Monclova, but as equipment was unavailable, the loan could not be disbursed until 1946.[87] Nonetheless, production began at Monclova in 1944 using an idle blast furnace and other parts which had been used in the US and which were dismantled and shipped to Mexico.[88] This is dramatically reflected in steel output which grew by 31 percent in 1945 alone, after having increased by only 22 percent over the period 1939–1944.[89] The Altos Hornos mill in its initial two years of production took military orders from the US and fabricated steel ship plates for the US Maritime Commission.[90]

In mid-1943 the US introduced a Decentralization Plan for the specification of import requests that required Latin American governments to compile lists of import recommendations to be submitted for review to the local US Embassy, which both assessed priorities and deleted any requests from blacklisted firms with Axis connections. The Embassy and the country's import agency were then to agree on a joint list of recommendations. The extent to which the recommendations were translated into actual imports turned on decisions by the US Board of Economic Warfare (later the Foreign Economic Administration) which in issuing export licenses took account of the supply situation in the US, the availability of transport, and the state of the war.

As the war drew to a conclusion, the US reverted to its support for free markets. Commodity prices were once again to be determined by world markets. The Latin American were encouraged to dismantle the controls and central organizations that they built at the urging of the US. In early 1944, as the Bretton Woods conference approached, the Latin American governments learned of the wish of the US to remove from the Decentralization Plan a range of items including petroleum products, motor vehicles, and repair parts for maintenance and capital equipment.[91] The State Department voiced its strong opposition to any attempt to replace national import recommendations with import licensing. The US Secretary of State Cordell Hull referred to the need for the 'progressive diminution and elimination of wartime controls . . . in anticipation of efforts to revitalize and augment international trade in the post-war period.'[92] American export controls, however, were to remain in force. Moreover, it was clearly stated that the 'rollback of decentralization should not be interpreted as indicating a general increase in supply.'[93]

Instead of support for social and economic initiatives in the Western Hemisphere following the conclusion of the war, flows were reduced to a trickle. The cynical observation that nations have interests, not friends,[94] seemed to be confirmed once again. As Mark T. Gilderhus observed:

> Preoccupied with the Soviet Union, the United States established priorites in other regions and thus violated Latin American expectations of large-scale economic aid and assistance. No Marshall Plan came about to repay Latin American nations for their wartime support, and disenchantment soon set in.[95]

The Latin American countries that had cooperated to the fullest with the war effort received a minimum of financial aid from the US in the form of loans, while substantial grant assistance from the US was directed to Europe and Japan, and later to Taiwan and Korea.[96]

Durable peace: lost in the Cold War

During the Cold War the US commitment to democracy fell prey to the 'anti-politics machine.' The understanding of the dynamics of democratic processes was apparently so superficial that there was a willingness to embrace 'anti-politics'—that is, the quest for efficient outcomes, even if the rights of citizens are trampled in the process. The advent of the Cold War and the anti-Communist witch-hunt in the US cast a chill over thought and action. The ink on the San Francisco charter of the UN was barely dry, when 'one-worldism' fell into extreme disfavor in the US.[97] It is useful to recall that even Harry Dexter White, the American architect of the IMF, was one of the early targets of the inquisition conducted by the US House Un-American Activities Committee.[98]

These were years in America when ideas even slightly at variance with the standard line were best kept to oneself. Nor was there much room for generosity left after the Marshall Plan. Hans Singer observes that even support for soft loans was regarded at the time as subversive: 'Those advocating soft aid for developing countries, specially when suggesting this be done under UN auspices, were often treated as outcasts and out to weaken the Free World.'[99] This view clearly reflects the length of the struggle for multilateral soft funding for developing countries, which culminated in 1960 in the creation of the International Development Association (IDA) under the wing of the World Bank, rather than a proposed UN Special Fund for Economic Development (SUNFED).[100]

No, the world was not yet ready for global redistribution or a world federation in the 1940s and 1950s. But until US Senator Joseph McCarthy transformed currents of anti-Communist sentiment into a full-blown witch-hunt, people had at least been earnestly exploring these ideas. The persecution of those with independent opinions during the McCarthy era drove any serious consideration of global social justice or even mention of it off the agenda for over four decades. One-world thinking ceased to be discussed not merely during the period of Congressional inquiries in the early 1950s, but until at least the fall of the Berlin Wall in 1989.

One of the most prominent of the early targets of McCarthy's witch-hunt was Owen Lattimore, the then Director of the School of International Relations at Johns Hopkins University. An attack on a scholar of Lattimore's standing initially led many to practice self-censorship. It was a simple matter for many to return to the comfort and safety of seeing only those solutions amenable to the independent actions of nation-states. Habits of mind born or reinforced in that period still impede our vision. The hesitancy about speaking freely generated by attacks such as that on Lattimore was intensified when the House Un-American Activities Committee asked for and received course reading lists from universities.[101]

The US provided extravagant financial and technical support and extensive encouragement to the world's most repressive dictators in return for their paradoxical pledge of allegiance to the 'Free World.' If the path advocated by Lattimore had been followed, rather than that of McCarthy and his sympathizers who lacked any real appreciation of democratic institutions, the record of the past half-century might well have been very different. For example, Lattimore wrote in 1941: 'We must have a policy that does not limit us to defending the possessions of the democracies, but pledges us to support and spread democracy itself.'[102]

In 1950, just four weeks after his last hearing before the Senate Subcommittee, Lattimore completed the manuscript of *Ordeal by Slander*, a work that is at once a wake-up call to the dangers of McCarthy's tactics and a spirited defense of democracy. In it Lattimore stated:

> Beyond the shores of our own country, all the many constructive possibilities of our foreign policy are being frozen by the cold war. The freeze is already so deep that nothing is left of foreign policy but the cold war itself. And yet it should be obvious that the cold war offers no solution either for our own problems or for the problems of the world.[103]

The promising convergence of ideas spawned by the years of global economic crisis and war is barely remembered today. It was swept aside almost totally during the anti-Communist crusade years in the US, when it was scarcely safe to even entertain private thoughts about altering the world order. Ellen Schrecker has described in detail the 'almost automatic sanctions [by private employers, including universities] on the people who had been described as politically undesirable' by Congressional hearings.[104] In that climate, 'open criticism of the political status quo disappeared,' as did consideration of topics imagined to be controversial.[105] The blinders with which we were fitted during the McCarthy years have kept us slavishly focused on national sovereignty for one-half century longer than is desirable for either humanity or the flora and other fauna of the Earth, a view that has been by expressed by Eisuke Sakakibara: '. . . the end of the Cold War released the world from a western civil war over differing versions of progressivism to confront the more fundamental issues of environmental pollution and the peaceful coexistence of different civilizations.'[106]

Conclusion

It was from Clarence Ayres, the patriarch of the University of Texas Economics Department and one-time editor of *The New Republic* during the 1920s, that I first heard the immortal phrase of the American psychologist and pragmatist philosopher William James 'a moral equivalent of war.'[107] Could economic development be the moral equivalent of war? Could the moral equivalent be world peace or global justice? The moral equivalent of war is a logical complement to Higgins' observation that economic development is a matter of commitment, not likely (in his view) to be as all encompassing as that required for a major war. Might there be lessons from the sacrifices and cooperation during hostilities that could be applicable to the quest for social, political, and economic development in the Third World? Can we imagine global justice or planetary sustainability becoming the moral equivalent for war? I submit that we are already on that path.

The wartime experience provides valuable lessons for countries now developing, but our examination suggests that recourse to self-reliant development is certainly not one of those lessons. The need for interdependence combined with resource reallocation (in peacetime) from the rich to the poor, a prescription embodied in variants of the 1970s call for a New International Economic Order, is an observation that clearly flows from this consideration of wartime economics.

During World War II, both economic ideology and democratic process took a back seat to getting the job done quickly and effectively. What was achieved then both domestically and internationally provides a striking example of what is possible when actors labor with a common cause. Shaping world common cause today, when the enemy is no longer the 'other' but the threat from our own excesses, is likely to require the strengthening, rather than abridgement, of inclusive democratic engagement.

What do these experiences tell us about the prospect for extending world order beyond present limits? Have times changed so that similar interests prevail throughout the world? A lesson that may be drawn is that even what might be regarded as 'premature' cooperation and utopian visions can serve a role in transforming the organizational and/or psychological environment. Grand visions serve as a catalyst and an inspiration. These may be put to either good use or ill: a united Europe gained by military conquest bears no resemblance in its trajectory to one forged through peaceful cooperation. Visions set the wheels in motion. They change perceptions, they alter focus, they change our sense of the possible.

Hirschman spoke of a 'hidden hand' in his observations about vast development projects that would have been abandoned had the difficulties ahead been known. Once one has embarked on overreaching projects, capabilities sometimes have a way of expanding. Individuals, institutions, and cultures do not stand still. The IMF is not the same institution today as when it was created. Richard Gardner argued in 1969 that with the expansion of country borrowing limits and the creation of SDRs, the Fund had grown to resemble Keynes' original vision. Others today would say that, in fact, the Fund has become the pivot of economic government of the world, but not at all in the positive sense that Keynes envisioned. The UN has grown and diversified to play an important role on a multitude of global issues. As Jeffrey Sachs observed in 2002, 'Despite a decade of criticism and budget cuts, the specialized UN agencies have far more expertise and hands-on experience than any other organizations in the world.'[108]

Time and again roads have diverged. While rhetoric consistent with our underlying values might have led to one approach, interests and realpolitik have taken us down a different path. The value of an examination of the wartime experience is to demonstrate that many avenues that are fiercely resisted today were considered entirely fitting and proper when one's fate was perceived to be in the balance. The wartime experience should serve to remind us that more can be accomplished and, in fact, has been when the determination was present. The wartime experience also suggests that major institutional initiatives may be our only way out of repeated impasses. Open agreements, openly arrived at and widely debated may be our only protection against those who seek to impose their imprimatur on the world.

Keynes concluded his proposal for an International Clearing Union by insisting that we need not be overcautious. He argued that 'a greater readiness to accept supranational arrangements must be required in the postwar world.'[109] If that was true 60 years ago, it is certainly and urgently true in the 21st century. For Keynes 'the winning of the peace' required what he called 'financial disarmament': an economic ordering of the world that would lead states 'to abandon that license to promote indiscipline, disorder and bad-neighborliness.' Indeed, we have been overcautious for too long with respect to the needs, rights, and privileges of the common person, which includes the constant reweaving of the intricate fabric of civilized society. To make a difference for the peoples of the world, the time has come to choose the less opportunistic, more just, less traveled road.

Notes

1. John Maynard Keynes, 'The International Control of Raw Materials', *Journal of International Economics*, 4 (1974), pp. 299–315. For two revised versions of the proposal, see also John Maynard Keynes, *The Collected Writings of John Maynard Keynes. Volume XXVII. Activities: 1940–1946, Shaping the Post-War World: Employment and Commodities*, for the Royal Economic Society (London: Macmillan, 1980), pp. 135–66 and 168–94.
2. Adam Smith, 'An Inquiry into the Nature and Causes of the Wealth of Nations' (1776), http://www.econlib.org/library/Smith/smWN.htm.
3. Albert O. Hirschman, 'Obstacles to Development: A Classification and a Quasi-Vanishing Act', *Economic Development and Cultural Change*, 13 (July 1965), pp. 385–93.
4. Woodrow Wilson, 'Fourteen Points' (8 January 1918), http://www.yale.edu/lawweb/avalon/wilson14.htm.
5. Max Lerner, *Ideas for the Ice Age: Studies in a Revolutionary Era* (New York: Viking Press, 1941), pp. 74–75. Emphasis added.
6. Sumner Welles, *The Time for Decision* (New York: Harper & Brothers, 1944), p. 374.
7. Hans W. Singer, 'The Terms of Trade Controversy and the Evolution of Soft Financing: Early Years in the U.N.', Gerald M. Meier and Dudley Seers, eds, *Pioneers in Development* (New York: Oxford University Press, 1984), p. 276.
8. James Meade, *The Economic Basis of a Durable Peace* (New York: Oxford University Press, 1940), p. 9.
9. Ibid., p. 10.
10. Ibid., pp. 184–85.

11. James Meade, *A Geometry of International Trade* (London: Allen & Unwin, 1952), p. 112. Emphasis added. In making the step from ordinal to cardinal utility, Meade went beyond the limits of Pareto optimality into terrain which is today thoroughly familiar to game theorists.
12. Jan Tinbergen, *International Economic Co-operation* (Amsterdam: Elsevier, 1945), p. 164.
13. Ibid., p. 17.
14. Ibid., pp. 17–18.
15. Jan Tinbergen, *International Economic Integration* (Amsterdam: Elsevier, 1954), pp. 150–51.
16. Jan Tinbergen, 'International Co-ordination of Stabilization and Development Policies', *Kyklos*, 12 (fasc. 3, 1959), p. 286. Tinbergen's renewed call for a World Treasury (and a World Central Bank) can be found in UNDP, *Human Development Report 1994*, p. 88.
17. C. Wilfred Jenks, 'Some Legal Aspects of the Financing of International Institutions', *Transactions of the Grotius Society*, 28 (1942), p. 88.
18. Ibid., p. 125.
19. Ibid., p. 93.
20. Theodore A. Sumberg, 'Financing International Institutions', *Social Research*, 13 (1946), p. 301.
21. Cordell Hull, *The Memoirs of Cordell Hull*, Prepared with the assistance of Andrew Berding (New York: Macmillan, 1948), p. 1625.
22. Quoted in Hull, p. 1625.
23. Atlantic Charter (1941), http://www.yale.edu/lawweb/avalon/wwii/atlantic: htm.
24. Hull, p. 1628.
25. Adolf A. Berle (Assistant Secretary of State 1938–44), who chaired the committee, added in his notes about post-war Europe: the creation of a monetary union and a communications union. Beatrice Bishop Berle and Travis Beal Jacobs, eds, *Navigating the Rapids, 1918–1971, From the Papers of Adolf A. Berle* (New York: Harcourt Brace Jovanovich, 1973), pp. 426–27.
26. Franklin Delano Roosevelt, *Franklin D. Roosevelt and Conservation, 1911–1945*, Edgar B. Nixon, ed. (Hyde Park, N.Y.: General Services Administration, National Archives and Records Service, Franklin D. Roosevelt Library, 1957), II, pp. 636–41.
27. D.E. Moggridge, *Maynard Keynes*: *An Economist's Biography* (London and New York: Routledge, 1992), p. 726.
28. John Maynard Keynes, *The Collected Writings of John Maynard Keynes. Volume XXV Activities*: *1940–1944, Shaping the Post-War World*: *The Clearing Union* (London: Macmillan, 1980), p. 189.
29. Ibid., XXV, pp. 189–90. Elsewhere Keynes merely observes *en passant* that a method is needed to employ surplus credit balances (ibid., XXV, p. 169). Such a provision could have been useful in redirecting large Japanese surpluses, an issue of concern in the 1980s or German surpluses in the 1960s. One example is given in the text.
30. Ibid.
31. See Bradford De Long's book review of Robert Skiddelsky's *John Maynard Keynes, Volumes I and II*, http://econ161.berkeley.edu/Econ_Articles/Reviews/skidelsky12.html.
32. Lionel Robbins, quoted in D.E. Moggridge, p. 721.

33. G.C. Peden, *Keynes, the Treasury and British Economic Policy* (London: Macmillan Education, 1988), p. 25.
34. Keynes XXV, p. 176 (para 9 of proposal for an ICU).
35. Ibid., pp. 186–88 (para 33).
36. Ibid., p. 190 (para 39)
37. Ibid., p. 328.
38. 'Proposals for an International Clearing Union', British Govt. Publication, Cmd 6437 (1943) cited in Herbert G. Grubel, *World Monetary Reform, Plans and Issues* (Stanford, Calif.: Stanford University Press, 1963), p. 55.
39. Keynes (1974), p. 307.
40. Ibid.
41. Ibid.
42. Ibid., pp. 307–08.
43. The text of the charter can be found at http://www.worldtradelaw.net/misc/havana.pdf.
44. A.F. Wyn Plumptre, *Three Decades of Decision: Canada and the World Monetary System, 1944–75* (Toronto: McClelland and Stewart, 1977).
45. William Diebold, 'The End of the I.T.O.', *Essays in International Finance*, 16 (Oct. 1952), pp. 11–23.
46. Warren F. Kimball, *The Juggler: Franklin Roosevelt as Wartime Statesman* (Princeton: Princeton University Press, 1991), pp. 132–33. See also Gaddis Smith, *American Diplomacy During the Second World War 1941–1945* (New York: John Wiley & Sons, 1965).
47. E.B. White, *The Wild Flag: Editorials from The New Yorker on Federal World Government and Other Matters* (Boston: Houghton Mifflin,1946), p. 41. See *The New Yorker* (21 October 1944) for original.
48. Ibid., pp. 62–63. See alternatively *The New Yorker*, 24 February 1945.
49. I.F. Stone, *The War Years 1939–1945* (Boston: Little, Brown and Company, 1988), p. 282.
50. Ibid.
51. I.F. Stone, *The Truman Era: 1945–1952* (New York: Random House, 1972), p. 12.
52. Ibid. In Kimball's words: 'Roosevelt treated the Soviet Union as an ally worth supporting, not an enemy or weak house of cards about to fall' and 'FDR's attempt to work with the Soviet Union makes more sense than the belligerent, confrontational approach that was the alternative.' p. 200.
53. Stone (1988), p. 282.
54. Benjamin H. Higgins, *Economic Development: Principles, Problems, and Policies* (New York: Norton, 1959).
55. Alison Gopnik, Andrew N. Meltzoff, and Patricia K. Kuhl, *The Scientist in the Crib: Minds, Brains, and How Children Learn* (New York: William Morrow, 1999).
56. William R. Keylor, *The Twentieth-Century World: An International History* (New York: Oxford University Press, 1984), pp. 222–23.
57. Ibid., p. 226.
58. *Department of State Bulletin* (19 July 1941), p. 41.
59. Ibid.
60. US Department of State, *Foreign Relations of the United States: Diplomatic Papers* (hereafter FRUS) (1940), V, pp. 524–48 contains correspondence detailing the negotiations. See also US Department of Commerce, National Production Authority (1953) *Materials Survey: Tin*, pp. 15.9 to 15.13.

61. FRUS (Washington: U.S. Dept of State, 1941), VI, pp. 452–64.
62. Ibid., pp. 578–96.
63. Welles for Hull to Chiefs of Mission in the American Republics, 12 December 1940, FRUS (1941), VI, pp. 149–51.
64. Ibid., p. 152.
65. FRUS (1941), VI, pp. 538–43.
66. FRUS, V (Oct. 1942), pp. 689–90.
67. FRUS (1942), I, pp. 565–86.
68. André G. Frank, *Capitalism and Underdevelopment in Latin America* (New York: Monthly Review Press, 1967), pp. 148–49.
69. Myron J. Frankman, 'North American Economic Cooperation: The Wartime Experience', *Canadian Journal of Latin American and Caribbean Studies*, 16 (no. 2, 1991), pp. 35–57.
70. Cited by David Green, *The Containment of Latin America: A History of the Myths and Realities of the Good Neighbor Policy* (Chicago: Quadrangle Books, 1971), p. 106.
71. *Time*, 38 (7 July 1941), p. 62.
72. Hull to Diplomatic Missions in American Republics, 30 August 1941, FRUS (1941), VI, pp. 171–72.
73. Ibid., pp. 171–72.
74. Ibid., p. 171.
75. Statement of Welles to Meeting of Inter American Financial and Economic Advisory Committee, 31 October 1941, Ibid., p. 182.
76. U.N., *Monthly Bulletin of Statistics* (Jan. 1947), p. 12.
77. Harold L. Ickes, *Fightin' Oil* (New York: Alfred A. Knopf, 1943), p. 144.
78. US Dept. of Commerce, Bureau of the Census, *Historical Statistics of the United States: Colonial Times to 1957* (Washington: 1960), p. 178.
79. *Foreign Commerce Weekly*, 10 (2 January 1943), pp. 12, 13.
80. Ibid., p. 18.
81. Corwin D. Edwards, 'Brazil's Economy in the War and After', in Seymour Harris, ed., *Economic Problems of Latin America* (New York: McGraw-Hill, 1944), p. 284.
82. 'The relaxation, weakening or absence of ties between metropolis and satellite will lead to a turning in upon itself on the part of the satellite ... Examples of such active capitalist involution are the industrialization drives of Brazil, Mexico, Argentina, India, and others during the Great Depression and the World War II, while the metropolis was otherwise occupied.' Frank, pp. 148–49.
83. Combined Mexican Working Party, *The Economic Development of Mexico* (Baltimore: The Johns Hopkins Press, 1953), p. 376. This severely understates the importance of imported capital goods as 'gross investment' includes far more than the cost of machinery. A more representative statistic is the share of imports in total capital goods supplies, which was two-thirds as late as 1950. Gerald K. Helleiner, *International Trade & Economic Development* (Harmondsworth: Penguin Books, 1972), p. 102.
84. Sanford Mosk, *Industrial Revolution in Mexico* (Berkeley: University of California Press, 1954), p. 279.
85. Ibid., p. 278.
86. Lloyd Gardner, *Economic Aspects of New Deal Diplomacy* (Madison: University of Wisconsin Press, 1964), p. 206 and Mosk, p. 86. The delay was partly

attributable to support which the oil companies enjoyed in the State Department. Roosevelt wrote the following to his Secretary of State in February 1943: 'I cannot see the relationship between the immediate need and the "clarification of general petroleum policy" .... The octane gasoline is solely for war purposes. The United Nations need it. They ought to have it.' FRUS (1943), VI, p. 455.

87. Mosk, p. 142.
88. Ibid., p. 141 and William E. Cole, *Steel and Economic Growth in Mexico* (Austin: University of Texas Press, 1967), p. 12. The US financed Volta Redonda integrated steel mill project in Brazil, which was to have been completed by 1944, experienced similar delays in obtaining equipment from the US. Operation of the Brazilian rolling mill began only in 1948. Werner Baer, *The Development of the Brazilian Steel Industry* (Nashville, Tenn.: Vanderbilt UP, 1969), p. 79.
89. Nacional Financiera, S.A., *Statistics on the Mexican Economy*, Mexico, 1966, p. 92.
90. Howard F. Cline, *Mexico: Revolution to Evolution 1940–1960* (London: Oxford University Press, 1962), p. 274.
91. Edward R. Stettinius Jr, to Certain Diplomatic Representatives in the American Republics, Washington, 12 February 1944, FRUS (1944), VII, p. 739.
92. Hull to White, Washington, 16 June 1944, FRUS (1944), VII, p. 1540.
93. Stettinius, FRUS (1944), VII, p. 739.
94. This has recently been rendered by Ignacio Ramonet as 'An Empire has Vassals, not Allies', *Le Monde Diplomatique* (Feb. 2003), p. 2.
95. Mark J. Gilderhus, 'An Emerging Synthesis? U.S.–Latin American Relations since the Second World War. America in the World', in M.J. Hogan, ed., *The Historiography of American Foreign Relations since 1941* (Cambridge: Cambridge University Press, 1995), pp. 434–35.
96. Between 1946 and 1961 the combined total of economic aid which Latin America received from the US was US$5.0 billion of which 80 percent was in loans. In contrast, Taiwan and South Korea received a combined total of US$5.2 billion of which 93 percent were grants. USAID.
97. I.F. Stone (1972), pp. 80–86. See also James M. Boughton, 'Harry Dexter White and the International Monetary Fund', *Finance and Development*, 35 (Sept. 1998), pp. 39–41
98. White, who had resigned as US Executive Director of the IMF owing to ill health in April 1947, died of a heart attack in August 1948, three days after he denied ever having had any Communist affiliation in his only appearance before the House Committee. See Stone (1972), pp. 48–50.
99. Hans W. Singer, 'The Terms of Trade Controversy and the Evolution of Soft Financing: Early Years in the U.N.', Gerald M. Meier and Dudley Seers, eds, *Pioneers in Development* (New York: Oxford University Press, 1984), pp. 296–97, n. 47.
100. Ibid., pp. 296–303.
101. Sigmund Diamond, *Compromised Campus: The Collaboration of Universities with the Intelligence Community, 1945–1955* (New York: Oxford University Press, 1992), pp. 121–22.
102. Owen Lattimore, *Ordeal by Slander* (Boston: Little, Brown and Co., 1950), p. 43.
103. Ibid., p. 226.

104. Ellen W. Schrecker, *No Ivory Tower: McCarthyism and the Universities* (Oxford: Oxford University Press, 1986), p. 9.
105. Schrecker, p. 39.
106. Eisuke Sakakibara, 'The End of Progressivism: A Search for New Goals', *Foreign Affairs*, 74 (Sept./Oct. 1995), pp. 8–20.
107. William James, 'The Moral Equivalent of war' (1906), http://www.constitution.org/wj/meow.htm.
108. Jeffrey Sachs, 'Weapons of Mass Salvation', *The Economist*, 26 October 2002, p. 82.
109. Grubel, p. 79.

4
World Public Finance

> It is neither necessary nor desirable that national boundaries should mark sharp differences in standards of living, that membership of a national group should entitle to a share in a cake altogether different from that in which members of other groups share.
>
> —Friedrich A. Hayek, *The Road to Serfdom*

The next step in the reconstruction of our mental map of world order is that of considering the creation of a system of world public finance. The focus of world public finance would be to raise revenue to pay for the operations of the global public sector, including their activities in support of global public purposes, that is, those activities that are deemed to have global impact and which are not amenable to the actions of states, either acting alone or in groups. Included in these public purposes would be development financing, efforts on behalf of greater global equity, and the provision of global public goods. Each of these functions tends to be a subject of separate sets of discourse with limited overlap. I contend that the time has clearly come to talk about both world government and world public finance and to talk about both in terms that the urgency of our multiple, interconnected global crises requires, rather than the present financially and organizationally minimalist approach which often separates one need from another and then labors to earmark specific, often voluntary, revenues for unique purposes such as preventing the spread of AIDS. Our present problem-focused approach sometimes involves the creation of a new unit or a new international institution for a designated objective. Commonly the total resources—financial, human, and institutional—will not be increased but rather diverted from previous uses, as when foreign-aid funds were redirected after the fall of the Berlin Wall to the countries of Eastern Europe and the former Soviet Union from those in the global South.

In fact, even applying the term 'public finance' to the world is still an unaccustomed viewpoint for most of us, as we commonly do not think in terms of world government and the two concepts (government and public finance) generally go hand-in-hand. I first encountered the term 'international public finance,' in the title of a 1963 article by Douglas Dosser.[1] The next occurrence of the phrase of which I am aware was almost three decades later in Ruben P. Mendez's (1992) major book on the topic.[2] A world-level perspective for public finance has not yet captured the imagination of the citizens and certainly not of policy-makers, who see greater international cooperation and new tax treaties as the only way ahead.[3]

I shall insist on two points in this chapter: If we are to have the global financial means necessary to meet our pressing global tasks, it must be within a system of world government. To be equal to the global tasks that require attention, we need to be speaking in trillions of dollars if we are at all serious about a systemic approach to heretofore intractable global imbalances. In considering what might be an appropriate budget for world government and associated global purposes, a useful starting point is the range of recommendations proposed in 1977 in the MacDougall Report to the European Commission on the role of public finance in European integration. As summarized by Timothy Bainbridge:

> When the report was written, total spending by the Community institutions was about 0.7 per cent of the Community's gross domestic product (GDP). 'Pre-federal integration' meant raising the latter figure to between 2 and 2.5 per cent. A 'small' Community public sector was reckoned to be from 5 to 7 per cent, and a 'large' something approaching 25 per cent of GDP.[4]

The world product has been estimated at around US$30 trillion. At present the budgets of our global organizations (principally the UN System, the World Bank, and the IMF) come to around $20 billion or 0.07 percent of world gross product. If we apply the MacDougall percentages to the global level, we find that the ratio for world institutions is one-tenths of that for the EC's public expenditure in 1977. A pre-federal budget for the world using the MacDougall Commission's ratio would be between $0.6 and 0.75 trillion; the budget for a small world public sector would be from $1.5 to 2.1 trillion; and a large world public sector, up to $7.5 trillion. These estimates are two orders of magnitude larger than the present combined budgets of the international public sector organizations. Even the underfunded EU has a budget limit of 1.27 percent of the combined gross product of the 15 member countries. If the budget for the international public sector were raised to the same percentage, the new total would be $420 billion.

Unless we are willing to think of a multifold expansion of global public sector expenditures, we are deluding ourselves about the financial needs of a peaceful, sustainable world order. Our present approach is one of meting out limited funds for global purposes with an eyedropper and then controlling their use as carefully as possible. When economists speak of agency, they are not using it in the sense of the empowerment of individuals or groups, but rather what is referred to as the 'principal-agent' problem. That is, if you delegate a task to someone, how can you assure that the task will be done expeditiously or even done at all? For those who are convinced that shirkers are lurking everywhere, the solution to the principal-agent problem is the building of elaborate systems of control rather than trust.

The trajectory of the idea of world public finance has largely been one of logical extensions consistently *not* being made owing to a range of ubiquitous default settings that limit our vision and our discourse. The principal limit is the nation as the customary unit of analysis. Another key assumption that has limited the vision of economists is that of the marginal productivity theory of income distribution, which allows us to regard efficiency and equity as necessarily going hand in hand: 'factors of production' under conditions of perfect competition are paid what they contribute to the value of the product they have helped produce. This distributional mechanism is at the heart of the standard Heckscher–Ohlin–Samuelson model of international trade, where free trade and free markets lead countries to specialize according to comparative advantage, which 'resolves all problems.' To be specific, given the appropriate assumptions, among which are a two country, two good, two factor of production theoretical model, free trade leads to the complete disappearance of between-country differences in the payment to each of the factors of production (land [or labor] and capital).[5] If one factor were labor, this would mean the wages in both countries would equalize as a result of trade. In the weaker forms of the model, wages would merely converge. The title of a recent article puts the message of the model more pointedly than the usual rendering of the results where all is for the best in the best of all possible worlds: 'Are your wages set in Beijing?'[6]

If inequalities between countries are, in effect, assumed away, then there is no need for global redistribution or even for a world fiscal authority. If the outcome of market transactions rewards production factors in accord with their contribution to the value of output, then no further consideration need be given to income distribution even within countries. If, on the other hand, there is no intersection of the reality set with the theory set, then we must be particularly circumspect about any leap of faith from our models to policy recommendations and certainly watchful with respect to the nature of policy outcomes.

Fiscal federalism

The notion of fiscal federalism was developed to provide economic insights into the fiscal management of already existing federal states. A major focus in that literature is on jurisdictional spillovers: positive and negative externalities, and public goods and bads. Until recently international spillovers were believed to be sufficiently limited in range so as to be amenable to ad hoc solutions by the few parties involved. Today many recognize the existence of significant negative externalities having global impact, some of which, like global warming and holes in the ozone layer, even threaten the survival of life on this planet.

The fiscal federalism writings take little note of the global domain. A survey of the major works in this area reveals that most early authors focused on the relations between central governments and subnational jurisdictions. Australian, Canadian, and German contributions to fiscal federalism are, as might be expected, quite prominent and, as might be expected as well, focus on relationships within these federal states.[7] Reviewing the varied experiences of federal states is a prerequisite for thinking about world order. The most notable extension of the concept of fiscal federalism beyond national jurisdiction is, of course, the EU. In fact, the MacDougall Commission report, to which I have already referred, considered quite carefully the experience of federal states in arriving at its recommendations for fiscal relations in an integrating Europe. Richard A. Musgrave, a leading authority on public finance, argued that in a multi-jurisdictional community redistribution should be a central function in order to remove gross inequalities in the balance of fiscal needs and capacities among provinces, but he excluded the possibility of redistribution from fiscal relations between sovereign jurisdictions based on voluntary association.[8] That is precisely why world public finance is insignificant today and why accord needs to be reached on building institutions and obligations at higher levels. Voluntarism simply cannot be counted on.

World fiscal federalism is a simple idea: mapping the funding and political authority over problems to the appropriately configured jurisdiction. As new problems arise and old ones evolve, the mapping changes as do the collective preferences of societies. In consequence, the functions and fiscal needs between levels of government from the local to the global are likely to be a matter for continuing re-negotiation. These are not matters that are settled once and for all. The essential focus of fiscal federalism is comparable in some ways to the idea of an optimum currency area (see Chapter 5): if markets and factor mobility map to the world, then that should be the locus of the currency. That is, if a single currency is counseled for an integrated market and the world is now an integrated market, it follows that all currencies should be replaced by one world currency.[9] In the case of public finance, the differing needs and preferences of lower level jurisdictions are best served and preserved by taxing and spending decisions influenced by their citizens.

Given the existence of interdependencies and spillovers, however, some degree of harmonization is required as is a system of compensatory transfers whose locus is at the world level. The extent of our global interdependence suggests that arrangements appropriate for a time when these interactions were limited should now cede some of their functions to global democratic institutions financed not by whim, but by legally constituted and enforceable taxes on individuals and corporations, and not by voluntary contributions on which recalcitrant nations (especially the most powerful) impose conditions prior to paying.

The most egregious example of the piper calling the tune is that of the US which has effectively muzzled the free speech and inquiry of the UN and American citizens working for the UN, the US Bill of Rights notwithstanding, in return for the promise of payments. An American Law passed in 1997 prohibits the payment of voluntary contributions by the US to the UN 'unless the President certifies to Congress 15 days in advance of such payment that the United Nations is not engaged in any effort to implement or impose any taxation on United States persons in order to raise revenue for the United Nations or any of its specialized agencies.' The phrase 'any effort' apparently is applied, in practice, even to discussion or the slightest printed reference to global taxes.[10] I was a witness to the troubling spectacle of a UN official, who is a US citizen, prefacing his remarks on the March 2002 Monterrey International Conference on Financing for Development with the comment that he was not going to use the 'T word.' It is probably worth reminding Americans that if the 13 Colonies had obstinately dug in their heels and prevented the granting of substantial revenue-raising power to their central government, originally denied under the Articles of Confederation, the US could have been an early example of a failed state (see Chapter 2).

When considering the social fractals of government and taxation, we would expect to encounter broadly homologous features at each level of jurisdiction. Details, of course, vary, but consistencies tend to predominate. This parallelism has yet to be achieved at supranational levels and least of all at the global level. When adding higher level or levels of jurisdiction and of public finance, one can reasonably expect a shift of revenues and expenditures to both higher and lower levels. Federal states will no doubt retain their distinctive arrangements. One small indication of the range of differences is provided by a ratio of the revenues (including transfers) of local governments to those at the regional and national levels. In 1999 the relationship for Australia was 1/6.6/9.8; for Canada 1/2.66/2.63; for Germany 1/1.6/4.3 and the US; 1/1.3/2.6.[11] These widely differing ratios represent the playing out of a complex set of variables, including the political. One can expect domestic democratic deliberations to continue to be an important element in preserving these difference, but newly created functions accompanied by taxing, spending, and transfer powers at the world level can be expected to alter some of the needs of states and localities and hence also bear an influence on these ratios. Rather than the prospect of a global leviathan, were a diminution of hostilities between countries to be a consequence of world government, one could reasonably expect a shrinkage of defense expenditure at the national and supranational levels of the system of public finance.

Global equity

Income is continuously redistributed both between and within nations in a myriad of ways with every transaction that occurs. It is redistributed through the prices of goods and services, both when they change and when they stay constant, through the actions of multinational corporations, through the action of cartels, through changes in interest rates, through nationalization of assets, and, rather minimally by comparison, through foreign-aid programs. The collusive actions by the OPEC states to raise oil prices in the 1970s had major distributive consequences, but so too did the constancy of crude-oil prices during most of the 1960s under the tutelage of the cartel of the Seven Sisters oligopoly oil-producing multinationals. In general, redistribution arising from the pricing of minerals is based on the combination of the historical accident of location of substances that have become economic resources and the bargaining relationship between countries and companies. The taxes, subsidies, and quantitative restrictions on trade imposed by individual national governments also have widespread distributional consequences in the world economy, as do laws governing property. The existence of tax havens is yet one further element in this by no means exhaustive list of factors exacerbating global inequality. One estimate places the wealth held in tax havens at $6 trillion or one-fifth of the no-doubt underestimated world gross product.[12]

National governments try to maintain some degree of equity between individuals and regions by means of provision of services, infrastructure, as well as direct payments, tax breaks, and/or subsidies. If one takes the Gini coefficient of inequality[13] as one measure of success of such efforts with respect to the income of households, one is far more likely to find relatively low Ginis (0.2–0.3) in the northern countries and Ginis reflecting high inequality (0.4–0.6) in southern countries. Even in the north, the continuous process of transaction-based regressive income redistribution has begun to run rampant where the commitment to equity has weakened or vanished. Data from the Luxembourg Income Study show that the Gini increased from 0.301 in 1979 to 0.372 in 1997 in the US, while in the UK it increased from 0.270 in 1979 to 0.345 in 1999.[14] Moreover, the US is the outlier among the industrial county members of the OECD on all six of the income inequality measures highlighted on the Luxembourg Income Study website.

At one time one could reasonably assume that at the national level there was a commitment to redistribution through taxation or benefits, or both. Globalization of economic activity has weakened the validity of that generalization, as has the writing of neoliberal thinkers, who have challenged the whole concept of redistribution. We have come a long way from Andrew Carnegie's Gospel of Wealth (1889) with its emphasis on one's obligation to live modestly and to use one's wealth fully for the benefit of humanity.[15] In recent years there has been a celebration of the notion that greed is good and the creation of what Robert H. Frank has called a 'Winner Take All' society.[16] Before one can make the case for redistribution globally, one must succeed in rescuing the concept and the practice at the local and national levels. Nor should we be turned aside in our determination by the facile arguments that redistribution is necessarily an eventual by-product of growth, free trade, community development, or, now, the provision of global public goods, followed by the counsel that one need only be patient.

Patience, indeed! The fact that income redistribution is no longer a topic of conversation in polite (read: elite) society, does not mean that it does not occur and is not implicit in today's political agenda. De facto *regressive* redistribution of income is central to support for the neoliberal agenda, whatever the public rhetoric may proclaim. It must remain implicit, however, because one can hardly affirm that one supports policies that have the effect of impoverishing most of the world's people, even if one is convinced that it is the will of the omniscient and omnipotent Market. Regressive redistribution of income is not just something that occurs as an explicit objective of public policy, although it may well be aided and abetted by public policy. Following Thurman Arnold, it is useful to think of *private* redistributive measures that are regressive in their effects, such as executive salaries in the US, in particular. Arnold made a distinction in 1937 between 'taxation' by private organizations which seems to be viewed as a pleasant way of paying tribute and the curious myth that permanent public improvements, conservation of resources, utilization of labor, and distribution of available goods are a burden on posterity if accomplished by an organization called 'government' which assumes public responsibility.[17]

Income is not redistributed globally in a systematic, predictable, progressive way at present. At the global level, discussion of an organized system of redistribution has not yet made its way to the negotiating table in any meaningful sense. The increasing calls heard during the 1980s for 'structural adjustment with a human face' may be offered as *prima facie* support for the contention that, on balance, the transactions of private and public actors have not favored global equity. The recent literature on global justice reinforces that case.[18]

While our income distribution data are the shakiest of our estimates, they paint a grim picture of widening gaps both between and within countries over at least the last two decades. I will not belabor the facts, the general trends of which are well known, but a few numbers are in order. For the global level, the United Nations Development Programme's (UNDP's) *Human Development Report* has been tracking regularly the rising world inequality as reflected by the growing gap between the 20 percent of the population living in the world's richest countries and the 20 percent living in the world's poorest countries. This ratio of the top fifth to the bottom fifth of the world's countries is estimated to have gone from 3:1 in 1820, to 7:1 in 1870, 11:1 in 1913, 30:1 in 1960, 61:1 in 1991, and 86:1 by the late 1990s.[19] You may have already seen the cover illustration of a champagne glass, with the narrowest of stems (and no base) used in the *Human Development Report 1992* to potently convey the sense the recent extremes of income concentration. The broad top of the glass represents the 82.7 percent of the world's income received by the residents of those countries accounting for the top 20 percent of world income, with the entire stem accounting for the remaining 80 percent of the population and 17.3 percent of the world income, of which the bottom 20 percent, in contrast, received only 1.4 percent of world income.

These numbers are now complemented by what Branko Milanovic in his January 2002 article in *The Economic Journal* calls the 'True World Income Distribution'; that is, estimates of income inequality based on household surveys from 91 countries.[20] His numbers confirm not only that world inequality is rising, but that inequality between nations is far greater than the inequality within nations. Milanovic estimates that the World Gini coefficient, adjusted for differences in purchasing power, increased from 0.63 in 1988 to 0.66 in 1993. If purchasing power parity adjustments are not made, then the World Gini for 1993 jumps to 0.805.[21] Of the 100 of so countries for which Gini coefficients are reported in the *Human Development Report 2001*, only two countries (Nicaragua and Swaziland) have Ginis as high as 0.60 and none as high as 0.66. Some of Milanovic's estimates are less dramatic than those published in the *Human Development Report* (HDR), but the picture is still one of vast inequality. For example, we learn that the richest 25 million Americans have a total income equal to that of the world's poorest two billion people.[22]

Detailed discussion of global income redistribution in the larger public interest has largely been like Sherlock Holmes' dog that did not bark in the night. One can identify several arguments whose logic strongly suggests that principles be extended beyond national boundaries. Yet, time and again, on this topic as on others, habits of mind seem to have prevented that line of demarcation from being crossed. One idea that is especially apt is the compensation principle, a concept from theoretical welfare economics, which involves winners bribing losers to obtain the acquiescence of the latter in the adoption of a policy that is not in their interest. In fact, the compensation principle can be likened to the practice of the matching of sets of concessions in tariff reduction bargaining in the framework of the GATT. Increased taxes on profits and/or the closing of tax loopholes (for example) could be regarded as compensation (when redistributed progressively) for agreement to the freeing of international trade. I have already referred in Chapter 3 to Meade's use of cardinal utility to demonstrate that compensating losers from free trade can bring the world to a maximum. Meade's point seems to have fallen on deaf ears. Today's students of international trade theory are unlikely to hear a murmur about the application of the compensation principle across national boundaries. Concerns about the environment, rather than free trade, led to similar recommendations, but on an ad hoc basis with no reference to theoretical underpinnings. Christopher Layton suggested in 1986, for example, that some of the Brazilian debt be retired in exchange for a commitment to preserve the Amazon rain forests,[23] an idea that led to a number of debt for nature exchanges. I will return to global equity in Chapter 6.

From foreign aid to global taxes

The foreign-aid writings of the post-World War II period are consistent in regarding aid as a *self-limiting activity* tied in with the transition from the less developed category to the developed category. During the 1970s a commonly invoked term was 'graduation': once a country crossed the magic line from developing to developed, it was expected that it would join the club of those providing official development assistance to those left behind. As none have graduated to the high income category listed in the World Development Report (WDR) since its inception in 1976 apart from Greece and Portugal, both members of the EU, the term has fallen into disuse.[24] For some time a number of OPEC countries joined the ranks of aid providers, but by 2000 only Kuwait, Saudi Arabia, and the United Arab Emirates figured among the shortlist of donors outside of the DAC of the OECD.[25]

In addressing the question of foreign aid, the parallel with income-redistribution programs within a nation-state is rarely drawn. It is, simply, absent from the foreign-assistance literature, which carries on with either national or regional blinders and fails to see aid as a step toward a permanent system of international transfers, in which the relative importance and even the cast of characters or the net recipients might alter over time. In a world of sovereign states, it apparently was simply regarded as unthinkable that net public transfers between jurisdictions would become permanently institutionalized. Nonetheless, there would appear to be no immediate plans for winding up the activities of the World Bank and the regional development banks. It would certainly appear that they anticipate that the 'less developed,' like the poor in the 19th century discourse (and today) will always be with us. To the extent that 'graduation' still exists it is with respect to whether a country has access to the World Bank Group's soft loan window at the International Development Association or must accept near-commercial terms on loans from the IBRD.

Since the publication of the Pearson Commission Report, *Partners in Development*, in 1969 we have had an agreed upon target of 0.7 percent of gross national product (GNP) for official development assistance (ODA) to be provided by the high-income countries.[26] This is a one-sided voluntary contrivance, which makes no mention of the relative entitlements of the recipients. The result is a system where some countries receive little on either a per capita or share of GDP basis. The net ODA receipts of India in 2000, for example, amounted to $1.5 per capita and 0.3 percent of its GNP, while the corresponding figures for Ghana, with a comparable human development indicator and per capita income (pci) (either actual or adjusted for purchasing power parity), were $31.6 and 11.7 percent.[27]

In the 1970s the development literature took a shift under the impetus of the International Labour Organization (ILO) and the World Bank to a focus on basic needs. With it came a major step in refocusing aid strategy on the elimination of poverty, which even were it to have been successful is not the same as eliminating the need for transfers within a federal system, whether it is a national or a global one. The foreign-aid debate has spawned many schemes for increasing the concessional financial flows to the Less Developed Countries (LDCs), but most of these have made no noticeable impact relative to the 0.7 percent target. It is important to add the qualification that 'concessional' is not, by any means, equivalent to 'without conditions attached.' Conditions abound and they are both significant and intrusive. Among the ideas that surfaced was David Horowitz's plan in the 1960s which involved an interest rate subsidy on commercial borrowings of the developing countries. In retrospect, that could have made a major difference to heavily indebted countries in the 1980s, when unprecedented interest rate increases inflated their debt service payments. Another proposal by Albert Hirschman and Richard Bird called for tax credits to individuals for voluntary contributions to foreign aid.[28]

A much-discussed proposal for linking the newly created SDR with foreign aid generated considerable excitement for a time in the 1970s, but both the SDR itself and any possible aid link have come to naught. When creation of the SDR was being considered, the principal problem being addressed was that of a shortage of international liquidity to use by Central Banks for the maintenance of stable exchange rates. SDR reserve assets created by the IMF were to be issued in a non-inflationary manner. In fact, the shortage of reserves was 'resolved' by the creation by private banks of Eurocurrency-denominated loans and any wholesale creation of SDRs would have exacerbated inflationary pressures. In the 30 years from 1970 to 2000 the value of SDRs created expanded by 8.2 times, while the value of total central bank reserves (excluding gold) expanded by 50.3 times. In fact, there has not been a new round of creation of SDRs since 1981, nor can there be without the agreement of the US. The total stock of SDRs had a value of $28 billion in 2000, slightly more than one-half the net value of bilateral official development assistance, with the latter amounting to only 0.22 percent of the combined GNP of the 22 DAC countries, well short of the three-decade old agreed upon target of 0.7 percent.

The numerous writings on foreign aid and the few on world taxation and income redistribution are two separate sets of discourse, with virtually no overlap. Writers on foreign aid have not embraced the viewpoint that predominates in the writings on global taxation. There are an elaborate set of issues in the foreign-aid literature—project vs program aid, grant equivalents, bilateral vs multilateral aid, aid effectiveness—which tend to shift attention away from the broader issues addressed by world public finance and even from the question of the adequacy of the current aid target itself.

Sayre Schatz described in 1983 a process that he referred to as socializing adaptation,[29] somewhat akin to John Kenneth Galbraith's notion of countervailing power. In Schatz's view this phenomenon of long-standing at the local and national levels, can now be observed in its manifold variations at the level of the world economy. A stereotyping of this concept, which is consistent with Schatz's presentation is that concessions to economic justice are introduced in the interests of keeping the world safe for capitalism:

> To be successful socializing adaptations need not be generous or freely accorded or sufficient to meet minimal human needs. Changes can be grudging, mean-spirited and stingy responses to problems that have become too painful to ignore. However, if they suffice to mollify dissatisfaction that jeopardizes the viability of the system, they constitute successful socializing adaptation.[30]

The 0.7 percent of GNP for foreign-aid target is one manifestation of socializing adaptation. Remarkably, we find this very modest objective reiterated once again in *A Better World For All*, an unprecedented joint document issued by the OECD, the World Bank, the IMF, and the UN in June 2000.[31] In 1998 the ratio of net ODA to GNP for the then

21 country members of the OECD's DAC was only 0.24, with the ratio for the US at a mere 0.10. The goal has been regularly attained only by Denmark, the Netherlands, Norway, and Sweden. In fact, even if that goal had been reached in 1998 it would have amounted to only US$150 billion (in contrast to the actual amount of US$52 billion) and had the money been allocated as unconditional grants in its entirety to those countries identified in the *World Development Report 2000–2001* as low income, it would have amounted to a mere $63 per capita for each of the 2.4 billion people living in those countries, a sum that would likely be insufficient to pay for an evening's dinner for one person, including wine and tip, in an upscale restaurant in any of the high-income countries of the world.[32]

Depending on largesse from today's 'dominant' countries with strings of conditionality attached seems hardly to be the manner in which to construct a planet-wide human partnership. That four institutions that function as would-be masters-of-the-world have nothing fresh to offer in the realm of world public finance than an obsolete formula for charity which is unequal to the tasks at hand belies their lack of serious commitment to building a peaceful and just democratic global order. That *A Better World for All* envisages reducing the share of those living on less than $1 a day from the current level of 1.2 billion people or 20 percent of the world population to 15 percent by 2015, suggests a lack of any sense of urgency. If as that report projects, world population were to grow only from 6 billion in 2000 to 7 billion in 2015 (an annual growth rate of 1.03 percent), there would still be 1.05 billion people living at less than one dollar per day in 2015.

In Chapter 3, I cited Owen Lattimore to the effect that the only US foreign policy was the Cold War. One side of US Cold War foreign policy was the very substantial allocation of grants first to Europe and Japan, and then to Taiwan and South Korea. We should not forget that there once was serious commitment to sharing with certain others: in 1949 alone during the Marshall Plan years, the US extended $6.3 billion in grants for economic purposes to countries in need (principally in Europe and East Asia), an amount which represented 2.5 percent of US GNP.[33] There is nothing quite like it in the records of recent 'generosity.' Within a few weeks of the Communist victory in Czechoslovakia in 1948, the Marshall Plan was through the legislative hurdles. Under the plan, between 3 April 1948 and 30 June 1952, 16 European countries[34] received a total of $13.2 billion, of which 88.6 percent were grants. Concern about communism in East Asia, brought vast sums in grants to Taiwan and South Korea. In military and economic aid, the two received $9.1 billion by the end of 1961; in economic aid alone, $5.2 billion. Of the $2.0 billion in economic aid that went to Taiwan 83.8 percent was in grants, while 98.5 percent of the $3.2 billion that went to South Korea was in grants. The facile generalizations about what was accomplished by these two tigers or Newly Industrialized Countries (NICs) have a way of forgetting the major economic boost that came their way through outright grants. The crisis focus of US foreign policy tended to divert attention from other parts of the world. By the time that Castro came to power in Cuba in 1959, US experience with confronting communism had evolved more parsimonious response patterns. The Alliance for Progress US aid program for Latin America launched by President John Kennedy in 1961 was from the outset far less magnanimous an enterprise, with $10 billion exclusively in loans pledged over a ten-year period, than the concerted attention given to Europe and East Asia. Generosity apparently required a more credible threat than that posed by a small Caribbean nation.

One of the earliest explicit references to the use of international taxation for financing world order appears in James Lorimer's *Ultimate Problem of International Jurisprudence*, published in 1884. For Lorimer the 'ultimate problem' is 'how to find international equivalents for the factors known to national law as legislation, jurisdiction, and execution?'[35] In sketching out his detailed answers to the question, Lorimer does not neglect finances:

> The expenses of the International Government shall be defrayed by an international tax, to be levied by the government of each State upon its citizens; and the extent of such tax shall be proportioned to the number of representatives which the State sends to the International Legislature.[36]

It is instructive to start with Lorimer, notably because he conceived of global taxes as one part of a complete framework of government activities at the global level. For Lorimer, global taxes were conceived as being contingent upon the existence of a higher level government. This is a crucial point: one can discuss at length the technicalities of global taxes, a global currency, global competition policy, and progressive global income redistribution, but they cannot exist until we are ready to establish a world government.

In the two decades prior to the publication of Lorimer's work, the organizations that were to become the International Telecommunication Union (ITU) and the Universal Postal Union (UPU) had been established, in 1865 and 1874 respectively. They were financed through membership assessments roughly keyed to benefits received. If one sees membership fees, whatever the basis of assessment, as a form of taxation, then we have in these organizations the beginnings on a most uncertain road to world public finance. The League of Nations was initially financed on a benefits-received basis, but that was quickly changed to a system approximating ability to pay based on an index combining government revenues and population, with the population of the largest European member as the upper limit, to prevent an undue burden on India and China.

There may well have been other proposals in the decades following Lorimer's work, but they would appear to have been consigned to intellectual limbo, scarcely meriting even a footnote. As already noted in Chapter 3, a flurry of writing occurred during World War II when considerable intellectual effort was turned to the question of organizing for world peace. Gunnar Myrdal writing in 1956 makes explicit his bias in favor of greater international economic integration and calls specifically for a 'world welfare state.'[37] By 1970 practicality seemed to have taken firm root in Myrdal's thought, for his 'World Anti-Poverty Program' contains little more than a plea for a shift from bilateral to multilateral assistance and the strategic counsel that aid will only receive popular support if the humanitarian dimension is emphasized.[38] By then Myrdal had discovered the 'soft state' and argued that 'much more important than aid . . . are the needed social and economic reforms within these countries themselves.'[39] Regrettably, the soft state characterization seems to have taken firmer root than his earlier pleas for greater equity. Reforms as a precondition for aid simply perpetuate the paternalistic relation between aid provider and aid recipient and may even exacerbate the difficulties of the recipient.

In law and political science, work was going on simultaneously on the financing of world government. The most noted of these is part of a highly detailed 'Proposed Revised Charter of the United Nations' drafted by Grenville Clark and Louis B. Sohn.[40] They proposed the creation of a World Development Authority directed by a five-person World Development Council. The Authority would channel 'grants-in-aid or interest-free loans' to developing countries for indispensable economic and social projects for which adequate financing is not otherwise available.[41] The Authority would be funded out of the general budget of the UN, which in their plan would be obtained through taxes earmarked by each member state for the UN. They called for each country to designate for the UN all or part of existing domestic excise, income, export, and/or import taxes up to a national limit of 2.5 percent of gross product and a world limit of 2.0 percent of estimated gross world product.[42] They emphasized the need for large and reliable revenues for the UN and, in turn, for development and noted that the national burden would be a relatively light one once disarmament is achieved.[43]

Taxes on beneficiaries of the existence of international order were proposed about the same time by the Commission to Study the Organization of Peace: they proposed that the UN receive a small part of the fees for international mail, passports, and visas as well as of tolls levied upon international waterways. They also proposed that the UN have either 'taxation powers or property rights over the actual and potential resources of the sea bed, Antarctica, and outer space.'[44]

Further discussion of new revenue sources for the UN System are contained in a 1964 volume written by John Stoessinger and his associates. Their survey ranges from the sale of postage stamps and greeting cards to a proposal for an international joint stock Cosmic Development Corporation to exploit the resources of outer space. Their main conclusions can be summarized as follows:

1. 'As a general rule, if a resource promises to yield revenue, states will tend to claim it. If they do not, it usually means that the resource is not only currently, but also potentially, useless.'[45]
2. '. . . [T]he resources of the frozen polar zones, of the oceans, and of outer space will not become substitutes for the failure of states to meet their financial obligations to the United Nations.'[46]

In the 1970s talk of international tax schemes began to be heard with increasing frequency. The passage of the UN resolution calling for a NIEO, with its plea for predictable, continuous, assured, and more substantial revenue sources for the LDCs, seems to have given impetus to the idea of global taxes. Nonetheless, the NIEO resolution made no explicit reference to international income redistribution as such and reiterates the 0.7 percent concessional aid target.

In 1969 a committee headed by Jan Tinbergen proposed that a 0.5 percent tax on the value of selected consumer durables be levied to increase the funds available for development finance.[47] A 1976 study coordinated by Tinbergen, Mahbub ul Haq, and James Grant merely lists a number of taxes which might be considered in order to increase the amount and automaticity of funds available for development and international income redistribution:

> tax on non-renewable resources, tax on international pollutants, tax on activities of transnational enterprises, rebates to countries of origin

> of taxes collected on the earnings of trained immigrants from Third World countries, taxes on or royalties from commercial activities arising out of international commons—for example ocean beds, outer space, the Antarctic region; and various proposals for taxing international civil servants, consumer spending and armament spending.[48]

Haq, in a separate study, which appeared the same year, discussed some of these taxes in greater detail and expressed his preference for an international income tax. He admitted that an income tax would pose the greatest challenge to national sovereignty and hence must be deferred until the time is propitious in favor of devices for taxing income indirectly.[49] Haq also singled out what he termed anti-humanitarian activities for taxation and included a 10-percent tax on arms expenditures.[50] In his discussion of international pollution, Haq drew the parallel with principles that are accepted at the national level:

> Whenever social diseconomies result on an international scale from the action of sovereign states, the United Nations should have the authority to impose a tax on such activities on behalf of the entire international community. The principle is a simple one. Its acceptance will require a revolution in mankind's thinking.[51]

Steinberg, Yager, and Brannon (1978), and Sunshine and Chaudhri (1981) are the first major studies to deal at length with global taxation. The former propose a national 'shadow tax' (that is, a payment required on the basis of estimated yields of hypothetical taxes, as opposed to an actual levy imposed by the UN on firms or individuals) to be levied on the GNP of nation-states; an arrangement that would convert the 0.7 percent concessional aid target into a formal obligation. They observe that shadow taxes not only would be a different way of calculating the obligation of countries to international organizations, but if substituted for existing assessments would not require any new formal international agreements.[52] The other sources of general revenue that they regard as most promising are the economic rents from deep-seabed mineral extraction and taxes on international trade and the international transfer of profits from international investments.[53] Other possible revenue sources discussed by Steinberg, Yager, and Brannon are taxes on both domestic and internationally traded oil, a tax on all hydrocarbons, taxes on international trade in mineral raw materials, taxes on oil spills, taxes on non-tanker cargo shipping, and taxes on offshore petroleum production.

Sunshine and Chaudhri[54] discuss many of the same taxes as are considered by Steinberg, Yager, and Brannon. Their article is a useful complement in that the emphasis is on the legal dimension and makes reference to existing precedents. Sunshine and Chaudhri envision, as do some others, that the funds raised through global development taxes would supplement, rather than replace, the components of current resource transfers. In common with other schemes, nationals of all countries, developed and developing, would pay their transaction-based taxes. Their exclusive emphasis on taxes for development stands in contrast to the work of Jenks, Sumberg, Clark, and Sohn who saw development as one of the international needs requiring finance, but not the sole purpose.

In the 1980 Brandt Commission Report we also find a listing of a series of international taxes.[55] The taxes mentioned would have been familiar to anyone following this literature at the time. The uniqueness of the approach taken is the insistence on universality of any revenue-raising program, no matter how modest at first, as being essential in the forging of global solidarity: 'We believe that a system of universal and automatic contributions would help to establish the principle of global responsibility, and would be a step towards the comanagement of the world economy.'[56]

To date, Ruben Mendez's *International Public Finance* (1992) is still the most comprehensive discussion of global taxes and global public finance. The engagement of Mendez with global taxation goes back at least to his involvement as a Chief Economic Adviser at the UN Conference on Desertification in 1977 and to proposals that he drafted at the time for 'international taxation and automaticity.'[57] His extensive contributions to advance the objective of world public finance include his participation in the Commission on Global Governance (1995) and to the volume published by the UNDP on Global Public Goods.[58]

The most discussed global tax proposal, after over one decade of neglect, is what has come to be known as the Tobin Tax on foreign exchange transactions. It originally appeared in a lecture presented by James Tobin in 1972 and was developed more fully by him in 1978.[59] Tobin's proposal for a tax on foreign exchange transactions was motivated by a desire to dampen speculative capital flows and to restore greater autonomy to national monetary policy. As Tobin's concern was to mitigate the 'predominance of speculation over enterprise,'[60] he expressed no interest in the disposition of the vast sums likely to be raised by an internationally uniform tax. He merely indicated that the proceeds collected by individual governments be paid into the IMF or the World Bank.[61] His concern was with altering behavior and not public finance. The Tobin Tax may well be the first proposal for a global tax that has spawned a worldwide movement: ATTAC, which originated in France in December 1998 and as of December 2002 had affiliates in 33 countries, with websites in 15 different languages and had over two millions hits on their home website (http://attac.org) in September 2002. Their acronym stands for Association for the Taxation of Financial Transactions in the Interests of the Citizen and their weekly web-based and e-mail-distributed newsletter 'Sand in the Wheels' is named after Tobin's stated intention for the tax, that of 'throwing sand in the wheels of international finance.' The publication of a volume devoted to the Tobin Tax (1996) under the aegis of the UNDP is doubtless the proximate cause for the hostile reaction of the US Congress to activity by the UN aimed at the promotion of any global taxes. Given the interest in the Tobin Tax, it is appropriate to remind the reader that he offered it 'regretfully' as a second best. For Tobin, the first best solution was 'a common currency, common monetary and fiscal policy, and economic integration.'[62] I will return to the Tobin Tax in Chapter 5 in my discussion of a world currency.

From common heritage to world public goods

In the 1970s the notion of the 'common heritage of mankind' was used in the discussion of global sharing of the proceeds from the extraction of seabed resources and the economic exploitation of outer space. Let us take the next logical step: a moment's reflection would tell us that virtually the entire world we live in today is based on a common heritage—written and spoken language, the food we eat, the clothes we wear, the very thoughts we think, not to mention the technological building blocks in the machines that surround us. Pablo Neruda acknowledged another dimension of the common heritage when he spoke of his indebtedness to Walt Whitman.[63] We are all indebted in countless ways and we all derive gain by standing on the shoulders of others. The notion of common heritage was doubtlessly applied primarily to seabed resources as a domain over which prior claims of sovereignty and property rights had not yet been established. Property rights themselves are part of our common heritage. The historical accident of national boundaries having been drawn as they happen to have been should not justify denying to the bulk of the world's population a share in the monetary gains resulting from the harnessing of our common heritage.

Yet in the very forum in which the notion of common heritage was being frequently invoked, a great sea grab took place, assigning resources not in relation to need, but rather in proportion to length of coastline and the richness of the resources located there. As William R. Cline pointed out, the creation of exclusive economic zones represented yet another extension of property rights, quite inconsistent with the notion of the common heritage.[64] As long as one's thinking about our common heritage is limited to what is no country's land, then that which is left as the common heritage is what little remains after all else is appropriated. The residual territorial common heritage is scarcely likely to provide the hoped-for revenues to finance global public purposes, among which is the quest for greater equity in the distribution of the world's income.

One can well appreciate that there was no inclination to include under the common heritage heading economic resources lying within national boundaries. Indeed, quite the contrary, at the very time that the notion of a common heritage was being invoked, not only were the OPEC countries capitalizing as fully as possible on their 'ownership' of crude-oil deposits, but, as already noted, territorial limits were being extended to expand the offshore rights of nations. Existing property rights in resources were to be maintained, while areas where property rights were not yet established were claimed by coastal states to prevent the potential for economic gain being lost to a Sea Bed Authority.

Is technology itself not part of the common heritage of mankind? Thorstein Veblen spoke of technology as being a 'joint stock of knowledge.'[65] Any technological advance builds on the pre-existing accumulated knowledge and tools. In *Reshaping the International Order* (1976) we find a suggestion for an even broader application of the common heritage concept 'to new domains such as mineral rights, science and technology, means of production and other sources of wealth.'[66] In terms of the present discussion, the important point is to invoke the common heritage principle to provide philosophical underpinning for the case for world taxation to finance both world development and the maintenance world order.

One can even think of social capital as part of our Common Heritage. In what was likely Nobel Prize winner Herbert Simon's last published paper prior to his death in February 2001, he put the case most strongly:

> I personally do not see any moral basis for an inalienable right to inherit resources, or to retain all the resources that one has acquired

> by means of economic or other activities. . . . When we compare the poorest with the richest nations, it is hard to conclude that social capital can produce less than about 90 per cent of income in wealthy societies like those of the United States or North-western Europe. On moral grounds, then, we could argue for a flat income tax of 90 per cent to return that wealth to its real owners.[67]

In fact, Simon went on to settle for a flat tax of 70 percent. For our purposes it is the idea rather than the rates that are of interest. The conceptual link between the common heritage and a guaranteed income to be paid to each of the world's people is developed in greater detail in Chapter 6.

One can also think of world public goods as part of our common heritage. Indeed world public goods and our Common Heritage can be thought of as partially intersecting sets. Charles Kindleberger observed in 1986 that international public goods are undersupplied in the absence of international government. For Kindleberger peace is the primary international public good, but he also identifies in the economic sphere 'an open trading system, including freedom of the seas, well-defined property rights, standards of weights and measures that may include international money, or fixed exchange rates . . .'[68] Ruben Mendez dealt at some length with global public goods in his *International Public Finance* (1992), in 1995 in 'The Provision and Financing of Universal Public Goods,' and in 1999 in 'Peace as a Global Public Good.'[69] The last few years has seen an explosion of interest in global public goods.[70]

The Global Public Goods volume produced by the UNDP contains a quote by UN Secretary-General Kofi Annan opposite the title page, which takes note of the characteristics of global public goods, observing that neither a single country on its own nor the global marketplace can provide them. He continues: 'Thus our efforts must now focus on the missing term of the equation: global public goods.'[71] Is it merely one 'term,' however all-encompassing, that we are missing? I fear that if we do not collectively break loose from our 0.7 percent of GNP psychological ceiling for ODA, then once again we will have to cut back on a range of ongoing activities as global public goods becomes the latest 'challenge' to be accommodated on a minimalist budget by crowding out last season's priority.

Consider the example of the new Global Fund to Fight AIDS, Tuberculosis, and Malaria, which, however meritorious, should be part of a larger endeavor to raise living standards and to address systemically public health. A larger mandate, depending on its scope, could certainly cost anywhere from tens to hundreds of billions of US dollars. The initial American government pledge was for $200 million. The Global Fund, as its name implies, is a charity. From the web-based US Department of State Fact Sheet on the Fund, one can go in two short clicks to a page where a contribution can be made to the Fund. Is charity the way in which we are going to deal with each of the world public goods? Jeffrey Sachs has expressed his discontent in a Special Report in *The Economist* (26 October 2002) titled 'Weapons of Mass Salvation.' He stresses that issues should be addressed by the UN at the appropriate scale: 'there must be no faking it with small-scale AIDS projects that might save one village while leaving whole nations to die. But true scale will cost money, especially from the United States.'[72] And so we come back, even with disease control as a global public good, to voluntarism and dependence on the whim of one country which in recent decades has tended to keep a tight rein on the non-military purse strings. Need more be said in favor of the case for world public finance with revenues from taxes collected worldwide on transactions, profts, income, and/or wealth?

Conclusion

In the 1950s and the 1960s when there was a wide margin for generosity, no steps were taken to establish a system of world public finance. We now find ourselves hard put even to maintain adequate welfare systems at home. The pressures of international competition are regularly invoked with the effect of breeding a mean spirit everywhere. If it is now every person for him/herself, thus bringing home the we/they dichotomous thinking previously limited to 'others,' what room is left for greater world solidarity?

With public sector activities under attack domestically, philosophizing about world justice finds few adherents. And yet it is only by global action that we can preserve what we hold dear at home. Highly productive activities must be adequately taxed for the global good of which we all partake, not just for the good of the jurisdiction where chance, tax incentives, or other circumstances have landed them.

The world market functions within a framework of law and is, in effect, a public good. If an open system is to be preserved from protectionist attacks, the addition of compensatory measures must be devised. Distributional equity must be treated as the reverse side of the free market coin. We should not speak of one without invoking the other, as balance between market activities and provision for well-being is essential for social harmony. In a society with broad-based participation, one is more likely to encounter skillful steering toward balance. Where no effective organization exists at the highest level, we are reduced to working on the global jigsaw puzzle with our hands tied.

World public finance is one part of a way out of our zero-sum game where each nation frantically competes its way into poverty wages and a devastated environment. The treadmill that nations and individuals find themselves on is one where there are few winners and a nation actually loses in important respects at the same time that it is said to be gaining. 'Who's counting' makes all the difference. My losses may be left out of your calculus.

If a long lead-time is necessary for us to accept a major organizational departure, then it is certainly not too early to begin speaking in earnest about word public finance and income redistribution. Central redistributive institutions, together with other executive, legislative, and judicial functions, as James Lorimer specified in the late 19th century, are required. Differing fiscal regimes will surely continue to exist, as they do in federal states at present. This is perfectly consistent with the writings on fiscal federalism or what the EU refers to as sudsidiarity, that is, functions should reside at the lowest level at which they can be efficiently performed.

Estimates of how much is likely to be raised by different proposed global taxes[73] are really beside the point at this stage, although, as I suggested earlier, we should be thinking about revenue targets of no less than one trillion US dollars. The key is clearly the matter of will: where there is a will, there is easily a way. When the perception becomes widespread that many key national objectives can be achieved only through global organization, then we can expect that these mechanisms will flourish. There is still scope for a certain degree of national policy independence, but the limits narrow daily. Building an umbrella of world government offers the promise of exchanging what Thomas Friedman calls the 'golden straight jacket' for additional freedom of action, which I shall elaborate on further in the next chapter. As Max Lerner observed: 'The truth is that the small states, and large as well, will have to surrender part of the *fiction of sovereignty* in order to get more of the reality of free national action.'[74]

The centrality of the nation as the unit of policy analysis in the social sciences has heretofore served as an obstacle by acting as a blinder to the potential for gain from world-level solutions. Yet our attachment to place can serve as an opportunity, once we perceive that extending the government and public finance fractals to the world scale may hold the key to preserving and enhancing what he hold dear at home. We must go beyond functional internationalism, international policy coordination, global summits, and world conferences. They may keep us headed in the direction of our desired outcomes, but they are not equal to the challenges we face.

Notes

1. Douglas Dosser, 'Towards a Theory of International Public Finance', *Kyklos*, 16 (fasc. 1, 1963), pp. 62–82.
2. Ruben P. Mendez, *International Public Finance: A New Perspective on Global Relations* (New York: Oxford University Press, 1992).
3. Jeffrey Owens, 'Taxation in a Global Environment', *OECD Observer* (1 March 2002), http://www.oecdobserver.org.
4. Timothy Bainbridge, *The Penguin Companion to European Union*, 3rd edn (London: Penguin, 2002).
5. Paul Samuelson, 'International Factor-Price Equalisation Once Again', *Economic Journal*, 59 (1949), pp. 181–97.
6. Richard B. Freeman, 'Are Your Wages Set in Beijing', *Journal of Economic Perspectives*, 9 (1995), pp. 15–32.
7. See, for example, David King, *Fiscal Tiers: The Economics of Multi-Level Government* (London: George Allen & Unwin, 1984); and Albert Breton and Anthony Scott, *The Economic Constitution of Federal States* (Toronto: University of Toronto Press, 1978).
8. Richard A. Musgrave, 'Theories of Fiscal Federalism', *Public Finance*, 24 (1969), pp. 521–32.
9. Marina von Neumann Whitman, cited in Charles P. Kindleberger, 'Government and International Trade', *Essays in International Finance*, 129 (July 1978), p. 1; and Kindleberger, 'International Public Goods without International Government', *American Economic Review*, 76 (March 1986), p. 5.
10. Ruben P. Mendez, 'Global taxation: The Rise, Decline and Future of an Idea at the United Nations' (Paris: Institut pour le développement durables et relations internationale, 2002), http://iddri.org/iddri/telecharge/fiscalite/mendez.pdf.
11. Calculations based on data appearing in IMF, *Government Finance Statistics Yearbook*, various issues.
12. Mark P. Hampton and John Cristensen, 'Offshore Pariahs? Small Island Economies, Tax Havens, and the Reconfiguration of Global Finance', *World Development*, 30 (2002), pp. 1657–73.
13. The Gini Coefficient is based on associating ranked income recipients (or families) from poorest to richest with their cumulative share of total income. The range of the Gini is from 0 (complete equality) to 1 (complete inequality, that is one income recipient receives the entire national income). In practice income Ginis usually range from 0.2 to 0.6. Recently the World Bank's *World Development Report* and the UNDP's *Human Development Report* have begun expressing the Gini as ranging from 0 to 100.
14. Luxembourg Income Study, http://lisproject.org/keyfigures/ineqtable.htm.
15. Andrew Carnegie, 'The Gospel of Wealth' (1899), http://xroads.virginia.edu/~DRBR/wealth.html.
16. Robert H. Frank and Philip J. Cook, *The Winner-Take-All Society: How More and More Americans Compete for Ever Fewer and Bigger Prizes, Encouraging*

Economic Waste, Income Inequality, and an Impoverished Cultural Life (New York: Free Press, 1995).

17. Thurman Arnold, *The Folklore of Capitalism* (New Haven: Yale University Press, 1962), p. xxvi.
18. Charles Jones, *Global Justice*: *Defending Cosmopolitanism* (New York: Oxford University Press, 1999). See also Darrel Moellendorf, *Cosmopolitan Justice* (Boulder, CO: Westview Press, 2002).
19. United Nations Development Programme, *Human Development Report 1999* (HDR) (New York: Oxford University Press, 1999), p. 3.
20. Branko Milanovic, 'True World Income Distribution, 1988 and 1993: First Calculations Based on Household Surveys Alone', *The Economic Journal*, 112 (2002), pp. 51–92.
21. Ibid., p. 72.
22. Ibid., p. 89.
23. Christopher Layton, 'One Europe: One World; A First Exploration of Europe's Potential Contribution to World Order', *Journal of World Trade Law*, Special Supplement No. 4, 20 (1986), pp. 332–33.
24. Singapore and Hong Kong also joined the high income category, but as both are city-states without the need to bear the costs of providing either infrastructure or social services to a hinterland (even a small one), I choose to regard them as constituting a separate category.
25. *HDR 2002*, p. 202.
26. Commission on International Development, *Partners in Development* (New York, Praeger, 1969). Commission chaired by Lester B. Pearson.
27. *HDR 2002*, p. 205.
28. Albert Hirschman and Richard Bird, 'Foreign Aid—A Critique and a Proposal', *Essays in International Finance*, 69 (July 1968).
29. Sayre Schatz, 'Socializing Adaptation: A Perspective on World Capitalism', *World Development*, 11 (1983), pp. 1–10.
30. Ibid., p. 4.
31. 'International Monetary Fund', 'OECD', 'United Nations', and 'World Bank Group', *A Better World for All* (2000), http://www.paris21.org/betterworld/.
32. If one were to change the dividing line between the low- and middle-income countries from $755 to $800, then China and Honduras would shift to the low-income category. The average aid per capita in my hypothetical scenario would fall to $42 for each of the 3.7 billion people.
33. US Agency for International Development, *US Foreign Assistance and Assistance from International Organization*: *Obligations and Loan Authorizations, July 1, 1945–June 30, 1961* (1962). The year 1949 refers to the fiscal year ending on 30 June 1949.
34. The Marshall Plan aid-recipient countries were Austria, Belgium, Denmark, Federal Republic of Germany, France, Greece, Iceland, Ireland, Italy, Luxembourg, the Netherlands, Norway, Portugal, Sweden, Turkey, and the United Kingdom.
35. James Lorimer, 'Book V. The Ultimate Problem of International Jurisprudence', *The Institutes of the Law of Nations*: *A Treatise of the Jural Relations of Separate Political Communities* (Edinburgh and London: William Blackwood and Sons, 1884), II, p. 186. See also C. Wilfred Jenks, 'The Significance Today of Lorimer's Ultimate Problem of International Jurisprudence', *Transactions of the Grotius Society*, 26 (1940), pp. 35–65.

36. Lorimer, vol. II, p. 287. There was to be one senator per three deputies sent by a State to Lorimer's proposed bicameral legislature. Each of the 'six great States—Germany, France, Russia, Austria, Italy, and England'—were to send 15 deputies. The 'smaller states' were to 'send a number proportioned to its international importance, as measured by population, area, free revenue, and the like, as these shall be determined by the representatives of the six great Powers' (II, p. 281).
37. Gunnar Myrdal, *An International Economy*: *Problems and Prospects* (New York: Harper & Brothers Publishers, 1956), p. 324.
38. Gunnar Myrdal, *The Challenge of World Poverty*: *A World Anti-Poverty Program in Outline* (New York: Vintage Books, 1970), p. xv.
39. Ibid. Myrdal does take the carrot approach to this reform, suggesting that virture—in terms of democratization of structures—should be rewarded as in the Swedish aid program (p. 372). The precondition of democracy for entry into the EC doubtless worked its magic in the Mediterranean.
40. Grenville Clark and Louis B. Sohn, *World Peace Through World Law* (Cambridge, Mass.: Harvard University Press, 1958).
41. Ibid., p. 331.
42. Ibid., p. 333.
43. Ibid., p. 340.
44. Commission to Study the Organization of Peace, *Strengthening the United Nations* (New York: Harper & Brothers, 1957), cited in John Stoessinger and Associates, *Financing the United Nations System* (Washington: The Brookings Institution, 1964), p. 266.
45. Ibid., p. 291.
46. Ibid., p. 292.
47. Report of the Preparatory Committee for the UN Development Decade, 4th session, 9 October 1969.
48. Jan Tinbergen, coordinator, *Reshaping the International Order*: *A Report to the Club of Rome* (New York: E.P. Dutton, 1976), p. 217. For a discussion of the brain-drain tax, see Koichi Hamada, 'Taxing the Brain Drain: A Global Point of View', in Jagdish Bhagwati, ed., *The New International Economic Order*: *The North–South Debate* (Cambridge, Mass.: The MIT Press, 1977), pp. 125–55. My proposal for a 0.1 percent tax on international capital movements was solely intended as a revenue-raising measure and applies to a portion of the tax base covered by the Tobin Tax, first proposed in 1972. Myron J. Frankman, 'Foreign Aid, World Government, and the Multi-National Corporation', paper presented at the Annual Meetings of the Canadian Economics Association (Winnipeg, 5 June 1970), p. 7.
49. Mahbub ul Haq, *The Poverty Curtain*: *Choices for the Third World* (New York: Columbia University Press, 1956), p. 196.
50. Ibid., p. 195.
51. Ibid.
52. Eleanor Steinberg and Joseph A. Yager, with Gerard M. Brannon, *New Means of Financing International Needs* (Washington, DC: The Brookings Institution, 1978), p. 196.
53. Ibid, pp. 195–96.
54. Russell B. Sunshine and Javade Chaudhri, 'Global Development Taxes: A Promising New Source of International Finance for Developing countries', *Columbia Journal of Transnational Law*, 19 (1981), pp. 407–53.

55. Independent Commission on International Development Issues, *North-South: A Program for Survival* (Cambridge, Mass.: The MIT Press, 1980), pp. 244–45. Commission chaired by Willy Brandt.
56. Ibid., p. 274.
57. Mendez (1992), pp. 4–8
58. Inge Kaul, Isabel Grunberg, and Mark A. Stern, eds, *Global Public Goods: International Cooperation in the 21st Century* (New York: Oxford University Press, 1999).
59. Tobin gives an example of the effect of a 1 percent tax (1974, p. 89; 1978, p. 155). Later he explicitly called for a tax set at 0.5 percent (*HDR 1994*, p. 70). For a discussion of a tax rate which would automatically vary with short-term interest rate differentials see Thomas Dernburg, *Global Macro-economics* (New York: Harper and Row, 1989), pp. 457–59.
60. Keynes as cited by Tobin (1984), p. 8.
61. Tobin (1978), p. 159. Tobin later added that the revenues could 'be devoted to international purposes and be placed at the disposition of international institutions.' Tobin in *HDR 1994*, p. 70.
62. Ibid., p. 154.
63. Pablo Neruda, in James Cockroft and Dale L. Johnson, eds, *The Chilean Road to Socialism* (Garden City: Anchor Press, 1973), pp. 140–41.
64. William R. Cline, 'Resource Transfers to the Developing Countries: Issues and Trends', in Cline, ed., *Policy Alternatives for a New International Order: An Economic Analysis* (New York: Praeger Publishers, 1979), pp. 343–44.
65. Thorstein Veblen, *The Vested Interests and the Common Man* (New York: B.W. Huebsch, 1919).
66. Tinbergen, coord. (1976), p. 123.
67. Herbert Simon, 'UBI and the Flat Tax', *Boston Review* (Oct. Nov. 2000), http://bostonreview.mit.edu/BR25.5/simon.html.
68. Kindleberger (1986), pp. 7–8.
69. Ruben Mendez, 'The Provision and Financing of Universal Public Goods', *Global Governance: Ethics and Economics of the World Order*. M. Desai and P. Redfern, eds (London: Pinter, 1995), pp. 39–59. See also, Ruben Mendez, 'Peace as a Global Public Good', in I. Kaul, I. Grunberg, and M.A. Stern, eds, *Global Public Goods: International Cooperation in the 21st Century* (New York: Oxford University Press, 1999), pp. 382–416.
70. See, for example, Kaul, Grunberg, and Stern (1999); Francisco Sagasti and Keith Bezanson, *Financing and Providing Global Public Goods: Expectations and Prospects* (Swedish Ministry of Foreign Affairs and the Institute of Development Studies, Sussex, 2001), http://www.ud.se/prefak/Document.jsp?DocumentID=43161; Ravi Kanbur, Todd Sandler, and Kevin Morrison, 'The Future of Development Assistance: Common Pools and International Public Goods', Overseas Development Council Policy Essay No. 25 (Baltimore: Johns Hopkins University Press, 1999).
71. Kofi Annan, cited in Kaul, Grunberg, and Stern (1999). p. ii.
72. Jeffrey Sachs, 'Weapons of Mass Salvation', *The Economist*, 26 October 2002, p. 82.
73. Among the estimates that have been produced at one time or another are those by Frankman (1970), Steinberg and Yager (1978), and Mendez (1992).
74. Max Lerner, *Ideas for the Ice Age: Studies in a Revolutionary Era* (New York: Viking, 1941), pp. 74–75 (emphasis added).

5
Get Ready for a World Currency

> Let us suppose that all countries had the same currency, as in the progress of political improvement they one day will have... So much of barbarism, however, still remains in the transactions of the most civilized nations that almost all independent countries choose to assert their nationality by having to their own inconvenience and that of their neighbours, a peculiar currency of their own.
>
> —John S. Mill, *Principles of Political Economy*

Humankind has come a long way since 'money' emerged as a device for facilitating the exchange of goods and services. Money has evolved, by an uncertain trajectory, from natural objects to human artifacts, to fiat money, to ledger entries, and to electronic impulses with or without tangible counterparts. Transactions have also coevolved to include face-to-face, multi-faceted encounters between buyers and sellers, and impersonal exchanges, often at a distance and often of financial claims not directly rooted in production processes. Those of us who awake to radio or TV broadcasts are greeted on the morning of each working day with a reminder of the global reach of money by market quotations from around the world—finance being one remaining empire on which the Sun never sets.

International financial markets have grown to encompass the globe, with transactions involving currency conversions once reported to have reached two trillion dollars per day.[1] A common observation is that growth in the number and value of financial transactions is partially related to the variety of financial instruments, the types of which have grown rapidly and beyond the control of major national regulators. To the diversity of instruments, must be added the role of the internet, which has given ready, low-cost access to information and ease of trading to many previously excluded from active involvement in global financial markets. With the internet has also come the first attempts at launching private electronic currency units.[2] The inventiveness of the financial sector in concocting new instruments might well be summed up by the maxim 'if it fluctuates, securitize it.'

The magnitude of financial flows occasionally dwarfs the capabilities of national central banks, even acting in concert with others, to mitigate effects. Information is instantaneous—approaching the assumption of 'perfect' information of the economist's model in its ubiquity, if not its trustworthiness. The ability of financial flows to overwhelm national policy departures, such as a new tax or controls on capital flows, has led many eager governments to scrap initiatives that gave financial markets the jitters well in advance of their intended implementation. Private bond rating services like Moody's have come to be regarded as having a near veto over the policy initiatives of states concerned with the possibility of capital outflows. Understanding the limits represented by the free movement of financial flows causes many policy-makers to tread lightly.

Much ink has been spilt over the mischief said to be created by free capital movements and integrated capital markets. In this chapter I argue that it is not capital movements as such that are necessarily problematic, but the context in which those capital movements take place. A central element of that setting is the continued existence of national currencies whose values can and do alter with respect to each other.

The Economist made the case for a world currency at least twice over the last two decades. It addressed the question editorially on 9–15 January 1988 and proclaimed on the cover of that issue: 'Get Ready for a World Currency.' Ten years later in 'One World, One Money' (1998) it renewed its statement in support of a single world currency, finding all the post-East Asian crisis proposals to be far too modest in light of the circumstances. In their words, 'In difficult times, people are allowed, even encouraged, to think the unthinkable,' which for them was a 'global currency union.' Readers were reminded of Richard Cooper's 1984 endorsement of a single currency for all the industrial democracies:

> This one-currency regime is much too radical to envisage in the near future. But it is not too radical to envisage 25 years from now, and indeed some such scheme or its functional equivalent, will be necessary to avoid retrogression into greater reliance on barriers to international trade and financial transactions. Moreover, it is useful

> to have a 'vision', ... some idea of where we would like to get to provides a sense of direction for the next steps.[3]

Cooper's 2009 target date may not be so far fetched. As *The Economist* (1998) went on to note, if the euro succeeds (which it clearly has), 'the case for a global currency union will seem much more interesting.' Nonetheless, few are even thinking about this vision. The present chapter is intended to provoke discussion of the matter. Scholarly treatment of the topic of monetary union pays scant attention to the accompanying need under such arrangements for government transfer payments from growing to declining jurisdictions or more generally from gainers to losers. The role of redistribution in a monetary union has not yet been explored in full detail at the planetary level. Even in the EU public fiscal transfers have been limited, but consequential, both before and since the introduction of the euro on 1 January 1999.

Freeing financial flows

A sustained decline in the value of world trade between April 1929 and February 1933 characterized the onset of the Great Depression of the 1930s. A well-known graphical representation of this by Charles Kindleberger shows the month-to-month decline as a converging spiral.[4] It was a time of the erection of countless barriers to both trade and payments. Given the bilateral nature of many of these policy measures, the US responded with a bilateral policy initiative: the Reciprocal Trade Act of 1934. In the face of a paucity of international initiatives, this was intended to restore most favored nation treatment to America's trading partners through negotiations with one country after another.

Freeing of trade was elevated by the US into a global project at the 1944 Bretton Woods Conference. For trade to flourish the war-torn countries had to rebuild and poor countries had to transform their economies: these were the twin objectives of the IBRD. In fact, the role of the IBRD in Europe was dwarfed once the American Marshall Plan was approved.[5] Equally necessary for trade to flourish, firms must be free of restrictions on their ability to pay for imports. Accordingly, the goal of restoring free payments for current transactions was incorporated into the Articles of Agreement of the IMF. Two categories were established for countries joining the Fund: Article VIII status and Article XIV status. Article VIII status called, among other things, for countries to free payments for transactions in goods and services.

The European countries were among those to avail themselves of controls on current payments permitted under the IMF's transitional Article XIV status. It was not until 15 February 1961, 14 years after the IMF began operations, on, that the six original members of the European Common Market accepted Article VIII status. In recent years the IMF has pressed forward beyond the limits of Article VIII to force on member countries the removal of controls on capital flows, a de jure capitulation of sovereignty that is not part of the Fund's mandate. Nowhere in the make-up of the Fund was the freeing of capital flows addressed. To date, rather than open up the process of reforming the Fund's Articles of Agreement, last done during the 1970s, freeing of capital flows was added to the list of conditions for borrowers that the Fund insists upon. Plans to propose an amendment of the Articles had been formulated in 1997, but are said to have been judged inopportune in light of the East Asian crisis.[6]

Modern monetary chaos

The 1950s and 1960s were a period of relative stability of prices and exchange rates in the industrialized countries. The exchange rate between the Japanese yen and the US dollar, for example, changed by only 1 percent between 1951 and 1970.[7] The calm economic seas for the major industrialized countries gave way to erratic exchange rate movements in the 1970s and beyond. Prices are said to serve as signals to economic actors in the elaboration of investment plans and in the choice of markets in which to either sell or buy products. However, when exchange rates can change substantially from night to day with the associated creation of competitive advantage for certain goods and services and the disappearance of that advantage for others, an extra element of uncertainty exists. Thorstein Veblen wrote in 1904 of the distinction between making goods and making money and pointed to the circumstances, arising from the interplay of technology and institutions, when making money might be the only reasonable option.[8] Three decades later John Maynard Keynes referred to the perils of capitalism of the casino:

> Speculators may do no harm on a steady stream of enterprise. But the position is serious when enterprise becomes a bubble on a whirlpool of speculation. When the capital development of a country becomes a by-product of the activities of the casino, the job is likely to be ill done.[9]

Observers of exchange rate movements since 1971 have likened movements of exchange rates to the erratic movement of stock market prices, remarking that explanatory variables have yet to be found that can account for the actual movements. While some observers have decried this volatility, others have celebrated it as yet another apparent triumph of market magic. The latter view surely reflects an inability or unwillingness to distinguish between salutary developments and pathological ones. Exchange rates are sanguinely described as essentially another set of asset prices, which can be expected to behave accordingly.[10] A study published by the IMF in 1994 contained the following judgment: '... a certain level of unpredictability is probably an inevitable character of unconstrained exchange markets. *However, this does not necessarily imply that all of the volatility that is observed is beneficial*.'[11] This benign judgment is vague as to specifics. Is most of the volatility beneficial or little of it? And beneficial to whom and under what circumstances? Between 1974 and 1994 there were 35 instances when variations of the yen/dollar exchange rate from the end of one month to the next was equal to or greater than 5 percent. It is worth emphasizing that an exchange rate is not the same category of asset price as is a company's share traded on a stock exchange. Indeed, a 10 percent variation in a share price may have little or no impact on the affairs of either the firm or the holder of the shares, while a 10 percent change in exchange rates affects the price of thousands of goods and services and even quite immediately the well-being of some of those whose livelihood depends on the profitability of those goods. Gyrating exchange rates can be likened to the children's game of snakes and ladders played with loaded dice and with very real pay-offs and losses.

The discontent with the distortions and uncertainties introduced by wildly gyrating rates led to a search in the 1980s for a way back to exchange rate stability. There were new advocates of a return to the gold standard, including Robert Mundell, who was later to win a Nobel Prize in economics. Others called for a multi-commodity standard. Talk of target rates was heard, somewhat reminiscent of the old fixed rates with a band of variation around them. John Williamson, who was one of the early proponents of crawling pegs in the mid-1960s, shifted, as circumstances changed, to the advocacy of crawling bands.[12] The countries of the European Common Market first formed the European Monetary System (EMS) in 1978 to try to carve out a stable situation at least between their member currencies. Whatever the judgment one may make of the success of the EMS in the pre-euro period, the world was still left with periodic extreme fluctuations in the value of various currencies. A more recent response has been to dust off a contrivance of the British colonial system, the Currency Board, with local currency backed 100 percent by foreign currency reserves and/or dollarization of the currency—in either event a 'permanently' fixed exchange rate.

We are beset by inertia, which depending on the circumstances can be a positive or a negative force. Inertia kept the BWS, with its commitment to fixed, but adjustable exchange rates, going until 1971 despite major strains. Discussions and conferences on international monetary reform in the preceding decade did little more than bring forth in the late 1960s a nearly stillborn electronic reserve asset, the SDR created by the IMF. Some saw the SDR as a precursor to a world currency, while others focused on the SDR as an important new source of development finance. In fact, the SDR turned out to be neither. The creators of the SDR hamstrung it from the outset. Rules for its issue are too cumbersome, arrangements governing its use are too elaborate, and limitations on its form are unduly restrictive. No wonder that it was marginalized during the unprecedented expansion of 'eurocurrencies,' which fueled the rapid growth of Central Bank reserve assets during the 1970s. At the start of the new millennium the SDR represented a scant 1 percent of the external reserves of the central banks of the member countries of the IMF.[13]

Inertia allows what Robert Triffin, one of the early advocates of European monetary union, calls 'the scandal of a non-system'—one that replaced fixed rates with erratically varying rates—to persist despite the associated costs and tensions. Instead of dealing with the heart of the matter, we resort to discussion of palliatives like the proposed Tobin tax on foreign exchange transactions or 'pounds of cure'—multi-billion dollar funds to limit the extent of major crises, such as in Mexico in late 1994 and South Korea, Indonesia, Brazil, and Russia in 1998.

In dispraise of exchange rate adjustment

It is not sufficient for countries to shift from flexible rates back to fixed rates with sporadic adjustment. The old arguments against adjustable pegs still hold: a fixed rate in need of a change in value represents a one-way option for those in search of quick gain. In such circumstances, even schoolchildren know which direction the change will take, the only question is how long a government can resist changing the rate. But to these arguments must now be added the considerable costs of currency devaluation in a highly interdependent world. Between 1950 and 1980 the share of imports to national product has increased in virtually every country. These imports often include both wage goods and producer goods (capital goods, raw material inputs, intermediate goods, and fuel). Raúl Prebisch, the first secretary-general of the United Nations Economic Commission for Latin America and later of the UNCTAD, already in 1951 envisioned the process of import substituting industrialization taking a country from one kind of external vulnerability to another as a country increased the dependence of its production on imported materials. A major devaluation can impart both generalized and sector-specific price increases, as well as depressing employment, investment, and growth for a period of time.

Devaluation has been and continues to be vastly overrated as an appropriate adjustment device. We have long analyzed devaluation as if it were just another marginal adjustment with virtually no spillovers to the 'rest of the economy.' Indeed, economic theorizing in general starts from the analysis of small changes and then pretends that it has insights to offer for policy in a world in which changes are not of a few percent, but of one or two orders of magnitude or more. The 1960s literature that advocated the crawling peg exchange rate adjustment policy for the industrial countries with a persistent surplus in their external payments started with the premise that a series of mini-revaluations that summed to 2 percent a year would be quite sufficient.[14] For many countries in the third world, exchange rate change is more likely to be in the range of 20–200 percent per year or even more. To even speak of spillovers understates the case: the shock effects of large devaluations tend to have significant economy-wide effects, including declines in a country's gross output. Exchange rate change is an unavoidable, blunt instrument, which is often resorted to by governments only when all other options available have been tried and failed.

Despite the experience of the 1970s and the 1980s, the view of economists remains mixed with respect to the efficacy of floating rates. We still find strong proponents of floating. Ronald McKinnon attributes the penchant for floating rates to the 'insular tradition in macroeconomic theory.'[15] And, as early as 1963, McKinnon pointed to the cost of that volatility to highly open economies; in his judgment small economies were best advised to maintain pegged rates or even, consistent with optimum currency area theory (see below), not to have a distinct currency.[16] As countries have become inexorably more open to foreign transactions, often as a result of prodding from the IMF and the World Bank, exchange rate adjustment becomes increasingly unsuitable as a policy tool. A small country, for example, is likely to see the local price of non-competing imported goods rise by the full amount of a devaluation.

McKinnon offered the judgment that as economies become more open, flexible rates 'become both less effective as a control device for external balance and more damaging to internal price stability.'[17]

McKinnon's severest criticisms of flexible rates and their advocates are reserved for the cases of the US and the UK. In his opinion, advocacy of floating exchange rates led to ill-chosen monetary policies for the US and the UK in the 1970s.[18] Exchange rates are both an asset price and an asset-pricing mechanism. The depreciation of the US dollar during the latter part of the 1980s not only provided a subsidy to US exporters, but also served to set the yen price of American assets at fire-sale levels. The numbers speak to a major (continuing) breakdown in international cooperation: using the end of year $/DM and $/yen values we find that at the end of 1984 (relative to the end of 1980) the US dollar had appreciated relative to the DM by 18 and to the yen by 39 percent. The pattern then radically reversed with the dollar depreciating relative to both by 103 and 152 percent (that is, the percentage increase in the number of dollars per DM and yen, respectively) in the six-year period between the end of 1984 and the end of 1990 (see also n. 8). The depreciated dollar prompted substantial inflows of foreign direct capital investment in the US with the 1989 peak value not being surpassed until 1996. Flexible rates are particularly inappropriate in a context in which international financial flows are highly mobile. Yet with each passing day international financial flows grow and there seems little doubt that many of these transactions have little to contribute to the efficient allocation of the world's resources.

When confidence in an economy depends on the stability of its exchange rate, the collective state of mind is of greater bearing than the so-called financial fundamentals. Worrying openly about a country's financial developments may be sufficient to set capital flows in motion. The US has continuously fretted about its role as banker to the world and yet it remains, judging from financial flows, a magnet for funds seeking safe haven. Its preoccupations with the adequacy of its gold stocks in the 1960s and about the confidence of foreigners in American assets and financial institutions helped precipitate the eventual collapse of the BWS. By talking a good game, Argentina and Chile maintained the confidence necessary to prevent major ripple effects of the 1994 Mexican devaluation. Indeed, Argentina was able to convince the world that its firm commitment to a 1:1 Peso–dollar exchange rate was both immutable and wise for the Argentine economy for several years, even though evidence to the contrary was steadily accumulating. In contrast, was it really Mexican economic mismanagement that led to the fall of the peso in 1994 or was it the very possibility of a major Mexican devaluation that fed a self-fulfilling sequence in the face of untoward political developments?

The cumulative cost of unsuccessful exchange rate defenses and the costs that follow large devaluations have rarely been estimated and go well beyond the easily measurable declines in imports, investment, and national product. It is, however, hard to imagine that it would be more costly to fix rates permanently and provide international transfers to compensate for resulting disadvantages. The discourse of economists who would appear to have moved from the maxim 'money matters' to one in which 'only money matters' generally obscures the societal distress occasioned by devaluation. In appropriating words from common discourse, providing them with technical content and then returning them with their transformed significance to the everyday realm where they circulate, the significance of adverse effects can be masked from view. The economist's use of 'real' does not align with common understanding of the word. The statistical 'real' refers to a price-adjusted measure. 'Real' was originally used in discussions of production to provide a measure of the volume of a country's output by adjusting for inflation. We now talk about real exchange rates, that is, rates adjusted by movements in a price-adjusted trade-weighted index. This may be a reasonable approximation in the context of low-inflation countries, but in using this as a shorthand measure of the performance of high- (or hyper-) inflation countries, one almost completely masks the major shocks involved. A stable *real* exchange rate may well be associated with a 10-, 100-, or even 1000- or more fold increase in the actual rate. The real rate may convey information about a country's trade competitiveness, but tracking changes in the actual rate gives an unmistakable view of a shock that may contribute to business failures and major changes in income distribution. Over the period 1987–94 there was a reported 39 percent appreciation of Brazil's real effective exchange rate for exports;[19] the change in the actual exchange rate was a depreciation that exceeded 10 million percent. One should not be lulled into a false sense of complacency about relative economic stability by data that focus on 'real' rates. The shock occasioned by large devaluations, such as those exceeding 40 percent per year should not be swept under the rug by statistical manipulations. This is a pervasively common and repetitive phenomenon particularly in the Third World and in the 'Transition' countries. We should not be led to imagine that because a few exceptional cases of supposedly 'good' performance can be invoked that this is the norm, that the good performance will persist, that it will still be viewed as positive in light of more careful examination and that attention should be diverted from major distress elsewhere.

As presented in Table 5.1, the figures for countries, other than the industrial country members of the OECD, with a population of 25 million or more provide a clear indication of the instability that has plagued the

Table 5.1 Ratio of changes in end of year exchange rates (originally expressed in home currency units/US$)

	1990/1980	2000/1990	2000/1980
Algeria	3.1	6.2	19.0
Argentina	»	1.8	»
Bangladesh	2.2	1.5	3.3
Brazil	»	»	»
China	3.4	1.6	5.4
Colombia	11.2	3.8	42.9
Congo DR	»	»	»
Egypt	2.9	1.8	5.3
Ethiopia	1.0	4.0	4.0
India	2.3	2.6	5.9
Indonesia	3.0	5.0	15.3
Iran	0.9	34.6	31.3
Kenya	3.2	3.2	10.3
Korea	1.1	1.8	1.9
Mexico	180.2	2.3	411.6
Morocco	1.9	1.3	2.5
Myanmar*	1.0	1.0	1.0
Nigeria	16.5	12.2	201.4
Pakistan	2.2	1.3	2.8
Peru	»	6.8	»
Philippines	3.7	1.8	6.6
Poland	206.3	4.4	899.7
Russia†		67.9	
South Africa	3.4	3.0	10.2
Tanzania	24.0	4.1	98.2
Thailand	1.2	1.7	2.0
Turkey	32.6	229.8	7482.1
Ukraine†		84.9	
Vietnam	»	1.8	»

Notes:
» greater than 10,000.
*Myanmar's currency is fixed in terms of SDRs, which is used here as the standard of comparison.
† Russia and Ukraine: rate change from 1992 to 2000.

Source: IMF, *International Financial Statistics Yearbook*, various issues.

poorer countries of the world in the past two decades. To keep the table relatively uncluttered, for cases where the ratio of exchange rate change over the period indicated exceeded 10,000 (even exceeding one billion in a single decade in the case of Brazil and the Democratic Republic of the Congo), I have substituted a symbol (») for the actual numbers. With the exceptions of South Korea and Thailand where the exchange rate merely doubled (roughly) over two decades and Myanmar, which has retained external controls, the record is largely one of the successive major shocks that doubtless have distorted resource use, rather than efficiently allocating them.

A governess in one of Oscar Wilde's plays advises her charge to skip the chapter on the fall of the Indian rupee, as it is much too shocking. Remarkably, accounts by economists of currency devaluations are rather bloodless narratives that tend to abstract from the human drama entailed. Of course, theoretical shocks are a common feature these days in open economy macroeconomic models, but these are nothing as compared to the social shock of a currency whose value falls sharply in external purchasing power. I occasionally ask my students in Montreal to think what life in Canada would be like if our dollar were to follow a path comparable to that followed by the Mexican peso. If our dollar were to fall during six years not to 60 American cents, but to less than one cent as occurred in Mexico between 1981 and 1987, might our celebrated amiability vanish along with the external purchasing power of our currency?

When trying to understand the causes of civil war, one should not overlook the fact that massive devaluation might just be an exacerbating element, not necessarily a determinant, but possibly of critical importance in helping to set one group against another. If the people jump on the bandwagon to support the overthrow of the government by a demagogue that too might be understandable. Their hopes may be misplaced, but desperation can play tricks with our judgment and our otherwise humane instincts. In trying to understand why 'Things Fall Apart' (to use the title of Chinua Achebe's novel), consider that an exchange rate in free fall may be accompanied by a society in free fall. The great tragedy is that we have an aid entourage and a monetary rules entourage, which, while claiming to pursue the same objectives, often work at cross-purposes. We labor mightily in good faith to eliminate poverty, through bilateral and multilateral aid, through the work of NGOs and through the work of countless aid workers, paid and volunteer. As signs of achievement are noted, along comes a devaluation that doubles the number of home currency units per dollar overnight and like a tidal wave sweeps away much of what is in its path. Whatever damage to the social sector was done by budget cuts during Washington Consensus-inspired structural adjustment, programs has been greatly exacerbated by a series of large devaluations, whose recurrence we seem to treat as being as immutable as tropical hurricanes. Corruption in such circumstances may be a survival response when all other lifelines are disappearing.

Putting abstract economic models and conditionalities above the needs of people is surely obfuscation. What is particularly scandalous about our current monetary arrangement, whether system or non-system, is that it is a framework that concentrates gains in the hands of the few and disadvantages the many. Equally scandalous is the general lack of attention by either scholars or policy-makers to the role of exchange rate adjustment in the generation of inequality. The system-wide shocks that are a built-in feature of a multi-currency world are cruel anachronisms if indeed the global economy is an optimum currency area, an idea that we will now consider.

The world as optimum currency area

John Stuart Mill reflected on a world currency over 150 years ago. One hundred years passed before a theoretical concept came into being that lends itself to the consideration of a single currency for the world. We owe to Robert Mundell the initial formulation of an Optimum Currency Area in 1961.[20] The world at that time having been one of relative exchange rate fixity and limited capital mobility, writers spoke of optimum currency areas as suited to regions which were limited in extent, whether sub- or supranational. Delbert Snider suggested that it was unlikely that a larger unit than a country would meet his conditions for an optimum currency area, which were:

1. A single monetary-fiscal authority.
2. Either a uniform distribution of productive resources or a high degree of factor (labor and capital) mobility.
3. A central responsibility for compensatory measures.
4. A certain minimum size and degree of self-sufficiency.[21]

Snider's list is explicitly more inclusive than that of others who have written on optimum currency areas: the criteria frequently go no further than factor mobility and a common monetary authority. Market-oriented economists have a tendency to assume that if factors are mobile, regional differences will disappear. Indeed much of this literature defines an optimum currency area solely in relation to factor mobility. If factors are immobile, an optimum currency area is deemed not to exist. By virtue of the definition of an optimum currency area and the assumption that markets work, the need to consider redistribution disappears. Even Richard Cooper in his 1984 espousal of a common currency for the industrial countries, could not bring himself to speak openly of income redistribution. Instead, he spoke guardedly and vaguely about the necessary fiscal measures:

> Balance of payments adjustment within this regime would be as easy, or as difficult, as it is between regions of the United States or any other large country today.... Fiscal policy in its various forms could be used to cushion such unemployment.[22]

But let me give credit where it is due. At least Cooper did not assume that the invisible hand would resolve imbalances. McKinnon, on the other hand, continues to speak of adjustment as being even swifter, smoother and more effortless than David Hume envisioned in his mid-18th-century essay 'On the Balance of Trade':

> among the financially open economies of the 1980s, trade deficits and surpluses are better balanced by offsetting automatically flows of private capital much like the balance achieved between Texas and California.[23]

McKinnon might have mentioned West Virginia and California, a pair considerably less illustrative of the omnisciently benevolent forces of the market.

Warren Smith asked in the 1960s whether there were sufficient economic policy tools for achieving what was referred to as external and internal balance.[24] With the fixing of exchange rates, in a world of high capital mobility, policy-makers at the national level lose two of those tools: the exchange rate and monetary policy. Fiscal policy and selective measures remain, but they are said to be constrained by the possibility of capital movements. Let it first be said that there is room to maneuver even within a context of constraints and it is incumbent on policy-makers to explore those constraints. More central to the case for a single world currency is the need to distinguish between international capital liberalization and capital volatility. In a world of either adjustable or floating exchange rates, liberalization and volatility go hand in hand. With the elimination of separate currencies, global capital movement per se should be no more troublesome than is capital movement today within national economies or within the euro zone. The hypermobility of capital is not to be resolved, as James Tobin suggested, by 'throwing sand in the wheels of international finance' but by eliminating once and for all the risk of exchange rate change.

The optimum currency area literature speaks of the need for a single fiscal authority. This may not be necessary, but some central redistributive mechanism certainly would be. As I suggested in Chapter 4, differing fiscal regimes would in all likelihood persist, as they do in federal states at present. This is perfectly consistent with the writings on fiscal federalism.

By 1976, with the world afloat and capital considerably more mobile than previously, Peter B. Kenen was arguing that the world as a whole should be considered to be an optimum currency area.[25] True to what has become the norm in these discussions, Kenen made no reference to transfers. Edward L. Morse even presented a viewpoint that suggests that a World Central Bank would remove redistribution from the agenda.[26] One wonders about the peculiar conditioning which makes it easier for an economist to think about global monetary policy than about global fiscal policy? Redistribution should be at the top of the socio-political agenda until it is so firmly institutionalized that differing human fortunes and particularly misfortunes are deemed to be justly compensated. Redistribution was on John Stuart Mill's agenda in his *Principles*: for him the production problem had been solved in the industrial countries, and it was time (in the mid-19th century) to tackle distribution. It is no less an issue today than when Mill was writing.

Changes in the workings of the world led to a 'new' optimum currency area literature in the 1990s. This literature is in my view more properly regarded as dealing with sub-global monetary union. It holds out the possibility that countries may wish to withdraw from a union. The writers associated with this work are concerned with monetary arrangements in Europe and in the former Soviet Union. Interestingly, it is not from those writing about the formation of monetary unions that the centrality of redistributive mechanisms and transfers finds most prominent expression, but rather in the writings of those examining the breakdown of monetary union, in particular, the Russian monetary union. Patrick Conway highlighted the importance of the failure of mechanisms to try to assure equitable redistribution in an essay published in 1995.[27]

Today we can add information about the dice-roll of devaluations with attendant distributional disasters in most of the newly independent states: figures of the sort seen in Table 5.1 tell a consistently bleak story of monetary instability. Taking as a starting point for the 11 members of the Commonwealth of Independent States either the end 1992 or 1993 (for the Kyrgys Republic, Turkmenistan, and Uzbekistan) and calculating the relative exchange rate change at the end of 2000, we find ratios running from a low (!) of 6.0 in the Kyrgys Republic to 78,667 in Belarus.[28] If the intent of those controlling the purse strings of the 'West' was to win new converts to the worship of marketplace magic, they could not have chosen a more peculiar way to do so.

Nobel-prize winner, former Chair of the President Clinton's Council of Economic Advisors and former Vice President and Chief Economist of the World Bank, Joseph Stiglitz has distinguished himself among the critics of globalization by his trenchant denunciation of the role of the IMF and the US Treasury in handling the East Asian crisis and in their position on many policy issues. Yet he, too, uses the economist's customary metric for judging a devaluation. In his remarks on 'Who Lost Russia?' he criticizes the IMF for delaying the devaluation of the ruble in 1998, which caused it to be larger than would otherwise have been the case.[29] He goes on to judge the devaluation a success in its effect on promoting exports and providing a price advantage said to have increased the production of import-competing goods. He further states that the ruble declined between July 1998 and January 1999 in 'real effective terms' by more than 45 percent.[30] In fact, the actual value of the fall, not adjusted using someone's statistical contrivance which may describe your reality, but not mine, was 72.4 percent. Using the reciprocal (as in Table 5.1), which tells us the number or rubles per dollar required relative to the starting point, the ratio at the end of January 1999 relative to the end of July 1998 was 3.62. In September 1998 alone the ruble per dollar exchange rate doubled. Stiglitz addresses the rampant increase in income inequality in Russia, but not in relation to this 'successful' devaluation.[31] In a world of adjustable exchange rates and mobility of funds across borders, there is no available policy option in our current system that protects the common person.

The absence of compensatory distribution that is highlighted as contributing to breakdown can, in like manner, be regarded as an impediment to the formation of monetary union. Concern about adverse distributional consequences has likely exacerbated the understandable fears of change among some of those asked to opt for union in the successive referenda in various European countries.

A national analogy

To what extent have nations, especially federal ones dealt with the problem of imperfect factor mobility? The answer is in a variety of ways which include both making markets work better, regulating markets, private non-market initiatives, and government policies at various levels, including transfers of both income and services from gainers to losers and uniform provision of state services to all. This process of adjustment to ever-changing differential fortunes of individuals, communities, industries, and regions is at the heart of political processes.

If we follow the logic of economics and push analyses to their limits, then we look beyond the nation to higher and lower levels. Some years ago, an ad for the state of California appeared in *The Economist* proudly announcing that California was the 6th largest economy in the world; while it is now the 7th, its gross state product was slightly over $1 trillion in 1998 (Table 5.2). We might want to reflect on that for a bit. Can anyone tell me with any assurance whether the state of California has a trade surplus or deficit with the rest of the world (including of course the other 49 US states)? What is its bilateral balance with the rest of the US? Has California's real exchange appreciated in the last few years? Should California institute controls on ostensibly volatile capital? Would the well-being of Californians increase if the state were to opt out of monetary union with the US in order to obtain monetary policy independence? While such calculations could be and no doubt have been made, these questions are not part of daily discussions and the Governor of California does not have to spend hours worrying about the state's exchange rate.

Were the levers of economic management to be moved to a higher level, those in the various nations of the world might find themselves in a California-like situation. In principle, Bolivia could blissfully be relieved of concern for its external payments and its ever-depreciating currency. Its government could then turn its attention to revenue raising

Table 5.2 California's rank among the 202 nations of the world (as listed in the World Bank, *World Development Indicators*)

	Rank	**G-8 countries smaller**
Area	53	Germany, Italy, Japan, UK
Population (1998)	31	Canada
Gross product (1998)	7	Canada, Russia

and expenditure, and negotiating with the next higher level of government the share of transfers for itself and its citizens.

Capital flows and the Tobin Tax

Estimates of foreign exchange transactions have placed these at anywhere between at least 1.3 and 2.0 trillion US$ per day. By the early 1970s James Tobin was speaking about the hypermobility of capital and urging the creation of a tax on currency trading.[32] Note that he was writing before the explosion in the variety of instruments, the rise of new banking centers and the widespread liberalization of capital flows that are at the heart of the today's hypermobility. These latter developments aggravate exchange market volatility, but the proximate cause for much volatility is the prospect of substantial windfall gains (or losses) arising from currency devaluation or revaluation.

When we consider the volume of daily foreign exchange trading together with its volatility, the question of recognizing pathological growth once again arises. Does the volatility and growth of foreign exchange trading contribute to either the efficient allocation of resources or the well-being of the human family? What is may not be what is salutary. I would suggest this is the case for foreign exchange markets. We have volatility that serves no public purpose and an addiction to the exchange markets that is harmful to our global community insofar as funds are diverted from production to speculation. Table 5.3 presents official figures from triennial surveys conducted by the Bank for International Settlements on foreign exchange trading giving some idea of the growing disproportion between foreign exchange trading and the values of world product and world trade in goods. The major

Table 5.3 Foreign exchange trading

	1986	**1989**	**1992**	**1995**	**1998**	**2001**
Market turnover (trillion $/day)	0.2	0.6	0.8	1.0	1.5	1.2
World exports (trillion $/yr)	2.0	3.0	3.8	5.1	5.4	6.3
World gross product (trillion $/yr)	14.7	19.7	24.2	29.0	29.3	31.9
FX trading/World exports	23.3	45.3	47.9	46.4	65.7	45.6
FX trading/World product	3.3	6.9	7.4	8.2	12.2	9.0

Note: I have used 240 trading days (20 per month), to annualize the daily turnover values.

Sources: Bank for International Settlements, *The Triennial Central Bank Survey of Foreign Exchange and Derivatives Market Activity*, various issues. IMF, *International Financial Statistics* and World Bank, *World Development Indicators*.

decline in turnover in 2001 has been attributed in part to the creation of the euro and to mergers of major banks and corporations.[33]

In a world in which financial markets are more integrated every day, have we reached the point where a major institutional departure is called for? Has the time arrived when John Stuart Mill's vision of a single currency is no longer such a bold departure? Is it now time to embark on the institution building that will rescue us from the problems associated with currency volatility? The rather abundant literature on the process of economic integration contains the consistent observation that the more integrated economies are the more extensive policy coordination needs to be. The experience of the 1970s and 1980s has clearly indicated that this is true whether one is talking of a regional grouping such as a common market or nations whose goods, services, factor, and financial markets are de facto more and more intertwined. In that respect the institutional framework created in the mid-1940s and the Pax Americana have succeeded so admirably in the task of freeing world trade and of freeing capital markets that dealing with major side effects, originally assumed away—a rising economic tide was supposed to raise all (seaworthy) boats—has now become an urgent matter.

The Tobin Tax on foreign exchange transactions, originally proposed by James Tobin in 1972 and then reiterated in 1978,[34] is an example of a partial measure originally proposed for a single purpose, that of discouraging speculative international financial transactions. The proposal was first rescued from oblivion by those who began to see the tax as a major source of funding for international development. Various estimates indicated that fabulous sums could be realized on the assumption that the tax, which was intended to dampen financial flows, would in fact not do so. (Were the tax to be successful, the flows would diminish and with it the revenues from the tax.) Even at 0.1 percent per transaction (0.5 percent is commonly suggested for the tax) and assuming the value of transactions actually taxed would be one-half of the current value, annual revenues would still amount to around $200 billion per year, which is slightly greater than what net official development assistance would be if the 0.7 percent of GNP target were to be attained by the industrialized countries of the OECD.

As the dangers of capital hypermobility became palpable, Tobin's argument for 'throwing sand in the wheels' of international finance became the object of serious consideration both among economists and policymakers. The capital flight stampedes from Mexico, Indonesia, and South Korea, among others in the past decade helped sustain interest in a transaction tax on foreign exchange deals. Ironically, these extreme circumstances are also instances where exchange rates changes (anticipated and actual) were of such a magnitude that a transaction tax of 0.5 percent on currency conversion would hardly have been a deterrent.[35]

The Tobin Tax proposal addresses symptoms, not causes. If exchange rates that are subject to variation are at the heart of capital hypermobility, then a tax would at best mitigate the problem in certain contexts. Tobin, himself, has made it clear that a world currency with supporting institutions would be preferable:

> A permanent single currency, as among the 50 states of the American union, would escape all this turbulence. The United States example shows that a currency union works to great advantage when sustained not only by centralized monetary authorities but also by other common institutions. In the absence of such institutions, an irrevocably unique world currency is many decades off.[36]

Unfortunately no one seems to be listening to such an apparently far-fetched idea. Moreover, Tobin, who might have used whatever measure of prestige goes with the Nobel Prize in economics by trying to bring to the fore discussion of a world currency, chose instead to cast his lot with the proposed tax on foreign exchange trading.

Flexible rates: reforming International Financial Architecture

Following the East Asian crisis of 1997–98 a frenzy of discussion of reforming the 'International Financial Architecture' was launched. Numerous studies were prepared, among which were the reports of three working groups prepared under the aegis of the Bank for International Settlements in 1998.[37] The US Congress established an International Financial Institution Advisory Commission(2000) chaired by Allan Meltzer, the New York-based Council on Foreign Relations commissioned an Independent Task Force under the direction of Morris Goldstein, and the IMF and the UN, not be left out, also produced reports.[38]

At the conclusion of extended reflection on a new financial architecture we find reaffirmation of the (pre-existing) theological divisions between advocacy of fixed and flexible exchange rates as one of the outcomes of the debate. Flexible rates are clearly gaining the upper hand and are endorsed by the Meltzer Commission, the Goldstein Task Force and the IMF. As the Goldstein Report puts it, 'The Currency Regime: Just Say No to Supporting Pegged Exchange Rates.' Following the course of flexible rates would likely skew economic activities even more toward the traded goods sector, particularly export goods. As with the exchange rate discourse in general, the recommendation ignores the income distribution effects of what for many third world countries will simply be a situation of continuously living with depreciating rates. As always, discussion of external payments focuses either on the rarefied level of abstract macroeconomic variables or on the interests of the elite actors directly affected by external transactions. George Soros, a member of the Goldstein Commission, in a dissenting view, took exception to a 'bias that permeates the report': precisely that of favoring those at the center of the global capitalist system and the disadvantaging of the countries at the periphery.

The last major episode of experimentation with patching up the fixed exchange rate aspect of the BWS in the 1960s and early 1970s, led to the creation of the SDR, to swaps between Central Banks, to a gold pool, to crawling peg exchange rate regimes, and ultimately to a partial demonetization of gold and the generalized floating of rates between industrial countries. Indeed the latter is one of the weaknesses of the current system, a point addressed by yet another Goldstein Report dissent, which included among its adherents C. Fred Bergsten, George Soros, and Paul Volcker, former Chair of the US Federal Reserve Board. They spoke of 'the complications for the conduct of any sensible exchange rate policy by emerging-market economies when the exchange rates [dollar, euro, yen] among their major trading partners move so erratically.' And so, the latest round in the debate leaves us with proposals that urge more tinkering to make an outmoded system work; as Roy Culpeper observed, the focus tends to be on plumbing, rather than architecture, whatever the rhetoric may be.

Fixed rates: dollarization

Countries that have endured successive economic crises may well be ripe to consider something completely different. There is no shortage of easy-to-apply miracle cures on offer. Full dollarization (defined as the use of a foreign currency by another country) is just such a form of snake-oil cure that may be worse than the disease. This goes beyond the notion of an ostensibly irrevocable peg to the US dollar (as was supposed to be case in Argentina) to actually abandoning one's currency (as in Ecuador). If resort to inflationary monetary policy is an irresistible urge for a nation's policy-makers, a logical solution might seem to be the abandonment of the national currency. However, dollarization without any compensatory transfers is a likely recipe for crisis and widespread pauperization in many of the countries considering this path. There may be a short honeymoon brought by stability of economic relations, but, more often than not, deflation, unemployment, and political tension will follow.

In support of dollarization, Panama has been shamefacedly invoked as a paragon of the advantages to be had through dollarization. The authors of the IMF's pamphlet on full dollarization invoke the example of Panama twice and refer to it within the same sentence as being 'the only sizable country with a history of using a foreign currency' and of being 'fairly small.'[39] This 'sizable' country, with a population of 3 million, also happens to have one-quarter of its population living on less than $2/day. The only 'distributional' costs of dollarization that are commonly identified are the insignificant one-time cost to the dollarizing country of buying up local currency in circulation and the loss of the seigniorage that results from the difference between the face value of currency and its cost of production.

Whatever ails the economy, dollarization is said to be the cure. Proponents of dollarization have even been working overtime to sell this idea in Canada. At least one study projects a 37 percent increase in GDP that would follow Canada's adoption of the US dollar.[40] Missing from the dollarization scenario are considerations of both equity and control, democratic or otherwise. In the Canadian context, mention is occasionally made of the possible creation of a 13th Federal Reserve district and bank; for smaller countries voice is assumed to be irrelevant. Moreover, the default setting which has been promoted by central bankers and the IMF is that of the indispensability of Central Bank Independence (CBI), a term used so often that it even has its own acronym. Independence from whom? An apolitical policy is an oxymoron. CBI is nothing more than a smoke screen for replacing democratic oversight with elite-technocrat control, the apparent necessity of which springs from the failings of our current system of a multitude of separate currencies. Moreover, even on 'economic' grounds, the case for CBI is dubious. As Stiglitz notes, there is 'scant evidence that countries with more independent central banks grow faster or have fewer or shallower fluctuations.'[41]

In fact, the benefits held out for 'full dollarization' (avoidance of currency crises, closer integration, avoidance of inflationary finance) are also the benefits that would apply to a world currency. Dollarization is the solution of political simplicity: no elaborate negotiations, no compromises, and no institution building are required. A world money, in contrast, if it is to avoid the pitfalls of our jerry-built currency system, must be the fruit of major commitment and major efforts to build global democratic federalism, as was the case with the embodiment of a number of federalist principles in the creation and continuing redefinition of the EU. Movements for monetary union recognize that the ultimate loss of sovereignty is to have no voice in the formation of policy. That is the heart of the task ahead: to build structures of global government that provide effective expression for the citizens of the World.

From euro to world currency

The European Union provides the ongoing example of the compromise, learning and adaptation involved in moving toward a unified supranational monetary and political area. Unlike many proposed supranational groupings, European integration has involved linguistic and cultural frontiers, as well as political ones. The EU's invocation of the notions of subsidiarity and mutual recognition seems to suggest that national policies need not be coordinated unless there are compelling reasons to do so. For those who cherish diversity, this is a positive omen. The essence of one's uniqueness need not be sacrificed on the altar of integration. On the other hand, some degree of harmonization is both inevitable and advantageous. One key lesson we can learn from the experience of the EU is the importance of having a vision of a possible future. Another lesson is that community-wide instruments and policies can bring substantial advantages. As John Pinder pointed out this was the case with the Common External Tariff which gave the then EC substantial bargaining power within the GATT.[42] The road to a single currency in Europe was an arduous one. Pinder was daunted by the complexities of monetary cooperation. Not long before the 1991 Maastricht Treaty, Jacques Delors, the President of the Commission of the European Communities, is said to have discarded the single currency option as politically unrealistic,[43] yet European Monetary Union was embodied in the treaty and eight years later the Euro was introduced. And that perhaps is the main lesson we can learn from the continuing evolution of the EU and the creation of the euro: what is 'unacceptable' today is not immutable, but subject to collective redefinition, as well as to being shaped by human agency. At what point can one expect the creation of a common world currency to be perceived as a priority step? The ongoing process in Europe could lead the way to a world currency. What must be perceived by Europe and the world is the advantage that a single currency conveys to all, especially when supplemented by redistributive measures in a framework of democratic federalism. The struggle to embody federalism more fully in the EU still continues and much remains to be accomplished in the area of redistribution.

As Europe has been in the vanguard of modern integration it has been the model for other regional initiatives. This was the case with trade integration and it is the case now with monetary union. Indeed, Rudiger Dornbusch, who was an economist at MIT and an influential voice on international monetary matters, declared: 'Convergence on regional monies is a no-brainer;...the burden is on the periphery to recognize and collect the bonus.'[44] I disagree. Periodic destabilizing adjustments between the regions would still be likely. Moreover, a unilateral embrace of a currency (which he recommends) without any prior commitment for appropriate timely and possibly extended support risks more cycles of deflation-induced mass unemployment followed by major financial crises as occurred in Argentina. Further, he misses the point: the important distinction in the case of the euro is that it is not a disembodied market solution, but rather one that is clearly embedded in a socio-political context of democratic decision-making, where offsets to adverse market outcomes can, in principle, be implemented.

In any event, our sights should be set higher. First, because what works for the EU augurs well for being writ large, that is, at the level of the world. And secondly, as I have tried to argue, the urgency of world poverty, the destruction of resources often related to the need of countries to pay their own way, and the intolerable injustices of the mix of global apartheid and of the migratory pull of differentials in life chances between rich and poor countries (see Chapter 6) require more than taking just the next sequential baby step in institution building, but rather pursuing a bold vision. The time has passed for replicating the European experience in other regions; now is the time to scale up to the world level, building on what we have learned. Without a world currency and world democracy, we remain within the framework of national competitiveness—a system of domination, rather than cooperation.

Robert Triffin argued that if the goals of exchange freedom and stability were truly taken at face value, then we would well be on the road to a single currency for the world.[45] Diagnoses are made and the next (giant) step seems clear, but analysts are too much the realists to embrace the logical conclusion. The nation continues to be the default setting for many in considering policy options. Barry Eichengreen's *International Monetary Arrangements for the 21st Century* seems to suffer from this mental impediment. His book starts with a quote by Richard Cooper, the last sentence of which is: 'Exchange rates can be most credibly fixed if they are eliminated altogether, that is, if international transactions take place with a single currency.'[46] Eichengreen goes on to say: 'The argument of this book is that contingent policy rules designed to hit explicit exchange rate targets will no longer be viable in the twenty-first century.'[47] Well? In fact, there is no chapter in Eichengreen's book on a world currency, nor is there an entry for world currency or suitable synonym in the index. Incredibly, while James Meade devoted a full chapter to a World Currency to be put in place after World War II,[48] Eichengreen, given a century-long interval to contemplate, seemed unable or unwilling to detach himself from today's 'realities' in order to explore the implications of a leap of imagination involving major institutional innovation.

A world central bank

Can the IMF and its SDRs be transformed into a world central bank and a world currency? The SDR is after all a centrally created reserve asset, albeit not the most popular of the reserve assets. Could the US dollar or the euro grow to be actually adopted by other countries with the concomitant transfer of responsibilities to a central monetary authority? The actual instrument does not matter, except that if it remains a national or regional currency then the gains from the operation of the system are likely to accrue disproportionately to the country or grouping whose currency is employed. It is the transfer of the management that is a critical element.

To make the IMF a vehicle for the achievement of a world currency requires changing its role. Some have spoken of the politicization of the IMF. In fact, the IMF was born politicized. The US has always had veto power on major issues in the IMF. As the relative economic strength of the US declined, the 80 percent special majority (20 percent veto), was no longer adequate to assure a US veto when quota revision was considered in the early 1980s. And so we now have an 85 percent special majority (15 percent veto). In principle, if the grouping of countries for voting purposes in the IMF were to be rearranged, a newly formed Euro group would also have a veto.[49] Multiple vetoes are a two-edged sword: they might either immobilize the Fund or turn it into a forum for serious horse-trading, which might better serve the international community.

The characteristics of the World Central Bank will take shape with the acceptance of the idea of moving toward a world currency. In the meantime, I contend that the notion of CBI whether national, regional or the IMF, must begin to be challenged. The standard presumption of economists that markets work and governments/politics do not, often leads to hasty policy conclusions of the 'believing is seeing' type. That is the case with respect to the supposed firmly established relationship between the degree of central bank political independence and the inflation rate: greater independence from political manipulation motivated by the quest for electoral gain is said to be associated with lower inflation rates. As James Forder has convincingly demonstrated, in the absence of agreement on how to measure central bank independence, competing measures give inconsistent rankings of independence.[50] A supposedly firm empirical relationship is exposed as an unsubstantiated assertion.

In a world in which democracy has become a hallmark, I believe that we must be aggressive to extend its practice to every nook and cranny of the public sector and the private sector as well. To accept the self-promotion by the Central Banks (and the IMF) that there should be a law unto themselves is to forfeit an important measure of control that had once devolved from the sovereign to the people. One does not build a democratic future by unthinking abdication of the rights of citizens. Happily, many voices have been raised questioning the single-minded concern of many central banks with inflation (occasionally even zero inflation).

Conclusion: closing the casino

The globalization of capital markets is not per se undesirable, indeed quite the contrary. What is undesirable is the dominance of financial flows that are motivated purely by the quest for speculative gains and which reach levels that are antithetical to the growth and welfare objectives of jurisdictions, not to mention human values. Have we not long since reached a situation in which preoccupation with exchange rates diverts the attention of governments from other tasks? Attention is focused on the exchange rate if it is a flexible one or on the balance of payments and export surpluses if the rate is a fixed one. These are the priority problems, in Albert Hirschman's words, which lead to the neglect of other problems.

To shut down the casino requires the permanent fixing of exchange rates as the first of two complementary steps on the way to eliminating separate currencies. The second step is the establishment of transfers to offset some of the uneven effects of the functioning of markets. Without the credible promise of compensating transfers willingness to join a currency union may be undermined.

My argument throughout this work is that an open trading system requires the addition of compensatory measures if it is to be maintained and, moreover, compensatory measures are a precondition for successfully moving to closer economic integration. In light of today's trade liberalization stampede, nothing less than global monetary integration would appear to be called for. If 'internationally defined conditions' are judged by many to produce intolerable outcomes, then steps should be taken to redefine those conditions. To only slightly overstate the case: if exchange rates no longer serve a useful role in guiding resource allocation, then it is proper to ask, 'Who needs them?' Redefining conditions to unify currencies and establish formalized international redistributive mechanisms is important for tipping the balance of incentives back from obsessive accumulation of personal wealth in favor of making goods and services (including artistic expression) and attending to human well-being. Such a change would free jurisdictions from the need for constant preoccupation with the balance of payments.

Many euro-like regional moneys would likely also see one region pitted competitively against another, when the world should be moving toward cooperative world-scale solutions. Given that building regional unions would likely require major attitudinal changes, we should not settle for a half-way house. If new institutions have to be built, let us build once and for all the institutional equivalents of Gothic cathedrals, so that future generations may marvel at our prescience, rather than our myopia.

Currencies are one symbolic element of our imagined national communities: a vestige of sovereignty which some of us resist parting with, even when the largest share of our transactions are increasingly electronic. Indeed, as far as the receipt of income is concerned, it is unlikely that anyone reading these lines receives a periodic cash payment in compensation for service rendered to an employer. And yet we struggle mightily, as Mill observed, to preserve separate currencies. As our consciousness of the interconnection of circumstances from the local to the global grows daily, so does our inclination to re-examine the default settings that limit our options. We are aware that national governments, while not impotent, are limited in their abilities to serve the needs of their citizens. A reflection of this awareness can be found in the title of a recent op-ed piece on the benefits of (European) federalism by Timothy Garton Ash: 'Joining the Continent To Unite the Kingdom.'

A utopian rarely spells out convincingly, if at all, how we get from here to there. As *The Economist* (1998) notes, 'Find the answer to that and the idea [of a global currency] would be thinkable.' The first step in getting from here to there is to challenge assumptions, suggest alternatives and open discussion. The path in democracies is rarely predictable and in the fullness of debate even the best ideas are often improved. What would a country require to willingly abandon an exchange rate? In Europe, a satisfactory answer to that question has been found by 12 of the current 15 EU members. What is necessary is not only a fuller appreciation of the limits of having a separate currency, but convincing commitments to provide compensation to those who may be disadvantaged by market outcomes. Perhaps the most attractive prospect of deeper political and economic integration is that of retaining and rebuilding local diversity and control that has been compromised by the imperatives of the 'golden straight jacket' and its complementary requirement that each nation pay its own way through export promotion.

The acceptance of a single world currency requires the renunciation of many nationalist pretensions, both symbolic and real. Whether the discussion relates to free trade, the role of markets, exchange rate arrangements, or other economic policies, unless there is serious democratically controlled global policy innovation, the outcome will likely be a situation where the devil shifts the locus of his/her operations from taking the hindmost to those in the front ranks. Governing for a stable world committed to renascence, not merely sustainability, requires that we begin in earnest on the next stage of institutional innovation: the reality of a world money and the institutional framework that goes with it.

Notes

1. *The Triennial Central Bank Survey of Foreign Exchange and Derivatives Market Activity* of the Bank for International Settlements, the only source for this data, reduced its figure for 1998 from $2.0 to $1.49 trillion in 2001, laconically noting in a footnote that the figures for 1998 were revised since the previous survey. Innocent mortals might imagine that a 25 percent adjustment that lops off half a trillion dollars might be worthy of at least an extra sentence in an era where some economic numbers serve as guide to policy. http://www.bis.org/publ/rpfx02t.pdf.
2. Benjamin Cohen, 'Life at the Top: International Currencies in the Twenty-First Century', *Princeton Essays in International Economics*, 221 (Dec. 2000).
3. Richard Cooper, 'A Monetary System for the Future', *Foreign Affairs*, 63 (Fall) (1984), p. 181.
4. Charles Kindleberger, *The World in Depression 1929–1939* (Berkeley: University of California Press, 1973), p. 172.
5. In the year prior to the approval of the Marshall Plan, the World Bank's first four loans were made to France, the Netherlands, Denmark, and Luxembourg. The amounts in million US dollars were 250, 195, 40, and 12. The World Bank speaks of the loan to France as one of the largest ever made by the Bank in real terms in its first fifty years.

6. Robert H. Wade, 'Capital and Revenge: The IMF and Ethiopia', *Challenge*, 44 (Sept./Oct. 2001), pp. 67–75.
7. The following comparison of the ratio of end of year exchange rates for five of the major currencies relative to the US dollar for the pre- and post-Bretton Woods periods show the greater exchange rate movement (degree of change shown by divergence from 1.0) for all but the French Franc in most of the latter decades than in the prior 20 years. A ratio below 1.0 denotes an appreciation of the subject currency relative to the US dollar. By way of comparison with Table 5.1, it is worth noting that if we look at the US$/Yen rate (rather than its more commonly referred to reciprocal) for the twenty years from 1970 to 1990, we would get a ratio of 2.7 for the depreciation of the dollar relative to the yen which is close to the exchange rate performance of Pakistan for the period 1980–2000 relative to the US dollar.

	1970/1950	**1980/1970**	**1990/1980**	**2000/1990**
Yen/US$	0.99	0.61	0.61	0.85
DM/US$*	0.87	0.54	0.76	1.12
UK£/US$	0.85	1.00	0.81	0.77
FrF/US$*	1.58	0.82	1.14	1.10
SwF/US$	1.01	0.41	0.73	1.26

* End of 1998 rate used, as the euro was introduced at the start of 1999.
Source: IMF, International Financial Statistics Yearbook.

8. Thorstein Veblen, *The Theory of Business Enterprise* (New York: Scribner's, 1904).
9. John Maynard Keynes, *The General Theory of Employment Interest and Money* (London: Macmillan, 1936), p. 159.
10. For example, the following appeared in an undergraduate textbook: 'exchange rates are asset prices and so considerable volatility is to be expected.'Paul Krugman and Maurice Obstfeld, 2nd edn, *International Economics: Theory and Policy* (Glenview, IL: Scott, Foresman, 1988), p.570.
11. Michael Mussa, Morris Goldstein, Peter B. Clark, Donald J. Mathieson, and Tamim Bayoumi, *'Improving the International Monetary System: Constraints and Possibilities'*, IMF Occasional Paper No. 116 (January 1995), pp. 18, 20 (emphasis added).
12. John Williamson, *The Crawling Band as an Exchange-Rate Regime: Lessons from Chile, Colombia, and Israel* (Washington, DC: Institute for International Economics, 1996).
13. The breakdown of reserves of the central banks of IMF member countries at the end of 2000 as reported in *International Financial Statistics* was:

Central Bank Reserves	**Billion US$**	**Share (%)**
Foreign Exchange	1916	84.7
Gold at Market Prices	261	11.5
Reserve Position in the IMF	62	2.7
SDRs	24	1.1
Total	2263	100.0

14. John Williamson, 'The Crawling Peg', *Essays in International Finance*, 50 (Dec. 1965).
15. Ronald McKinnon, *An International Standard for Monetary Stabilization* (Washington, DC: Institute for International Economics, 1984), p. 13.
16. Ronald McKinnon, 'Optimum Currency Areas', *American Economic Review*, 53 (1963), pp. 717–25. See Henry Wallich, *Monetary Problems of an Export Economy: The Cuban Experience 1914–1947* (Cambridge, MA: Harvard University Press, 1950), for a rudimentary cost–benefit evaluation for Cuba of not having its own currency.
17. McKinnon (1963), p. 719.
18. McKinnon (1984), p. 13.
19. Ricardo Ffrench-Davis and Manuel Agosín, *Managing Capital Flows in Latin America*, UNDP Office of Development Studies, Discussion Paper No. 8 (1995).
20. Robert Mundell, 'A Theory of Optimum Currency Areas', *American Economic Review*, 51 (Sept. 1961), pp. 657–65.
21. Delbert Snider, 'Optimum Adjustment Processes and Currency Areas', *Essays in International Finance*, 62 (Oct. 1962), p. 15.
22. Cooper (1984), p. 181.
23. McKinnon (1984), p. 18.
24. Warren Smith, 'Are There Enough Policy Tools?', *American Economic Review*, 55 (Mar. 1965), pp. 208–20.
25. Peter B. Kenen, *Capital Mobility and Financial Integration: A Survey*, Princeton Studies in International Finance, 39 (1976).
26. In Fred Hirsch , Michael Doyle, and Edward L. Morse, *Alternatives to Monetary Disorder* (New York: McGraw-Hill, 1977).
27. Patrick Conway, 'Currency Proliferation: The Monetary Legacy of the Soviet Union', *Essays in International Finance*, 197 (June 1995).
28. The full list follows: Armenia, 267; Azerbaijan, 94; Belarus, 78,667; Kazakstan, 23; Kyrgystan, 6.0; Moldova, 30; Russia, 68; Tajikistan, 477; Turkmenistan, 2,613; Ukraine, 852; and Uzbekistan, 250. IMF, *International Financial Statistics On Disk*, and Economist Intelligence Unit, *Country Data Online*.
29. See 'Who Lost Russia?' (Chapter 5), in Joseph Stiglitz, *Globalization and its Discontents* (New York: W.W. Norton, 2002), pp. 133–65.
30. Ibid., p. 149.
31. Ibid., pp. 153–55.
32. James Tobin, *The New Economics One Decade Older*, Eliot Janeway Lectures, 1972 (Princeton: Princeton University Press, 1974).
33. Bank for International Settlements, *The Triennial Central Bank Survey of Foreign Exchange and Derivatives Market Activity* (2002), http://www.bis.org/publ/rpfx02t.pdf.
34. James Tobin, 'A Proposal for International Monetary Reform', *Eastern Economic Journal*, 4 (1978), pp. 153–59.
35. See Paul Bernd Spahn, 'The Tobin Tax and Exchange Rate Stability', *Finance and Development*, 33 (June 1996), pp. 24–27, and a dissenting comment from Janet Stotsky, 'Why a Two-Tier Tobin Tax Won't Work', *Finance and Development* (June 1996), pp. 28–29.
36. UNDP, *HDR 1994*, p. 70.

37. These reports which dealt with Transparency and Accountability, Strengthening Financial Systems, and International Financial Crises are all available as pdf files for download at http://www.bis.org/publ/othp01.htm.
38. International Financial Institution Advisory Commission (2000), *Report* ('The Meltzer Report'), March (Washington, DC), http://www.house.gov/hec/imf/meltzer.htm; Morris Goldstein, *Safeguarding Prosperity in a Global Financial System: The Future International Financial Architecture. Report of an Independent Task Force* (Washington: Institute for International Economics,1999); International Monetary Fund (2000), 'Report of the Acting Managing Director to the International Monetary and Financial Committee on Progress in Reforming the IMF and Strengthening the Architecture of the International Financial System' (April 12), http://www.imf.org.external/np/omd/2000/report.htm; and UN, 'Towards a new international financial architecture', *Report of the Task Force of the Executive Committee on Economic and Social Affairs of the United Nations* (New York, 21 January 1999). For a critical analysis of several of these reports see Roy Culpeper, 'Systemic Reform at a Standstill: A Flock of "G's" in Search of Global Financial Stability' (Ottawa: North-South Institute, 2000) (June), http://www.nsi-ins.ca/download/Gs_eng.pdf.
39. Andre W.Berg and Eduardo Borensztein, 'Full Dollarization: The Pros and Cons', *Economics Issues*, 24 (Dec.) (Washington: IMF, 2000), p. 5.
40. Justine Hunter, 'US Dollar Could Lift Our Economy 37%', *National Post* (19 May 2001).
41. Stiglitz, p. 43.
42. John Pinder, 'Integrating Divergent Economies: The Extranational Method', Michael Hodges and William Wallace, eds, *Economic Divergence in the European Community* (London: George Allen & Unwin, 1981), p. 198.
43. Commission of the European Communities, pp. 11–12.
44. Rudiger Dornbusch, 'Fewer Monies, Better Monies' (Dec. 2000), http://econ-www.mit.edu/faculty/dornbusch/papers.htm.
45. Robert Triffin, 'The International Monetary System in the Year 2000', Jagdish Bhagwati, ed., *Economics and World Order; From the 1970's to the 1990's* (New York: Macmillan, 1972), p. 192.
46. Barry Eichengreen, *International Monetary Arrangements for the 21st Century* (Washington, DC: Brookings Institution, 1994), p. ix.
47. Ibid., p. 4.
48. James E. Meade, *The Economic Basis of a Durable Peace* (New York: Oxford University Press, 1940), pp. 35–57.
49. The twelve euro countries are currently 'represented' by eight different Executive Directors. If grouped together, their combined vote would come to 23.0 percent. Pascal Lamy, among other EU officials, has spoken of the desirability of having one EU voice in each key policy area. Some of the groupings defy common logic. Spain and Ireland are each in groups whose other members are all in the Western Hemisphere. They are 'represented' respectively by Venezuela and Canada. You are encourged to check http://imf.org/external/np/sec/memdir/eds.htm.
50. James Forder, 'Central Bank Independence: Reassessing the Measurements', *Journal of Economic Issues*, 33 (1999), pp. 23–40.

6
Worldwide Real Freedom for All

> When speaking of real-freedom-for-all, we must mean it: for *all*. In other words, we must pursue the objective of introducing substantial redistributive mechanisms on a world scale, indeed ultimately an individual basic income at the highest sustainable level for each human being.
>
> —Philippe Van Parijs, *Real Freedom for All: What (if Anything) can justify Capitalism?*

> Everyone has the right to a standard of living adequate for the health and well-being of himself and of his family, including food, clothing, housing and medical care and necessary social services, and the right to security in the event of unemployment, sickness, disability, widowhood, old age or other lack of livelihood in circumstances beyond his control.
>
> —Universal Declaration of Human Rights, Article 25(1)

The roots of my advocacy of a planet-wide citizen's income can be traced back to at least two elements from my early professional experience in the latter half of the 1960s. One influence was a volume edited by Robert Theobald on a guaranteed income that formed part of a debate on the possibility of introducing a negative income tax in the US at that time.[1] The other was the discourse that continues to this day about providing adequate financial support to developing countries. I have come to believe that a basic income guarantee extended to all members of the human family, not just to those in one country, could bring these two elements together.

Voluntarism has been the consistent principal answer to the allocation of funds to developing countries: since at least the late 1960s each of the richer nations was to provide 0.7 percent of its GNP for ODA. That target has been repeated over and over again for more than three decades, including in the 1974 UN General Assembly resolution on a New International Economic Order and, more recently, in June 2000 in the joint OECD, World Bank, IMF, and UN statement, *A Better World for All.*

The voluntary 0.7 percent ODA target made sense when it was first suggested. Nonetheless, it should have been regarded primarily as a device to prime the pump of northern generosity, which it failed to do (see Chapter 4). For it still to be restated today must be seen as reflecting a scandalous lack of any real sense of urgency as to the plight of the world's poor. As I shall argue below, our sights are set far too low. Rather than thinking of the cost of global sustainable development in terms of millions or billions of dollars, it is time that we began to consider an *annual* price tag of trillions.

Why trillions? Because to date everything else has been inadequate to cope with the problems of poverty throughout the world. In 1978 Robert S. McNamara, the then President of the World Bank, wrote in his Foreword to the first *World Development Report* that despite a 'quarter century . . . of unprecedented change and progress in the developing world' 800 million people continued to be trapped in absolute poverty. His remedy was substantial acceleration of growth in the developing countries, without which, given population increase, 'numbers of the absolutely poor will remain unacceptably high even at the end of the century.'[2] In fact, that is precisely the case: 1.2 billion people were reported to be living on less than $1 per day and another 1.6 billion living on less than $2 per day in 1998.[3] Think about it: after one-half century of freeing of trade and commitment to fostering development, 2.8 billion people, constituting 47 percent of the Earth's population, are living at the material, political, and social margin. The preceding facts suggest that, whatever the rhetoric, solidarity has decreased rather than increased in recent decades and that the results of our efforts to close the income gap between the rich and the poor have been either inadequate and/or inappropriate.

Even more scandalous has been the devastating ascendancy of neoliberalism with its assignment of blame to poor people and poor nations for what is, in effect, their inability to prosper in a contest between those with unequal capacity and access, where the rules of the game have been established (and not consistently honored) by those controlling most of the world's monetary wealth. Neoliberalism puts economic 'imperatives' at the center of a hegemonic discourse that best serves the world's elites. The work of Thomas Paine is often cited by those supporting the introduction of basic income provisions. I, too, shall invoke Paine: not, however, *Agrarian Justice* where he makes the case for sharing of income, but rather *The Rights of Man* (1791) where his words can be applied to life under neoliberalism:

> The original despotism ... divides and subdivides itself into a thousand shapes and forms, till at last the whole of it is acted by deputation ... against this species of despotism, proceeding on through an endless labyrinth of office till the source of it is scarcely perceptible, there is no mode of redress. It strengthens itself by assuming the appearance of duty, and tyrannises under the pretence of obeying.[4]

Today's victims of downsizing, re-engineering, and structural adjustment will recognize the plaintive 'the deficit made me do it,' as one expression of a social fractal akin to that described by Paine. The hindmost victims of the neoliberal tyrannies of our time, like the deserving poor of old, must demonstrate their worth if any assistance, however meager and conditional, is eventually to come their way.[5]

If we are at all concerned about the persistence of worldwide poverty and all the symptoms associated with it, we need to think boldly, give free reign to our imagination, and actively work together to shape an alternative discourse. One of the earliest notions I encountered as a social scientist was that of 'institutional lag': as a result of the Cold War and neoliberalism, we are at least 60 years behind in our thinking about shaping democratic global institutions. That is the 'double movement' à la Karl Polanyi or countervail à la John Kenneth Galbraith needed to reign in capitalist excesses, which even Friedrich Hayek included in his expressions of concern about the totalitarians in our midst.[6]

In Chapter 4 some of the available data on growing global income inequalities were given. Just so that the magnitude of disparities in wealth and influence are not forgotten, bear in mind that the income of the world's richest 1 percent was said to be equal in 1993 to that of the world's poorest 57 percent and that the top 25 million (or 10 percent) of income recipients in the US received as much as the world's poorest 2 billion (43 percent).[7] Even more startling are the comparisons that have been made between the world's wealthiest and the income of those at the bottom. *Forbes Magazine* reported in 1998 that the assets of the world's three richest individuals exceeded the combined GNP of all the least developed countries and that the assets of the world's 200 richest people were greater that the combined income of 41 percent of the world's people.[8] We are a long way from Jean-Jacques Rousseau's ideal for his Good Society, that 'in respect of riches, no citizen shall ever be wealthy enough to buy another, and none poor enough to be forced to sell himself.'[9] Indeed, we have reached the point where rich individuals can 'buy' organizations (including political parties) and even countries.

Social reproduction

Production and distribution are interdependent sides of a single relationship. In earlier drafts of this chapter I followed the long-standing conventional production–distribution dichotomy; I always placed the emphasis on distribution and insisted on its complementary relation with production. In this regard, I regularly invoked John Stuart Mill, who observed in his *Principles of Political Economy* in the middle of the 19th century: 'It is only in the backward countries of the world that increased production is still an important object: in those most advanced, what is economically needed is a better distribution...'[10] Progressive income redistribution, by altering consumption possibilities broadens the market for a wide range of goods and services that are basic to well-being, while narrowing somewhat the market for elite goods and services.

We can view production–distribution relationships as matters of social provisioning. Progressive redistribution can also be seen as altering life chances, by enhancing personal capabilities, as Amartya Sen and Jean Drèze have reminded us.[11] The capabilities perspective strongly suggests that the appropriate framework in which production and distribution should be situated is that of 'social reproduction': reproduction of healthy, wholesome human beings; reproduction of society, reproduction of peace, civility, creative expression, joy. Changing the framework in which we view production and consumption conforms to Karl Polanyi's notion of re-embedding the economy within society, which is one of the two concepts that guide my thinking in this chapter. The other is what Philippe Van Parijs calls 'real freedom for all': universal monetary entitlements which offer the promise of both liberating individuals from penury and restoring to them both dignity and the possibility of choice of life options. In an age of globalization both these concepts must be universalized.

If we regard societal reproduction as a sacred trust, insofar as it celebrates the uniqueness and value of each individual and the integrity of community, then we must consider paying the price and we must consider the strategies. In the words of Eduardo Suplicy, in the subtitle of his book espousing an income guarantee, 'the exit is by the door.'[12]

That is, after trying to reduce poverty by a multitude of roundabout schemes, it is time to try the one approach which should have been obvious from the outset: providing an income guarantee to all. In fact, the door is not the 'exit' but rather the threshold to a distinct worldview. Once the perspective of an unconditional income guarantee is embraced, the entire discourse surrounding poverty elimination is transformed. Much like Dorothy who leaves black and white Kansas behind and arrives in the brightly colored Land of Oz, the intellectual and practical landscape on the income guarantee side of the threshold is humanely transformed.

The centrality of the facilitation of social reproduction is consistent with the belief that informs this work, namely, that world problems require world solutions; anything less necessarily perpetuates injustice which carries with it a train of untoward consequences, among them periodic eruptions of genocidal violence. There is nothing new in these sentiments, nor are they foreign to the field of economics. Nobel Prize winning economists James Meade (1940) and Jan Tinbergen (1945) were among those who wrote about global approaches to economic organization, including redistribution, during World War II.

If we believe in 'real freedom for all,' then freedom must be accorded to people as human beings and not solely on the basis of their role as human capital or labor. Building peace and freedom is incompatible with our currently advancing movement toward a world of great walls, armed guards, and surveillance cameras monitoring attempts to cross borders.

Entitlement was once a perfectly respectable word to describe social provisioning arrangements on whose merits a jurisdiction had reached a consensus through democratic processes. In recent years entitlements have come to be regarded to be the source of societal problems and are alleged to foster a culture of dependence. The disappearance of safety nets has created a culture of deprivation. Remarkably, little scorn has been directed at the entitlements and even unbridled greed of the dependent rich. Instead, additional tax cuts were directed their way in the US and elsewhere.

Writings advocating a minimum income for all refer variously to a guaranteed income, social dividend, basic income, citizen's income, universal allocation, or negative income tax. While differing in design, all address the desirability, if not the right, of all people to a guaranteed minimum annual share of the revenues of political jurisdictions. The intellectual record of these proposals date back at least to 16th century and include the argument of Thomas More that a minimum income guarantee would reduce the number hanged for stealing food.[13] At the time of the French Revolution, Thomas Paine advanced a plan which dissociated in part reward from effort and recognized as a 'right and not a charity,' the just claim of all to a share in the produce of the soil, which he regarded as being originally the common property of the human race.[14] In the middle of the 19th century John Stuart Mill spoke of our common inheritance.[15] Mill addresses the right to a share of the product. While he spoke of the 'just claim of the individual to the fruits, whether great or small, of his or her own industry,'[16] he envisioned a time when 'the conquests made from the powers of nature by the intellect and energy of scientific discoverers, become the common property of the species, and the means of improving and elevating the universal lot.'[17] Matthew Arnold addressed the question of a 'just claim' and insisted that this reflects no more or no less than a societal choice, which is always subject to modification. In a manner similar to that of Paine and building on Mill, Thorstein Veblen referred to our 'joint stock of knowledge.'[18]

We continue to try to resolve the problem of distribution by tackling production, implicitly invoking either the marginal productivity theory of income distribution or trickle down, two of the assumptions whose use circumvents discussion of income distribution. In the economic analysis of the atomistic firm, benefits are distributed to the 'factors of production' in relation to their contribution to the product. That is, whether it is recognized or not, the default setting in economic analysis: 'factors' receive as compensation what they have directly contributed to output and that is all there is to say about the matter. But who is to be compensated for the free gifts of the environment, for the existence of a system of laws, stable money, and contract enforcement? And is there any consideration to be given to the contribution of civilization, broadly speaking, that provides the opportunities for us?

Production cannot be ignored, but it surely must share center stage with distribution and the two must be seen as inextricably intertwined. Moreover, we must not be blind to the fact that the 'resolution' of neither the production nor the distribution 'problem' rests within the hands of a single country. Neither can the question of full employment be solved by national policies, which, in any event impinge on foreign countries to the extent that resort is made to trade and transaction controls, export subsidies, and/or exchange rate devaluations.

As for 'trickle down,' the Universal Declaration of Human Rights affirms that 'Everyone has a right to life, liberty and security of person' (Article 3). These rights, in my view should be sought directly and not as some hoped-for residual of the pursuit of other objectives. The most direct mechanism available for securing the 'right to life' is through the establishment of a planet-wide citizen's income.

More recently, in the 1960s and 1970s, the 'common heritage of mankind' was used in the discussion of global sharing of the proceeds from the economic exploitation of regions that are not part of the territory of any sovereign state (*res nullius*). As was pointed out in Chapter 4, the consideration of offshore areas as part of our common heritage led to a fiscally defensive extension of national territorial claims.

In the mid-1970s we find a suggestion from Nobel Prize winner Jan Tinbergen for an even broader application of the common heritage concept 'to new domains such as mineral rights, science and technology, means of production and other sources of wealth.'[19] In terms of the present discussion, an important point to note is that an open-ended interpretation of the common heritage of humanity can be invoked to provide philosophical underpinning for the case of a global system of taxation[20] to finance both the maintenance of international order and a worldwide system of entitlements intended to universalize concretely the 'right to life.'

Expenditures in support of global equity and global order can also be thought of as investments in the maintenance and expansion of our global joint stock of knowledge. Paul Streeten made this argument in 1972, suggesting that there is a harmony of interest between the fulfillment of basic needs and the pursuit of sustainable growth:

> It is not only a *moral* duty to enable human beings, wherever born, to develop their facilities, but it is in the *interest* of all that these human resources should be fully developed, so that, instead of being a drain on the world's resources, they may contribute to their growth.[21]

No less than four Nobel Prize winning economists (James Meade, Milton Friedman, James Tobin, and Herbert Simon) have all espoused one version or another of a minimum income guarantee and another Nobel prize winner, Amartya Sen, has insisted on the centrality of entitlements. The essential rationale is quite simple: all earned income takes advantage of pre-existing institutions, knowledge, communication, and transportation nets, which are part of what is commonly regarded as social capital. While social capital, like so many concepts, is generally spoken of in a national context, it can also be viewed from a global perspective.

To the extent that each of us is a common beneficiary of the cumulative global process of civilization, we are entitled to some reasonable monetary dividend and those who reap the greatest monetary gain should be subject to charges for the use of the collective social capital of our increasingly globalized society.

While a citizen's income is an indispensable component of social reproduction, the role of the state and the community does not end there. Provision of merit needs (among which are education, health care, and systems of public health) and public goods and the maintenance of a range of existing social supports are essential. While this might be obvious, Milton Friedman, in his espousal of a negative income tax for the US, envisioned that it would be more than amply financed by eliminating all existing welfare programs.[22]

Humanity unbound

A Citizen's Income sufficient to assure a reasonable level of subsistence to all worldwide could have a profound effect on the entire socio-political economy. It may be unrealistic to imagine that its absence stands between us and a new renaissance, but benefits observed in experiments and in actual applications provide ample basis for some of the optimism. The abolition of means tests for entitlements would alone restore respect to those who have to bare intimate details of their lives in order to remain on welfare roles.

While a citizen's income is not equivalent to wages for housework, insofar as all receive the income, it could, if set at a sufficiently high level, allow one to engage in highly valued, but presently unremunerated, care activities without the economic need to earn one's sustenance.

Time devoted to unpaid activities, for which a lack of remuneration is currently a distinct barrier and a basis for social exclusion, might expand significantly. A partial listing of such activities include household work, voluntary activities, democratic political participation, creative endeavors, cultural representations, sports, and learning. As John Collett observed from personal experience: 'participation in society does involve having a disposable income—something that benefits do not provide.'[23]

Voluntarism in particular might receive a significant boost from the creation of a citizen's income. The vast majority of the students that I advise in the International Development Studies program at McGill University would, I believe, be on their way right now to do volunteer work with NGOs in Africa, Asia, or Latin America if they were recipients of a citizen's income and would also probably abandon their part-time school year jobs in favor of volunteer work with NGOs in Montreal. Instead, many are shut out of voluntary participation by the need to work throughout the year in whatever unskilled job is available to finance their education.

Indeed, in today's neoliberal context, voluntarism is often either exclusionary and/or exploitative. For example, student internships are increasingly offered with neither remuneration nor any allowance for living and travel expenses. I know of at least two McGill students who were offered unpaid summer internships with the UN in New York. One desperately sought funding sources; the other resolved to work evenings and weekends as a server in a New York restaurant to be able to take advantage of the opportunity. When voluntarism excludes those who cannot shoulder the financial burden, it does not serve as a source of solidarity. While a citizen's income would not completely level the playing field of possibilities and opportunities, it could reduce the slant significantly.

Writing in 1969, Buckminster Fuller fully imagined that within a decade an income support scheme would come into being. He preferred to speak of it as a 'life fellowship in research and development or in just simple thinking.' He firmly believed that this would allow each person to 'be able to dare to think truthfully and to act accordingly without losing his franchise to live.'[24] For Fuller, an income guarantee has the potential to unleash both human creativity and 'humanity's unique capability—its metaphysical capability.'[25] Breaking an individual work-subsistence link, like breaking a country's export-survival link, may be the key to unleashing creative imagination and enabling a joyful people-centered socio-economy by removing the props from mind-deadening activity.

To return to Streeten's observation about the fullest development of human resources, another advantage of a citizen's income is that it could also permit students to pursue education to the limit of their interests and not to the limit of their finances as increasingly is occurring. It bears noting as well that late entry into the labor force has been our most sensible solution to youth unemployment. I explicitly reject dead-end jobs at rock bottom wages as being a 'solution.' If anything, it is a Pandora's box to increased societal ills.

The societal fractal that encompasses the values necessary for the introduction of a planet-wide citizen's income would also likely extend to prioritizing education and its public financing. Expenditures on schooling are no longer a sacred cow as they once were and when budget cuts come, education comes under attack. This reflects a short-sighted preoccupation with the monetary value of national product, rather than a concern with the quality of a society and the many indirect costs of not educating citizens. A bumper sticker that I saw in the US proclaimed: 'If you think education is expensive, consider ignorance.' To which one might add the societal costs in the short and long run of high dropout rates, youth crime and punishment and lost human potential. Well-staffed and equipped schools are likely to be much cheaper than increases in law enforcement officers, prisons, and confinement costs. When prisons and security services are celebrated as one of a country's major industries, it is time to pinch oneself and ask where have we lost our way. This returns us to the argument in Chapter 4 about the necessity of a system of world public finance that ends tax competition between jurisdictions and eliminates tax havens and the array of tax avoidance schemes that have been cooked up to escape civic responsibility.

Funding a planet-wide citizen's income

The actual form that a citizen's income might take is not the issue at this juncture; it is the principle that needs to gain wide acceptance as a superior approach to social reproduction and planetary sustainability. It is, nonetheless, instructive to show the economic feasibility of a planet-wide citizen's income (PWCI). One recent variation by Patrice Spadoni proposed setting a citizen's income at no less than 50 percent of a country's per capita income.[26] A phase-in arrangement for a planet-wide citizen's income intended to narrow the global income gap might set the initial annual, unconditional stipend to all at some lower fraction of the world per capita income. By this criterion every man, woman, and child on the planet, irrespective of status, would be entitled to this stipend related to the world per capita income as a birthright. While a truly universal entitlement, paid to rich and poor alike, involves higher direct outlays than either targeted grants or a negative income tax, it may be the least expensive in terms of associated administrative costs, least stigmatizing, and most effective in reaching those in need by choosing not to discriminate. Administrative costs are also held down by avoiding the need to monitor whether an individual's income-earning activities and revenues have changed.

Embracing the income redistribution implications of taking global solidarity seriously will not 'break the bank.' A citizen's income equal to 20 percent of the world average per capita income in 1999 of around \$5000[27] would come to \$1000, equivalent to about \$2.74 per day, an amount that would be more than double the income of half the world's population. By this expedient, no one would remain below the \$2 per head poverty line. While there might be some inflationary impact, this is by no means a necessary outcome. There would be a shift in the profile of goods demanded and a certain shift from savings to consumption, but there is no a priori reason to believe that a major inflationary impact would result, given the levels of unused capacity and idle labor in the global system.

At a level for a planet-wide citizen's income of 20 percent of the world per capita income, the total bill for a universal program would have been US$6 trillion out of an estimated world income of around US$30 trillion. To put this into perspective, let us refer to Branko Milanovic's figures on the 'true world income distribution.' He found that in 1993 the top 25 percent of world's persons accounted for 77.7 percent of the world's income, the top 15 percent accounted for 63.0 percent of total income and the top 10 percent for 50.8 percent of total world income.[28] I have done trial calculations for financing a universal global program set at 20 percent of world per capita income per person per year out of taxes levied solely on the top 25 percent of the world's income earners, on the top 15 percent and on the top 10 percent. I opt here to suggest that levying supplementary taxes on the top 10 percent of the world's income recipients could easily finance a planet-wide citizen's income. If the financing fell exclusively on the top 10 percent of income recipients, then, it would require a tax burden of an additional 39 percent of the average income of the world's highest income recipients. In recognition of the steepness of the World's Lorenz curve of income inequality, reflecting sharply higher incomes in each of the highest income segments, I have fashioned an example with supplementary income-tax rates that go from 35 percent of gross income for that 5 percent of the population between the 90th and 95th percentile, to 40 percent for the next highest 4 percentile, 45 percent for those in the top 1 percentile. Given that the citizen's income is provided to all, one needs to consider the net tax payment as a share of income. As shown in Table 6.1, these go from an average of 29 to 37 to 43 percent for each of the three top cohorts. These estimates of the tax burden required for an introductory level universal citizen's income are well below either the 90 percent social capital estimate of Herbert Simon or the 70 percent flat tax level that he proposed (see Chapter 4). Moreover, my example involves a supplementary tax that falls only on those 600 million individuals in the world's richest households.

Kevin Phillips, who has written extensively and critically on the concentration of income and wealth in the US notes that in the 1950s there were six different marginal tax brackets for those in the top 2 percent of

Table 6.1 Hypothetical tax proceeds for funding a worldwide citizen's income

	Population (in billion)	**Share of world income 1993**	**Income (in trillion US$)**	**Tax rate %**	**Proceeds (in trillion US$)**	**Net tax/pci**
Top 1%	0.06	9.5	2.85	0.45	1.3	0.43
Next 4%	0.24	24.2	7.26	0.40	2.9	0.37
Next 5%	0.30	17.1	5.13	0.35	1.8	0.29
Sum	0.60	50.8	15.24	0.39*	6.0	0.35*

* Average.
Source: Calculations based on data appearing in Milanovic (2002).

the income distribution, reflecting the steepness of the slope of income differences in that category. He proposes to return to that kind of distinction with a six or eight bracket policy. He provides an example with a 40 percent rate at one million dollars and a 56 percent rate at $50 million.[29]

In the absence of evidence to the contrary and given the likely level of error in estimates of both world income and its distribution, it is reasonable to treat income recipients and households as equivalent. A further word is in order about estimates. The widely cited figures about population living under $1 and $2 per day, which represent close to one-half of the world population in 1998 would give, by generous estimate a combined income of these low-income recipients of $1.33 trillion or 4.4 percent of total world income, rather than the 8.5 percent estimated by Milanovic. Other things being equal, that would suggest even higher concentration of income at the top and that lower supplementary tax rates might be sufficient to finance a planet-wide citizen's income at the dollar value used here. As Milanovic's figures are based on survey data, reasonable doubt can be raised about how forthcoming the richest are about their income from all sources.

Milanovic's figures placed the 1993 purchasing power parity adjusted income of the richest 1 percent at 9.5 percent of world income; while comparable figures for the US in the late 1990s, attributed 17 percent of that country's income to the richest 1 percent.[30] Alternatively, holding to the proposed 20 percent of per capita income target for a PWCI, a truer (and higher) estimate of world income (and per capita income) would lead to a higher PWCI. A significant gap in inequality measures exists between Milanovic's estimates of the ratio of the income of the top 20 percent to the bottom 20 percent, which, reading from his graph is likely about 33:1 in 1993 as opposed to the figure reported for 1991 of 61:1 (and which was reported to have risen by 1997 to 74:1) in a UNDP *Human Development Report*. This reinforces the view that there is room at the top for financing a planet-wide citizen's income. Of course, reconciling 'room' and 'will'—the task at hand—will not be an easy one.

We are not talking here about confiscatory levels of taxation. This is the kind of effort that is required if we generalize our concerns about poverty, equity, and inclusion to the world level. A reminder of the change in order of magnitude relative to ODA is appropriate: had the 0.7 target been realized it would have yielded US$150 billion, while the actual amount was US$52 billion, roughly one-hundredth of the amount required for a universal stipend set at 20 percent of the value of average per capita world income.

An example focusing on a country where net recipients would predominate is that of the largest European country, the Russian Federation. The per capita income of Russia is reported to have been $2270 in 1998. The transfer to each of the Russian people of $1000 per year would, if this had been in place at the time, have come to $138.8 billion, which can be contrasted to receipt by Russia of official development assistance of $1.0 billion ($7 per capita) in 1998 and net private capital flows of $19.3 billion. In fact, the unconditional hypothetical transfers would have amounted to 76 percent of Russia's total outstanding external debt of $183.6 billion, the management of which carries with it countless externally imposed conditions.

The intent here is not to minimize the effort that would be required to implement any such scheme, but rather to illustrate that the magnitudes involved are not unrealistic. The far, far more difficult roadblocks are the preconceptions that first lead to an insistence that individuals and countries must earn their living and then lead to blaming the victims when their earnest efforts fall short.

Starting the process

The period between 1965 and 1978 held great promise particularly in the US for the introduction of a negative tax, which tops up actual income to a specified minimum. This effort came to little except for some four pilot projects in the US over the period 1968–80 and one in Canada (1975–78).[31] As Richard Darman observes with regard to the US research projects relating to the negative income tax and other social programs: 'most of these experimental efforts were abandoned before they could deliver—often before they were fully financed.'[32] While most of the US negative income tax studies involved a two or three year horizon, members of a subgroup in the Denver and Seattle study were to be monitored for a 20-year period, but were cut off after nine years.[33] Widerquist and Darman share a similar view, summed up in Darman's words: 'When the legitimacy of a governmental role is denied, there is little interest in improving it.' Numerous prominent thinkers contributed to the policy discussion, including Milton Friedman. At the time it looked very much like an idea whose time had finally arrived, but it was not to be despite its supporters across a wide portion of the political spectrum. The subsequent shift to the right in North American politics has pushed the idea into deep storage and some economists would like to jettison completely the income tax on which the proposal was centered.

Nonetheless, one functioning citizen's income is to be found in the US. For the past 20 years the state of Alaska has administered a basic income allocation to all men, women, and children who are residents of the state. The Alaskan program has its origins in the fortuitous circumstances of the state (or rather legally the ensemble of its citizens) owning oil fields providing an abundance of revenues, rather than a resolve to increase taxes in the name of equity. The variable once-a-year allocation which is based on a five-year moving average of the price of oil has regularly been over $1000 per year recently and has been as high as $1900.[34] An Associated Press account relates that Alaska is the only one of the 50 US states which registered an improvement in its income distribution.[35] With its population of 600,000, which is 0.2 percent of the total US population, it does represent a well-established experience, not experiment; a case worthy of note.

In recent years interest in a Basic Income has gathered considerable momentum, starting in Europe, where it is regularly discussed among a number of writers, who issue a periodic newsletter and have been holding regular biennial conferences of BIEN, the Basic Income European Network, ever since the founding meeting in 1986 at the Hoover Chair for Economic and Social Ethics at the Université Catholique de Louvain in Louvain-la-Neuve, Belgium. The authors of all the papers in the 1986 BIEN Proceedings were from Europe. At the 9th Biennial meeting of BIEN held at the ILO in Geneva in September 2002, every continent was represented and there was a distinct feeling that the door was opening to modest initiatives that could lead in time to full-blown national programs and eventually to a planet-wide citizen's income.

Of the three global economics policy initiatives that I am proposing in this book, a planet-wide citizen income is the one that least involves a scaling up of actual national policies to a global level simply because such programs do not yet exist. All countries have some mixture of policies making up a social safety net, which occasionally includes some form of financial entitlement, generally not of as broad application as a universal national citizen's income. Introducing a generous income guarantee only in the richer countries of the world would simply exacerbate the problem of global apartheid. Other things being equal, immigration would become even more attractive and border restrictions would doubtless increase. Given global income differentials and the ethical case for meeting the needs of the poorest first, the needs of those whose incomes are below $2 per day should surely take priority, were our responses not influenced by local and national citizenship loyalties. I hasten to add that individual countries wishing to exceed the planet-wide stipend, which should have first priority, would be free to do so.

To help build momentum for a planet-wide income, wealthier countries should be lobbied by proponents of income guarantees as to the advantages of strengthening existing income supports at the national level, which might lessen resistance to an eventual planet-wide uniform system. Residence requirements would presumably suffice to prevent any increments in petitioners for immigrant status above existing levels. On the other hand, piecemeal change can be the enemy of more radical change and, as well, in these circumstances might undermine any embryonic sense of global solidarity.

The world's countries which have the greatest disparities in wealth as reflected by a Gini coefficient of inequality of 0.4 or greater and/or a ratio of the richest 20 percent to poorest 20 percent of 7.5 or higher might be strongly encouraged (and supported) to initiate national guaranteed income programs. These inequality measures might be highlighted the way the under-five mortality rate (U5MR) has been highlighted by UNICEF, which uses those rates to rank countries of the world. Of the developing countries for which data is available, Brazil, Chile, Mexico, Uruguay, Costa Rica, Guatemala, Panama, and Malaysia are all characterized by high levels of income inequality that surpass my suggested standard. Brazil has begun work in this regard, including the introduction of an income supplement contingent on school attendance.

There are many ways to go from A to B. If we are serious about eradicating global poverty, then we must begin to imagine solutions and begin to implement steps directed toward minimizing the extremes of global inequality. As for financing, we need not resort to gimmickry: the tried and true societal solution is the progressive taxation of income and profits. One of the stylized facts of public finance prior to the advent of neoliberal globalization was that as jurisdictions gained experience in the management of public finance and built social solidarity, one observed a shift in the reliance for public revenue from taxes on transactions to taxes on income and wealth. It is high time to return to a commitment to progressive taxation.

In considering the basic income, one should keep in mind distinctions between entitlements in cash and in kind. These are clearly not interchangeable. There is a need for the provision of public and merit goods free of charge and of a cash income. Providing one does not solve the problem of the provision of the other. Social policy is never a matter of one magic bullet.

The expanding world of work

The specter of wide-scale unemployment has been present at least since the beginning of the Industrial Revolution. It is a topic that occupied the attention of many including Karl Marx in the 19th century who spoke of a reserve army of the unemployed and John Maynard Keynes in the 20th century.[36] The international dimension of full employment was already under discussion in the 1930s and James Meade (1940) and Thomas Balogh (1945) were among those who commented during the war years on the international dimension of full employment. In fact, the international conference in Havana whose 1948 treaty called for the creation of the ITO was devoted to trade *and* employment and the first substantive chapter of the Havana Charter deals with employment. The first article reads as follows:

> The Members recognize that the avoidance of unemployment or underemployment, through the achievement and maintenance in each country of useful employment opportunities for those able and willing to work and of a large and steadily growing volume of production and effective demand for goods and services, is not of domestic concern alone, but is also a necessary condition . . . for the well-being of all other countries.[37]

For I.F. Stone, writing at the time of the creation of the UN, preservation of the peace was the international dimension of full employment in the US: '. . . failure to achieve full employment would also provide the right emotional climate for imperialist adventures: disillusioned veterans, renewed isolationism, xenophobia, fascist movements. In such an atmosphere whatever is achieved at San Francisco would become worthless.'[38] Fifty-seven years later, writing at a time when the sound of war drums again filled the air, Robert R. Reich, a former US Secretary of Labor, also linked jobs and global security: 'If we fight for fuller employment and economic justice, for better jobs, decent work, and fight against poverty, we will be fighting the circumstances in which terrorism can flourish.'[39]

In the middle of the 19th century John Stuart Mill wrote: 'If Manchester, instead of being where it is, were on a rock in the North Sea (its present industry nevertheless continuing), it would still be but a town of England, not a country trading with England; it would be merely, as now, a place where England finds its convenient to carry on her cotton manufacture.'[40] If today we 'choose' to have our stereo equipment produced in Malaysia or China, does it matter? In the case of the more urbanized countries of the world, north and south, direct engagement in the production of goods employs a smaller percentage of the total population with each passing day. What does matter are the many consequences of the loss of associated employment and tax revenues and our ability to respond individually and institutionally to such changes. A planet-wide citizen's income and world public finance from which profits could not legally escape could make a significant difference.

Part of the significance of Mill's statement relates to the extent of separation of production and distribution of income, as opposed to their direct link in basic neoclassical economic analysis. The locus of production and jobs is always subject to change, for a variety of reasons, which may have nothing to do with the rootlessness of foreign investment. Changes in production techniques, changes in transportation costs, change in communication, reduction of tariff barriers, and cost differentials all can lead to the shutting of local industry and its replacement by production elsewhere. This has been witnessed throughout human history. What has been missing is a systematic global flow of compensatory financial transfers (and a single fixed exchange rate) both to ease the adaptation to change and to minimize the necessity for countries to bid competitively to attract foreign investment or production contracts in order to earn foreign exchange.

The world witnessed a succession of pilot projects of sorts with the growth of export production in Japan and then in the first four Asian NICs (Hong Kong, Singapore, South Korea, and Taiwan),[41] then from export processing zones around the world. The concomitant disappearance of jobs in the north was doubtless but a tiny foretaste of what the 'opening' of China means for job security in the rest of the world. These have had an impact on employment and tax revenues both at the local, regional, and national levels in many northern countries. Associated with these developments have come difficulties in maintaining social safety nets, exacerbated politically by the demands for privatization of public services.

What does matter crucially if we have one world market for labor is that arrangements exist for providing offsets as pre-existing jobs disappear. The outliers on the upper end of the generosity scale in the provision of social benefits are among the first to be buffeted by the winds of change associated with the flight of jobs from certain industries. Offsets that may have existed have been cut back. Winds of change and winds of opinion have combined to reduce national welfare programs around the globe.

Growing concentration of income has narrowed demand in consumer markets and downsizing of governments has reduced jobs directly as well as indirectly through effects on demand. That there is a perceived shortage of jobs should be seen as the result of a failure of social imagination under the hypnotic influence of neoliberal principles, which demonize the public sector. Today's societies have ample scope to expand employment in the full range of people-centered activities in education, health care, caring professions, public service, sports, and the arts. The scope for ever-expanding employment is there, we need to truly prioritize what the ILO calls 'decent work' for all by insisting on income guarantees that will expand demand for goods, services, and the associated job creation in their provision (production and distribution), and expansion of public sector funded and/or operated activities in the social sector.

Over six decades have elapsed since the publication of the first edition of Colin Clark's *The Conditions of Economic Progress*, in which one finds countless international comparisons of changes in economic structures. That work is remembered today mainly for the conclusions he drew about the role of the tertiary or service sector as a follower on the road of socio-economic transformation: 'the most important concomitant of economic progress . . . [is] the movement of working population from agriculture to manufacture, and from manufacture to commerce and services.'[42] Following Clark it was commonly held that the rapid growth of service employment in developing countries is not only premature, but prejudicial, in that it serves in various ways as a drag on progress. The contrary view sees the growth of the service sector, by providing income and adding to demand, as playing a dynamic role in the transformation of developing countries[43] and, I would add, the world.

Since the start of the Industrial Revolution there has been an unprecedented growth of total world employment and revolutionary changes in the structure of employment. Andrew Maddison estimates that between 1700 and 1998, the share of total employment in agriculture in the UK fell from 56 to 2 percent, while service sector employment increased from 22 to 72 percent.[44] World population has grown vertiginously since 1750 and with it has grown total world employment in spite of or, more properly, in association with technological change. It is only in some of the world's poorest countries that the number of those employed in agriculture is still growing (while the share is falling) and in most countries of the world, the service sector accounts for at least half of total employment. While the number of production workers worldwide is still growing, this is no longer true in many countries and production jobs are likely absorb worldwide an ever-diminishing share of the annual additions to the world's labor force.

In Tanzania, for example, with over 80 percent of the labor force still in agriculture, urban population has been growing at more than twice the national population growth rate for the past 25 years. In only 2 (Myanmar and Ethiopia) of over 90 low- and medium-human development countries listed by the UNDP in its *Human Development Report 1995* did the share in agriculture not fall between 1965 and 1990–92. The extent of the relative (and absolute) decline in the agricultural labor force over that period of at least 25 years in some countries has been nothing short of revolutionary.[45] You need scarcely be reminded that the relative shift out of agriculture in the developing countries is occurring in a context of extremely rapid population growth, hence the absolute numbers to be 'absorbed' in either industry or services give government economic planners nightmares.

Agriculture is still protected, subsidized, and supported in a myriad of ways; ways which seem to attend to the needs of some farmers, but which do not assure that the needs of the hungry are met. We continue to support agriculture not necessarily because of intrinsic economic merit, but rather because it is (was) a way of life. Or we support agriculture because it is unthinkable for a nation to be vulnerable to unreliable external circumstances. Or we support agribusiness because it cloaks itself in the virtues of national self-sufficiency and/or resolving world hunger. If agriculture (and associated rural communities) is indeed a way of life, then financial gain (which may not be equivalent to efficiency of production in meeting nutritional requirements)[46] need not be the key consideration to agricultural survival.

If at all we are serious about choice, then let people have a real choice where they wish to live and what they wish to produce and not an ersatz one where the choice is rural squalor with few public services vs urban opportunities. A fair choice needs to be provided rather than a choice that is forced. However, one should not delude oneself into imagining that the historic pull of urban diversity is going to be fully overcome by the provision of a universal basic income. The words of David Hume are as true today as they were in the middle of 18th century:

> The more these refined arts advance, the more sociable men become: nor is it possible, that, when enriched with science, and possessed of a fund of conversation, they should be contented to remain in solitude, or live with their fellow-citizens in that distant manner, which is peculiar to ignorant and barbarous nations. They flock into cities; love to receive and communicate knowledge; to show their wit or their breeding; their taste in conversation or living, in clothes or furniture. Curiosity allures the wise; vanity the foolish; and pleasure both.[47]

Human occupation and remuneration is in the hands of society, including global society, for, to paraphrase Harry Pearson[48] and expand the implicit: 'The society has no surplus labor, if it is so organized.' The last clause is critical: if prevailing myths, conventional wisdoms, and associated public policy are firmly hitched to the star of expanding *industrial* employment, then unemployment is more likely to be a worrisome ever-present and spatially ubiquitous problem.

The trajectory of the share of industrial employment in the industrial countries may well provide a gauge of what can be expected in the LDCs as a group and worldwide in the way of labor absorption in industry. If one considers only the countries which are presently in the avant-garde in the historical movement to remove people from the soil, the following picture emerges. For those 11 industrialized countries which had less than 20 percent of their labor force in agriculture in 1960,[49] we notice a very striking pattern: eight registered declines in the share of employment in industry over the period from 1960 to 1978.[50] During the decade of the 1960s Belgium and Sweden recorded absolute declines in industrial employment, while since the mid-1970s they have been joined by Germany, the Netherlands, Switzerland, and the UK.[51] One must add that only a portion of the employment in industry is engaged in direct production of goods. The decline in share of the labor force in industry continued to decline for all of the 11 during the period from

1980 to 1995 and only three maintained the level of the labor force in industry: Australia, Canada, and Denmark. In the US, the industrial labor force was down by 1.3 million, while in the UK the industrial labor force fell by 2.1 million or over 20 percent.[52] In any industrial enterprise, a share of total employment will be engaged in a range of front office, research lab, warehouse, and other jobs. Some of the change in employment structure has been a reflection of increased specialization, generally involving contracting out for production or services to separate firms. While part of this may reflect increasing specialization and increasing efficiency, there is also an escape from responsibility toward employees. In shedding workers, one may also be depriving those workers of benefits and rights, which once lost cannot be regained. The loss of benefits associated with 'good jobs' has, of course, been exacerbated by the cut back in public support programs in many jurisdictions.

It is important to stress that having almost reached the limit as far as the departure of labor force from agriculture is concerned, these countries are now experiencing relative declines in the industrial labor force and some are already experiencing the net expulsion of labor from industry. The basic fact of life that a substantial proportion of new jobs throughout the world are already and will be in the service sector must be fully understood by policy makers and by society at large. Our ability to foresee the effects of far-reaching changes in technology, even on employment, has always been flawed. Is our foresight necessarily any more perfect now as we cross the threshold of the computer and robot revolutions?

A detailed analysis of service sector employment in any of the countries of the North provides an instructive clue to emerging job patterns in the world. In the US, for example, in 2000 there were 362.5 people employed in the service sector for each 1000 population. To give but one example of the scope for absorption of trained professionals, which of course entails an increase in the employment of those needed to do the training and to assist the professionals. The average number of doctors per 100,000 people in the 20 highest human development countries in the 1990s was 300. The number in India was 44.[53] To close the gap would require that India train 2.5 million new doctors. This exercise could be repeated for other countries and other occupations. Suffice it to say, there is ample scope for finding 'decent work' for the world's people to complement a citizen's income and to give the meaning to life that comes from active engagement with others.

Consider next employment in public administration in Brazil in 1970, which amounted to 12.5 per 1000, of which at the state and local level the proportion appears to have been 3.8 per 1000.[54] A comparison with levels in the US in 1967 indicates that while federal employment levels per 1000 did not differ that dramatically (13.7 in the US as opposed to 8.7 in Brazil), there was an overwhelming difference at the local level. Were Brazil to have increased its public employment in 1970 at the state and local levels to just one-third of the 1967 US level of 44.5 per 1000, slightly over 1 million jobs would have been created with a resultant absorption of 3.4 percent of the *total* Brazilian labor force. Discussions of balanced regional development and basic needs give inadequate attention to the need for the expansion of vigorous local governments which can provide an effective counterweight in the national political arena to the interests based in the dominant regions. The salutary effect of spreading democratic openness to local levels is itself meritorious.

A further word or two about basic needs would seem appropriate. The *World Development Report* of the World Bank in 1980, 1990, and 2000 all focused on human development and the task of abolishing absolute poverty and gave special attention to education, health, and nutrition. This same focus is found in *A Better World for All*. Improvement in all three areas would require substantial increases in service employment and concomitantly in the 'current', as distinct from capital, expenditures of governments.[55] Certainly any advice from the World Bank and the IMF that government budget growth should be kept in check is clearly going to be at cross purposes with the concern for human development that had been expressed by both the Bank and the Fund.

Ending global apartheid

One major consequence of the growing disparities in income is the growing inducement to international migration. Migration is not solely about income differentials; it is also about lifestyle and the human condition. There may be little that can be done to stop the exodus from rural areas until it has largely run its course. International migration is a different matter. Those who leave their country of origin more often than not do so by virtue of the force of circumstances and often with regret, given that it means leaving behind one's friends and family and familiar surroundings and given also that it may mean having to learn a new language and even having to try to revalidate professional credentials, not to mention the fact that one has likely internalized national loyalty through potent symbols and through the educational system.

Anthony H. Richmond in his *Global Apartheid* sees no peaceful alternative to mass migration. In his words: 'we must all learn to live with ethnocultural diversity, rapid social change, *and* mass migration. There is no peaceful alternative.'[56] How quickly we can all make this adjustment may depend on our individual economic security. When jobs disappear, when the future seems highly uncertain, then the identifiable 'other' becomes the enemy and the social learning that Richmond calls for does not occur.

Among the responses to unemployment and slow growth in the industrial countries in recent decades has been the tightening of immigration regulations, changes in definitions of citizenship, and rights to residence. Borders have become more permeable to the movement of good, services, and capital, at the same time that ability of the common individual to immigrate and even to travel across national boundaries is being increasingly circumscribed. The May 1997 *Le Monde Diplomatique* chronicled the enactment by many French municipalities of prohibitions on the right of residents even to house foreign visitors overnight.[57] Restrictive immigration policy would appear to be simultaneously one of the last bastions of sovereign power and of officially sanctioned racism (parading under the banner of economic necessity).

The 1948 Universal Declaration of Human Rights proclaims the asymmetric right of everyone to leave any country, but not to enter any country other than his own. The only right to freedom of movement that is affirmed therein is limited to the confines of one's own country. However pathbreaking the Universal Declaration may have been, it is nonetheless the work of a past epoch, when voice belonged almost uniquely to national governments and not to the people.

It is only by dealing directly with the enormous international disparities in income, life chances and human rights that one can expect to alter the nature of international migratory flows in a non-repressive and non-restrictive manner. By taking direct action to deal with the push factors influencing international migration, we may well be able to bring about the dismantling of barriers and create a world where people will be free to move (or not) as they please.

Conclusion

A social dividend or citizen's income holds out considerable promise, but it cannot stop at national boundaries as presently defined. The task of the modern age is to generate social product; physical product is potentially under control. Distribution of income in cash and kind must be placed squarely on the agenda. Amidst what is generally described as a crisis, the way ahead must be sought in redistribution as an essential part of building an equitable world order.

We are not marching into the future looking into a rearview mirror, but rather limping, if not actually backtracking, and by doing so we compromise the future. National sovereignty is but a shadow of what it once meant, yet sovereignty is still invoked as a prop for agricultural protection. Hostility between 'us' and 'them' dominates our thoughts; cooperation, the necessary corollary of a multiplicity of interdependencies, is not an ingrained habit of mind. What holds for agriculture, now also holds for industry. On balance, jobs in industry are disappearing daily. The national response to job loss in industry is to offer various incentives to firms, notably tax breaks, subsidies, and/or protection from foreign competition. Rather than harnessing the productive potential of technology to make the world work for 100 percent of humanity, we insist on maintaining national industries operating at levels that assure high unit costs.

The focus (in the words of C. Wright Mills[58]) is on biography, not history: new jobs are (for now) being created in the everywhere burgeoning service sector, which includes the even faster growing information-based activities. A broad-based worldwide citizen's income offers the promise of sustaining the generation of wealth and with it the creation of jobs and the maintenance of the global tax base.

The changing pressures on national actions and alterations in patterns of work create an urgent need for a reconsideration of the nature of national sovereignty and of the work-income link. Such an examination is necessary if socio-political and economic reorganization for sustainable development is to be achieved. What is important is that people have the opportunity to lead fulfilling lives, not that a particular kind of job is preserved long after it has ceased to have a rationale for existing. Well-being should not be tied to particular jobs in either the public or private sector.

A planet-wide citizen's income supported by a global system of public finance could free individuals and nations from the pursuit of environmentally and socially destructive policies pursued in the name of competitiveness. In the words of Philippe Van Parijs, one of today's foremost advocates of the introduction of national income guarantee systems, a universal social dividend would provide 'real freedom for all.'[59] In my view, the achievement of a worldwide socio-economic system in which people matter requires the shaping of a political system in which people matter, namely the crafting of democratic institutions and practices at all levels from the local to the global.[60]

In a market economy, entitlement to income is related in part to property rights, relative bargaining power, market conditions, legal constraints and position within a family. Without property, job or family, one's claim on a share of a community's flow of income may be limited or even nonexistent. And even one's claim to a limited share may be subject to severe restrictions and limitations. In effect, if one does not 'earn a living', one may not have the 'right to live.'[61]

As the 'right to life' is part of the task of building global social justice, we should be affirming world citizenship politically, socially, and economically by crafting a global system of guaranteed entitlements to income, goods, and services which would be supportive of the development of human capability. I contend that the exclusion and inequality generating effects of free-market globalization-from-above requires that a worldwide system of entitlements to services and income be created if our collective commitment to the preservation of human rights, including worldwide freedom of movement in the fullest sense (including the 'real freedom' not to migrate), is to be respected and if world peace is to be preserved.

A social dividend can serve to take the pressure off the family. The young, previously forced to join the workforce, particularly in the poorest strata of the poorest societies would more likely be able to stay in school. Individuals wishing to stay at home would not be forced to go out to work, when valuable work at home or in the vicinity involving social reproduction requires attention. Those with dead-end jobs would not be forced to stay against their will. To espouse free labor markets without some compensatory measures is to consign many workers to a shrinking living standard, if not near bondage. Regrettably, that is all too often precisely the counsel that is offered today.

Solidarity, community, acceptance, and respect extending beyond the local and the national to the global are infectious sentiments and practices that cannot be contained once they begin to take root. They are the keys to the fractal geometry of the partnership model that embraces the common humanity of all. These sentiments have the potential, as in the quote from Thomas Paine earlier in this chapter, to divide and subdivide 'into a thousand shapes and forms' in a virtuous profusion. That is truly our millennial task: to displace despotism, benevolent or otherwise, with a partnership culture that unleashes the creative, rather than the destructive, potential of all humanity.

Notes

1. Robert Theobald, *The Guaranteed Income: Next Step in Economic Evolution?* (Garden City, N.Y.: Doubleday, 1996).
2. Robert S. McNamara, 'Foreword', World Bank, *World Development Report 1978* (New York: Oxford University Press, 1978), p. iii.
3. *A Better World for All*, p. 2.
4. Thomas Paine, 'The Rights of Man', Mark Philp, ed., *Thomas Paine: Rights of Man; Common sense; and Other Writings* (Oxford: Oxford University Press, 1995), p. 20.
5. 'The [US] Internal Revenue Service is planning to ask more than four million of the working poor who now claim a special [earned income] tax credit to provide the most exhaustive proof of eligibility ever demanded of any class of taxpayers.' Mary Williams Walsh, 'I.R.S. to Ask Working Poor for Proof on Tax Credits', *New York Times*, 25 April 2003.
6. Friedrich Hayek, *The Road to Serfdom* (Chicago: University of Chicago Press, 1944). John Kenneth Galbraith, *American Capitalism: The Concept of Countervailing Power* (Boston: Houghton Mifflin, 1952). Karl Polanyi, *The Great Transformation: The Political and Economic Origins of Our Time* (Boston: Beacon Press, 1957).
7. *Human Development Report 2002*, p. 19.
8. United Nations Development Programme (UNDP), *Human Development Report 1999* (New York: Oxford University Press, 1999), p. 38. See also Lant Pritchett, 'Divergence, Big Time', *Journal of Economic Perspectives*, 11 (1997), pp. 3–17.
9. Guy Standing, 'About Time: Basic Income Security as a Right', Paper presented at 9th Biennial Congress of the Basic Income European Network (BIEN), Geneva 12–14 September 2002, http://www.bien.be/Archive/Congress/Geneva2002.htm.
10. John Stuart Mill, *Principles of Political Economy*, 5th London edn (New York: D. Appleton & Co., 1865), II, p. 338.
11. Jean Drèze and Amartya Sen, *Hunger and Public Action* (New York: Oxford University Press, 1992).
12. Eduardo Matarazzo Suplicy, *Renda de Cidadania: A Saída é Pela Porta* (São Paulo: Cortez: Fundação Perseu Abramo, 2002).
13. Phillippe Van Parijs, *Short History of Basic Income* (2003), http://www.bien.be/BI/HistoryBI.htm.
14. Thomas Paine, 'Agrarian Justice' (1796), Mark Philp, ed., *Thomas Paine: Rights of Man, Common Sense and Other Political Writings* (Oxford: Oxford University Press, 1995), pp. 417–19.
15. John Stuart Mill, *Principles of Political Economy*, 5th London edn (New York: D. Appleton & Co, 1865), I, pp. 321–38.
16. Mill, Book IV, Ch. 6, § 2, p. 330.
17. Ibid., p. 332.
18. ThorsteinVeblen, *The Vested Interests and the Common Man* (New York: B.W. Huebsch, 1919), pp. 56–59.
19. Jan Tinbergen, coordinator, *Reshaping the International Order: A Report to the Club of Rome* (New York: E.P. Dutton & Co., 1976), p. 123.
20. Myron J. Frankman, 'International Taxation: The Trajectory of an Idea from Lorimer to Brandt', *World Development*, 24 (May 1996), pp. 807–20.

21. Paul Streeten, 'A New Look at Foreign Aid', *Frontiers of Development Studies* (New York: John Wiley & Sons, 1972), p. 301.
22. Milton Friedman, *Capitalism and Freedom* (Chicago: University of Chicago Press, 1962).
23. John Collet, 'Participation-Personal, Organizational and Service User Perspectives', Paper presented to conference 'From Vancouver to Vladivostok: University Voluntarism for a Participative Society', organized by Helsinki-España Network, Santander, Spain, 28 June 2001, http://www.humandimension.com/foros/correo/John%20Collet%(Manchest).doc.
24. R. Buckminster Fuller, *Operating Manual for Spaceship Earth* (New York: Simon & Schuster, 1969), pp. 107–108.
25. Ibid., p. 108.
26. Basic Income European Network News Flash no. 8, March 2001.
27. As estimates of world income and even population are subject to a considerable degree of error, little is lost by rounding and it avoids conveying spurious accuracy and with no loss to the arguments being advanced. World per capita income was reported by the World Bank to have been $5179 in 1999.
28. Branko Milanovic, 'True World Income Distribution, 1988 and 1993: First Calculations Based on Household Surveys Alone', *Economic Journal*, 112 (2002), p. 73. In the absence of evidence to the contrary and given the likely level of error in estimates of both world income and its distribution, it is reasonable to treat income recipients and households as equivalent.
29. Kevin Phillips, 'Too Much Wealth, Too Little Democracy', *Challenge*, 45 (Sept./Oct. 2002), pp. 6–20.
30. Ray Boshara, 'The $6,000 Solution', *The Atlantic Online* (Jan./Feb. 2003), http://www.theatlantic.com/issues/2003/01/boshara.htm. Another sharp contrast between Milanovic's figure and those of the US for the top one percent of the distribution: Milanovic's 1993 figures for a world income of $30 trillion would translate into an average income for the richest of $48,000, while the US Internal Revenue Service (IRS) reports the annual gross income that marks the bottom of the one percent category as $293,000. Just for the record, in terms of concentration of income (and power) 10,380 corporations (or 0.2 percent of those that filed US tax returns) with assets over $250 million accounted for 81.6 percent of corporate net income in 1999. One can reasonably conclude that there is ample scope for taxing the world's top one percent and that our estimates of income within that bracket are woefully low.
31. Karl Widerquist, 'A Failure to Communicate: The Labour Market Findings of the Negative Income Tax Experiments and Their Effects on Policy and Public Opinion', Basic Income European Network, 9th International Conference, Geneva, 2002.
32. Richard Darman, 'Riverboat Gambling With Government', *New York Times Magazine* (1 December 1996).
33. Widerquist (2002).
34. Scott Goldsmith, 'The Alaska Permanent Fund: A Basic Income in Action', Paper presented at 9th Biennial Congress of the Basic Income European Network (BIEN), Geneva, 12–14 September 2002, http://www.bien.be/Archive/Congress/Geneva2002.htm.

35. United States Basic Income Guarantee Network (USBIG), *USBIG Newsletter*, 3:18 (2002), http://www.usbig.net.
36. See also Bertrand Russell, *In Praise of Idleness: and other essays by Bertrand Russell* (New York: Norton, 1935).
37. Final act of the United Nations Conference on Trade and Employment Havana Charter for an International Trade Organization (1948).
38. I.F. Stone, *The War Years 1939–1945* (Boston: Little, Brown and Company, 1988), p. 277.
39. Robert B. Reich, 'The Challenge of Decent Work', *International Labour Review*, 141 (2002), p. 115.
40. Mill, II, p. 256.
41. For a discussion of the unique nature of the experience of the 'Gang of Four,' see William Cline, 'Can the East Asian Model of Development be Generalized', *World Development*, 10 (1982), pp. 81–90; and Fernando Fajnzylber, 'Some Reflections on South-East Asian Export Industrialization', *CEPAL Review*, 15 (December 1981), pp. 111–32.
42. Ibid., p. 176.
43. See, for example, Myron J. Frankman and Edwin Charlé, 'Employment in the Service Sector in Sub-Saharan Africa', *Journal of Modern African Studies*, 11 (1973), pp. 201–10.Werner Baer and Larry Samuelson, 'Toward a Service-Oriented Growth Strategy', *World Development*, 9 (June 1981), pp. 499–514; and Albert Berry, 'A Positive Interpretation of the Expansion of Urban Services in Latin America, with some Colombian Evidence', *Journal of Development Studies*, 14 (January 1978), pp. 210–31.
44. Angus Maddison, 'Economic Growth and Structural Change in the Advanced Countries', in I. Leveson and J. Wheeler, eds, *Western Economies in Transition: Structural Change and Adjustment Policies in Industrial Countries* (Boulder: Westview Press, 1980), p. 95
45. Those that experienced a decline of 30 percentage points or more in the share of the labor force in agriculture:

	1965	**1990–92**	**%-age point change**
Lesotho	91	23	68
Botswana	88	28	60
El Salvador	58	11	47
Zambia	79	38	41
Algeria	57	18	89
Korea, Rep. of	55	17	38
Iraq	50	14	36
Colombia	45	10	35
Malaysia	58	26	32
Honduras	68	38	30

Source: UNDP, *Human Development Report 1995*, pp. 176–77.

Another 14 countries experienced declines of between 20 and 29 percentage points during the same period, including four countries with a population currently of more than 100 million: Turkey, Mexico, Brazil, and Nigeria.

46. See Vandana Shiva, *Water Wars: Privatization, Pollution and Profit* (Toronto: Between the Lines, 2001).
47. David Hume, 'Of Refinement in the Arts' (1752), http://www.econlib.org/library/Hume/HumeEssArts.html.
48. Harry Pearson, 'The Economy Has No Surplus', in Karl Polanyi, Conrad M. Arensberg, and Harry W. Pearson, eds, *Trade and Market in Early Empires: Economies in History and Theory* (New York: Free Press, 1957).
49. Australia, Belgium, Canada, Denmark, the Federal Republic of Germany, the Netherlands, New Zealand, Sweden, Switzerland, the UK, and the US.
50. *WDR, 1980*, p. 147.
51. Maddison, p. 48
52. World Bank, *World Development Indicators On Disk 2001*.
53. UNDP, *HDR 2002*, pp. 166–69.
54. Fundação Instituto Brasileiro de Geografia e Estatistica, *Anuário Estatístico do Brasil* 1978 (Rio de Janeiro, 1978), pp. 148–55.
55. I am convinced, as I have argued in Chapter 4, that many of the poorest countries may well be incapable of making the necessary expenditures unless a system of automatic international financial transfers is established.
56. Anthony H. Richmond, *Global Apartheid: Refugees, Racism, and the New World Order* (Toronto: Oxford University Press, 1994), p. 217.
57. Philippe Videlier, 'Immigration et conscience citoyenne: L'honneur de désobéir', *Le Monde Diplomatique* (May 1997), p. 17.
58. C. Wright Mills, *The Sociological Imagination* (New York: Oxford University Press, 1959).
59. Phillipe Van Parijs, *Real Freedom for All: What (If Anything) Can Justify Capitalism?* Oxford, Clarendon Press, 1995).
60. Myron J. Frankman, 'No Global War? A Role for Democratic Global Federalism', *Journal of World-Systems Research*, 3:2 (1997), pp. 321–38.
61. Fuller, p. 118.

7
Peace and Justice Indivisible

> Every extension of the area of effective internationalism, every growth of the international mind by co-operative practice, will diminish the danger of an undue preponderance of power remaining in the hands of a great State, or a group of States, inclined to exercise unjust dominion or oppressive exploitation over weaker members of the social union or over unrepresented peoples.
>
> —John Hobson, *Towards International Government*

> Universality means taking a risk in order to go beyond the easy certainties provided us by our background, language, nationality, which so often shield us from the reality of others. It also means looking for and trying to uphold a single standard for human behavior when it comes to such matters as foreign and social policy.
>
> —Edward W. Said, *Representations of the Intellectual*

Indivisible is a marvelous word. For one who was born and raised in the US, that word was used once every school day in the pledge of allegiance to the US flag: 'one nation indivisible.' It meant little, if anything, until I learned about the mid-19th-century American Civil War. Even then the connection was not made, as the pledge was recited, but never studied as a historical document. More recently I have heard the word used in the context of global rights and particularly the Convention on the Rights of the Child, endorsed by all but two member states of the UN.[1] It was only at that point that the word struck me as having remarkable potency insofar as it has come to be associated with universal values, as opposed to an implied threat to a region that once wished to withdraw from a political union.

The phrase 'peace is indivisible' has been attributed to Maksim Litvinov, the principal Soviet delegate to the World Disarmament Conference in Geneva in 1932. Indivisibility does not stop there: a document deposited under the foundation stone of the ILO headquarters in Geneva reads: 'Si vis pacem, cole justifiam.' If you desire peace, cultivate justice. Aase Lionaes concluded her presentation speech for the award of the Nobel Peace Prize to the ILO in 1969 by remarking: 'Just as peace is indivisible, so also is justice.'[2] Our world, too, is indivisible. It is only we humans who seem beholden to lines drawn in the sand and reified first on maps and then in barbed and electrified wire fences and/or cement walls. The rest of creation pays no heed to these spatial delimiters. The collective realization that appears to be attaining critical mass at the start of the 21st century is that the time has arrived to take global indivisibility seriously.

Eric Hobsbawm may have been premature in describing the 20th Century as a short one, extending from 1914 to 1991, that is, from the start of World War I until the dissolution of the Soviet Union.[3] Implicitly this was a period of either World War or the possibility of World War. For him, the emergence of a unipolar world system in 1991 represents the 'end' of a short century. While it is too soon to be sure what name will be applied to the pre-emptive war of the US-led coalition in Iraq in 2003, at least one writer has spoken of it as the last war of the 20th century. A sign seen at demonstrations in 2003 proclaimed: 'War is Terror.' If we are to act on the many shared values of the peoples of this world, the time is ripe to eliminate war, not merely by outlawing or defining it as an absolute last resort, but rather by getting serious about eliminating the causes of war, if we are truly distressed by the associated unavoidable human tragedies that wars entail and the legacies of hate that they create.

In the three preceding chapters I have considered existing economic arrangements that exacerbate both economic inequalities and the poverty of some nations. It is common these days to speak about failed states, when we should instead be speaking about a failed global economic system. Our current system of global economic governance is guided by neoliberal principles of minimal government and maximal individual responsibility, implicitly pretending that concentration of economic power carries no consequences with it for economic, social, or political outcomes. I have proposed major initiatives as corrective measures: a single world currency, global public finance, restoring progressivity to income and profit taxes (nationally and globally), and instituting an unconditional PWCI set at a level in excess of the income of over one-half of the world's population. These are radical initiatives whose introduction is urgent. These are not simple questions of technical economics; these are deeply political and ethical questions. Moreover, these suggestions imply an agenda for political institution building at the global level.

More generally, I suggest that filling in all levels of the global organizational hierarchy is essential. For example, further supranational cooperation in various regions may be seen as a prerequisite for and a complement to global action. I do not have answers on either the trajectory, the timetable, or any of the specifics of getting from here to there. What I can offer is the certainty that if humanity is not merely to survive, but to continue to flourish on this planet that we will surely have to see the development of a PWCI (or its equivalent), which, in turn, will require some form of global government. The precise details are not the crux of the matter, a shared vision is. Widespread belief in the vision is an essential ingredient for its eventual achievement and for setting in motion deliberations on design.

Paradoxically, the uniqueness of nations may be best preserved by recognizing which of the tools of sovereignty are amenable to local control and which have long since passed from effective control. A viable renewed social compact may only be attainable if national governments appreciate the need to build global governmental structures. The vision that looks to a world of regional blocs is worth pursuing, as we have learned from the example of the EU, but building institution at multiple levels contemporaneously is what we have done throughout at least in the 20th century. It is never either/or; always both/and. The world is indivisible—economically, socially, politically, and especially environmentally. The spatial consequences of the technical changes in the 20th century have been revolutionary in the fullest sense of the world. The car and the plane have made every corner of the earth readily accessible to an important part of the world's population. The electronic media provide an instantaneous link available in principle to every home and workplace regardless of location. In this world sovereignty must be rethought, for it no longer is what most leaders and followers still imagine it to be.

A global civil culture is evolving, growing daily in front of our very eyes. For ideas as sweeping as those of global social justice, global federation, global redistribution, and global democracy to take hold requires a lengthy period of discussion and growing familiarity with the concepts. Academics have to work out their theoretical models—which is happening with a veritable deluge of writings on a panoply of global themes, which were not being addressed even five years ago. Business leaders have to do the reckoning of the cost advantage of paying the price for the restoration of civility. Schoolchildren need to study the history and practice of our common, yet variegated, civilizational history. In our time, NGOs are the added ingredient, the catalyst that is projecting humane global order and global government onto the agenda and quickening the pace by doing so.

We have now to build a world of cooperation, to rediscover the cooperative modes of the past, and to remove from the pedestal the wars whose central point was the 'other' as threat. We need to recast the pantheon of the founders of the modern world. We need to celebrate the peacemakers and the lawgivers as the giants of the human drama, rather than those whose method embraced the spilling of blood. Every era has its appropriate revisionism. Ours is well underway, but much urgent deconstruction and subsequent building remains. We shape our own myths and are shaped by them. The giants of peace are as much to be celebrated today, as were the giants of war yesterday.

During the Cold War our commitment to democracy fell prey to the 'anti-politics machine.' Our understanding of the dynamics of democratic processes was apparently so superficial that we were willing to embrace 'anti-politics'—that is, the quest for efficient outcomes even if the rights of citizens are trampled in the process.[4] Anti-politics and the quiescent citizen were reinforced by neoliberalism and by the war on terrorism that followed the events of September 11. The democracy which is honored today is at best procedural democracy (although even low voter turn out is simply shrugged off as a fact of life) and certainly not substantive democracy. We urge free elections in countries around the world, on the one hand, but insist on a set of policies that, in the absence of substantial supporting financial flows, create conditions that virtually condemn fledgling governments to failure.

In spring 1994 we celebrated the holding of free multi-racial elections in South Africa and its shift to majority rule, the product of lengthy campaigns both inside and outside of South Africa. When will we take the extraordinarily giant step beyond the three-century old nation-state dominated system (effectively superpower dominated at present) toward free multi-racial elections worldwide? Is it not what Vandana Shiva calls monoculture of the mind[5] that leads most of us to shrink from even entertaining such a notion?

If we embrace universal suffrage at the global level, several important corollaries emerge. Those with a platform for which they want support must labor to secure it. Any concern about the ability of the newly franchised to exercise that right in a responsible way should be translated into a changed viewpoint on the question of extending educational opportunities to those previously both illiterate and disenfranchised. The politics of competing interests replaces the anti-politics of technical experts and institutional overlords.

Once we embrace the indivisible world as inclusive, egalitarian, and ours, then the whole set of institutional arrangements that are (or should be) part and parcel of a state will almost naturally be extended to the globe, much as King João of Portugal felt obliged to install a range of royal amenities in Rio de Janeiro when Rio became the capital of the Portuguese empire following the Napoleonic invasion of the Iberian Peninsula. What we must do is discard the implicit and explicit national blinders in many of the current approaches to economic, social, and political challenges. Novel problems demand novel approaches, ideally consistent with our humanitarian values and the urgency of the needs at hand. Trickle down, like justice delayed, is justice denied.

Democratic global federalism

Between 1943 and 1946, E.B. White wrote a series of editorials in *The New Yorker* magazine supporting democratic federal world government. In his editorial of 1 June 1946, he wrote:

> World government is an appalling prospect. . . . Certainly the world is not ready for government on a planetary scale. In our opinion, it will never be ready. The test is whether the people will chance it anyway—like children who hear the familiar cry, 'Coming whether ready or not!' At a Federalist convention the other day, Dean Katz of the University of Chicago said, 'Constitutions have never awaited the achievement of trust and a matured sense of community; they have been born of conflicts between groups which have found a basis for union in spite of deep suspicions and distrusts.' The only condition more appalling, less practical, than world government is the lack of it in this atomic age.[6]

In fact, the issue is not whether we shall be governed globally, but rather by whom and on what basis. The international realm is not one of anarchy as the realists would have us believe, but rather one of order: of rules, procedures and accepted norms of behavior associated in part with what are termed 'international regimes,' each dedicated in principle to a separate functional domain. Global government is not something that is to be created, but rather something to be altered in the public interest.[7] The 'government' of the globe is currently configured by a shifting set of ill-coordinated actors: among them the one remaining superpower and, to a lesser extent, other strong states, as well as powerful individuals and a number of large multinational corporations and financial institutions. Robert Cox has summed up our current system of global governance with the phrase *nébuleuse*, although Cox apparently limits the term to the international organizations.[8] *Le Monde Diplomatique's* phrase *les nouveaux maîtres du monde* is doubtless a more apt characterization.[9]

Our current system of global government is one of rule by the few. While an increasing number of the world's countries are procedural or even substantive democracies, global government is far from democratic. Moreover, those international institutions where diverse voices are heard are precisely those with not only the least power to act on matters of substance, but with the most precarious financing. Imagine what the circumstances of any national government would be today if it had to rely for its funds on a combination of voluntary assessments and proceeds from the sale of greeting cards. Without both cooperation and funding by the US, actions approved in the UN General Assembly are essentially dead letters. The mid-1970s General Assembly resolutions creating a NIEO and that proclaiming the Rights and Duties of States were both doomed by the de facto veto (that is, non-cooperation) of the US before they were even approved. In the International Monetary Fund the US has had a de jure veto on matters requiring a special majority (of first 80 percent and later 85 percent) of the weighted votes since the Fund was created at Bretton Woods based largely on the American drafted proposal. The ability of the US to block increases in country quotas (the source of the Fund's own resources) has been a key element in the conversion over the years of the IMF from a credit union to a powerful global financial watchdog.[10]

Institutional arrangements at the national level to raise taxes, pay for public services, regulate money supply, and perform a multitude of other functions were commonly established at an early stage in the spatial integration of countries, long before they were as integrated economically as the world as a whole is now. Today, these national institutions are increasingly threatened by what Robert Gilpin calls the crisis of national welfare capitalism in a non-welfare international capitalist world.[11] We live in an integrated world economy with few effective control mechanisms to provide offsets to the varied national impacts of global economic activities. Indeed, governments, acting in response to external constraints, pursue strategies that reinforce some of the adverse national consequences. Drainville has elaborated on this in his description of global accumulation being validated politically by state-bound democracies and on their ability to strike social compromises. Drawing on Desmond King, Drainville describes how citizens are called upon to embrace economic rationality and 'lead the assault on . . . the social rights of citizenship.'[12]

People cannot be counted on, however, to faithfully function indefinitely in a manner consistent with the interests of global accumulation. As the divergence-widening effects of the current scheme of global governance with its supporting national manifestations become more and more obvious, reactions begin to set in. One common reaction is to point to 'others' as being the threat to one's job. But immigration controls are not a solution to the employment problem, which is only one of a range of human interactions which can only be dealt with successfully by collective action on a global scale. The insistence that national solutions be sought to problems generated by global accumulation is essentially a recipe to 'divide and conquer.'

The Latin Americans have invented a word to describe a procedural democracy where participation is not merely limited, but actively suppressed: a *democradura*—hard democracy.[13] Are we not already seeing the signs of an emerging *democradura* in a number of northern countries as the ability to maintain social programs erodes? The limits on state action arising from the (real or anticipated) hypersensitivity of financial markets has led to what Susan Strange has called the end of opposition from established parties.[14] One hastens to add that where opposition does remain, it is treated as a dangerous fringe that unrealistically refuses to accept the new and (ostensibly) immutable circumstances of state limits. Immutability was best summed up by Margaret Thatcher's refrain: 'There is no alternative,' immortalized in the acronym TINA.

Paradoxically, if we are to save the world from breakdown occasioned by capitalism, we must once again save the capitalists from their global excesses, just as the earlier creation of national welfare states saved the capitalists from their excesses at the national level. The same logic that propelled the creation of the welfare state and liberal democracy at the national level, now must be extended to the global level, not with the express purpose of making the world safe for capitalism, although that may be the effect, but rather to make the world safe for the common person, safe for civil rights, safe for our children and grandchildren, safe for the flora and the other fauna.

A 'well-being state,' whether national or global, requires a structure of government to shape the programs, to finance them, and to respond to changed circumstances. The difficulty which presently confronts us is that our ability to act at the global level is severely restricted by an institutional framework with limited responsiveness, owing to the recalcitrance that is a correlate of the hegemonic neoliberal discourse and to the frequent US refusal to be bound by global accords that are deemed to limits the exercise of its interests. We are limited as well by the misperception that trying to solve problems at the national level is wholly appropriate for most issues.

We have a two-speed or multi-speed Europe. Not all the EU countries have yet chosen to adopt the euro as their currency and not all have chosen to endorse the Schengen convention. Nonetheless, the construction of the EU continues. In a like manner we have a two-speed world. If this was not made abundantly clear by the non-adherence of the US to the Kyoto protocol, the International Criminal Court, the Convention on the Rights of the Child, the Convention banning anti-personnel mines, the Convention on the elimination of all forms of discrimination against women, among other international conventions, it was certainly proclaimed by the US initiative to launch a war in Iraq in 2003 without the explicit approval of the UN Security Council. Nonetheless, the countless efforts to build one peaceful world do continue and must. As in the case of the EU, the door must be open for latecomers to participate throughout and to be welcomed with open arms whey they are ready to adhere as a coequal of those already on board. As the dominator model continues to lose ground as an organizing principle for conduct, the world's single superpower may eventually see the many advantages of not acting as if it is from Mars.[15]

The acceptance of functional globalism, of the sort described in 1943 by Daniel Mitrany,[16] that pretends that most issues of global significance are purely technical and best left to experts, represents another major limit. In fact, few problems are purely technical. Wherever there is a human dimension to a decision, discretion and preferences enter into play; we leave the realm of the exact and enter the realm of the political. To capitulate to the claims that only the experts can decide, for example, as in the current conventional wisdom regarding independence of central banks[17] and of the IMF, is to concede to a select group sovereign rights, which few of the world's remaining monarchs even exercise. Political problems require political solutions within a context where a range of opinions can be heard. Those that are global problems require global political solutions.

The idea of global government is hardly new. To give but a sample, we can trace the idea back to Immanuel Kant, John Hobson, Leonard Woolf, and Harold Laski.[18] In 1925 Laski was already arguing that world government was one of the implications of modern conditions and that federalism would be the most appropriate form.[19] Democratic global federalism is also an idea that has been around for a while. At the time that official representatives in San Francisco in October 1945 were but a few days away from signing the UN charter, *The New York Times* carried a front-page account of a conference in Dublin, New Hampshire whose distinguished delegates signed a declaration calling instead for global democratic federalism.[20]

What are new are the urgency and the possibility for bringing the project into being. Consider the logistics of bringing together the American Founding Fathers in Philadelphia in 1776 or the Fathers of Canadian Confederation in Charlottetown, Prince Edward Island in 1867. Even bringing delegates to San Francisco in 1945 was a major undertaking. To physically convene today a representative cross section of the human population would be child's play compared to these earlier assemblies. We have already witnessed several instances of the gathering of appreciable numbers of citizen delegates to unofficial meetings that have paralleled major world summits. To 'convene' the likeminded electronically is even simpler and quicker, as well as being a prerequisite for eventual face-to-face encounters. To create a basic web page is almost as simple today as producing one page of text. Accessing information on your cause and urgently spreading the word may require no more than a couple clicks on the keyboard of a computer.

If we achieve global democratic federalism, the eventual form will reflect the outcome of lengthy political processes, with variations from one level of the hierarchy to another and from one jurisdiction to another at the same level. There is no reason to believe that existing differences in federal structures between countries will disappear, nor any way to predict what form will emerge at the global level. We might see a greatly strengthened UN, but this is unlikely to help us much with our dilemmas born of neoliberalism, unless there is a major sea change in the visions of national governments.

Democratic global federalism is a potential framework that may allow the maximum of freedom for the parts. Enrique Leff has spoken about filling a vacant space. World level government is such a vacant space. We have an international space filled with the UN and its affiliated agencies, but we do not have global government where the people have a voice. A Global Peoples Assembly that would provide the UN with a bicameral legislative structure might well be a possible scenario. Citizen involvement and a global assembly of representatives of the world's people could be an important counterweight to a system where states have the sole voice.[21] Take heart, that failing of the current system has been perceived and several initiatives are already under way to create a global peoples assembly which could evolve into one house of a bicameral legislature, with the General Assembly of the UN being another. Citizen action on a global scale is already seizing the day; Andrew Strauss identifies the Assembly of the United Nations of Peoples, Citizen Century, and the Global Peoples Assembly Movement as groups which are already at work to provide a citizen's voice.[22]

Let us not be timid about democratic global government and the quest for its achievement and let us not underestimate its appeal to the peoples of the world. Nor should we be discouraged by merely attaining a foot in the door. Strauss reminds us that the European Parliament and even the English Parliament both grew in importance from largely symbolic origins.[23] The point of democratic institutions is precisely not to freeze important elements of the structure of government indefinitely because of the de facto or de jure veto of a key player and to recognize that their influence can grow (or wither) with use (or disuse).

Citizenship: the noblest avocation

Redemocratizing a society where a widespread anti-politics perspective prevails is a job for all of us; a job that will require our whole-hearted energies. It is a job that will require imagination and the harnessing of every opportunity to build networks and to involve especially the energies of the young. Democracy is not something that one learns to value through the customary educational obstacle course, but rather is a process that one grows to appreciate through experiences in working with others in a context where participants are given voice. Indeed, many of the institutions within our democratic societies are still essentially anti-democratic and at risk of becoming more so. In the words of Ursula Franklin: 'When work isn't shared, the instruments of cooperation—listening, taking note, adjusting—atrophy like muscles that are no longer in use.'[24] David Korten has spoken of democracy as something we do, not something we have. This basic message must be learned and relearned.

Jane Jacobs, in talking about technical innovation, suggests that it comes not from those in control of the existing monopoly—neither the electric typewriter nor the instant camera came from the established companies in those domains.[25] In a like manner one might argue that the impetus for global government as opposed to international cooperation may not be expected to be high on the agenda of states that perceive the few remnants of sovereignty slipping through their fingers. The prospects for direct citizen action to help craft a global system to either supplement, complement, or replace existing mechanisms, as appropriate, should not be underestimated. The history of human civilization is the story of a succession of social inventions. Each step in the human drama has represented an unprecedented initiative, a leap of the imagination calling for collective action or approval. To create a global peoples assembly would be yet another in a long line of social innovations. A succession of NGO meetings have coincided with global summits and have addressed the same general topic, but often from an entirely different perspective from that taken by the official national delegations. These represent an important precedent pointing to the possibility of a more permanent democratic assembly.

As André Drainville observes, 'there is something radically important about conceptualizing the world economy as a social space in the making.'[26] The very act of describing serves to alter; the act of naming can create. To see our current situation as one of exclusionary global governance is to raise the possibility of action. Drainville speaks of reconstructing, reimagining, and remapping world politics.[27] That is precisely the task: to create a real 'world politics' which would give substance to a phrase that has long been a misnomer. What we label today as world politics is actually the realm of anti-politics, of the experts and of the diplomats whose instructions carefully delineate their limits.

Those who reject supranational government as escapism would appear to be affirming that citizen participation is a well-established reality in most of the world's democracies and that citizens acting through their governments are equal to the task at hand. In fact, democratic deficits are ubiquitous and have been growing with the advance of neoliberalism. To the best of my knowledge democratic deficits are not measured, not reported, and not the object of serious criticism in the way that government budget deficits are. Indeed were national democratic deficits to be reduced markedly, the hysteria concerning fiscal deficits and the size of the state might well be dispelled as an outcome of the resulting public debates. The use of the phrase 'democratic deficit' has been an important catalyst in provoking steps to revitalize local and national politics. For it is not only regional citizens and world citizens that are to be created, but true national and local citizens must also be either created or recreated. Mitrany suggested that 'the performance of a number of common functions is the way to create a normal community.'[28] For too long now we have been witnessing the disappearance of common functions, a phenomenon chronicled for the US by Robert Putnam in his work on the decline of social capital.[29] Our challenge is to create a world in which the number of common functions performed by individuals is markedly expanded in order to swell the ranks of the politically active *at all levels*.

The task confronting the peoples of the world is the major one of changing perceptions of the nature of our current reality and then changing behavior to join in and create public debates at all levels and to engage in political action. Civil society must either be created or strengthened everywhere. The democratic deficit is partly of our own making insofar as we have ceased to behave collectively. Our myopia, cynicism, withdrawal, avoidance of collective responsibility, and deference to authority and technical experts have been carefully nurtured by an educational system in the service of nationalism. H.G. Wells spoke of the evils of nationalism and of education distorted by those who choose to use nationalism for personal advantage.[30] Most of us are products of an educational system that has done its best through passive learning to neutralize knowledge and of a society with an anti-political bent.

The construction of meaningful world citizenship is not likely to be a direct by-product of 'globalization from above.' Indeed, meaningful citizenship at whatever level is not likely to result from the activities of the power elites who tend not to focus on participatory democracy, but rather on 'good governance.' Those who speak of governance do not necessarily equate the term with either government or democracy. The Co-Chairs of the Commission on Global Governance (Ingvar Carlsson and Sridath Ramphal) were quite emphatic in their Foreword to *Our Global Neighborhood*, the Commission's 1995 report: the report was about global governance and not global government. In their view world government would necessarily lead us to an even less democratic world than we have.[31] This same message was embodied in the title of a book edited by James Rosenau and Ernst-Otto Czempiel in 1992: *Governance without Government*.

The construction of meaningful world citizenship is taking place daily. 'Globalization from below' with its daily cross-border, cross-cultural interactions, is the incessant process by which our mental images are being altered. Conscious perceptions may not matter in the early stages of formation of our sense of planet-wide interdependence. The process is in motion and the participants may only be dimly aware of the transition of which they are currently part. We have yet to recognize the opportunities that are arising daily. There are limits to the role of civil society at all levels, especially at the global level, but the frontier of action is an ever-changing one. In an era of positive feedback, particularly nourished by electronic communications, those limits can change swiftly; witness the events following Perestroika and, less than five years later, the fall of the Berlin Wall.

To get from here to there will require major efforts to spread the word: we live on one small planet and we are one people with a common culture. We may speak different languages, we may have distinct local customs, we may look different, but we are one. Those of us committed to saving local autonomy, must support efforts to strengthen the global umbrella. Elise Boulding has written of crafting a global civil society.[32] The time has come to craft as well the global democratic federal structures of government to go with that. If individuals become citizens instead of onlookers, then the prospect of the public and the political spaces becoming far more active venues could well mean the death of expert-driven exclusionary anti-politics where decisions currently masquerade as technical necessities.

NGOs and global citizenship

John Dryzek has pointed to the growth of non-state actors engaged in free discourse as one of the salutary developments of our epoch.[33] Chief among these non-state actors are the NGOs. While NGOs are a challenge to 'business as usual' at levels of government from the local to the national, their activity can be seen as possibly leading the way to the creation of deliberative democratic institutions at the global level. The extensive activities and networking of tens of thousands of NGOs represent an ongoing important stepping stone in the broadening of world politics and in the construction of world citizenship. Their achievements should renew our hope that what appear to be oppressive and unchanging structures are in reality processes in motion and that perception should strengthen our resolve to continue our collective efforts.

Non-governmental organizations play an increasingly important role, both on their own and in activities that complement those of the UN system. Participation in the work of NGOs can be seen as a response to exclusion, to alienation, to the dissolution of social bonds, to the weakening of other voices on the social horizon and, quite simply, to a concern for the public interest. The UN, for its part, values the work of the NGOs and appreciates having a vocal constituency at the very moment when opinion in some countries, abetted by neoliberal propagandizing, has turned against the UN.[34] The NGOs and the UN need each other.

Non-governmental organizations can also be seen as a response to a loss of voice as union power has declined and as a response to unmet local needs. Existential problems do not disappear when a plant closes and a union no longer has an opposite number to which to appeal. NGOs tend to provide an open environment, particularly for female advancement. NGOs can be seen as providing elements of society with the kind of voice that unions provided during the most successful periods of their existence. NGOs may well be the only voice remaining to speak for societal interest on behalf of the geographically dispersed. NGOs can in some respects be much broader in involvement than unions and may cut across various societal dividing lines, which have otherwise become formidable obstacles to societal unity. There is, of course, ample room and need for both NGOs and unions and they no doubt have many overlapping concerns, most notably the focus on imbalances in power and influence.

Non-governmental organizations may, at an early stage of their individual development, offer flexibility and multi-faceted approaches, but they are neither inherently immune from organizational sclerosis nor from critical dependence on key committed individuals. These problems are common to human institutions and not unique to NGOs. Similarly, NGOs could well become a yea-saying pillar of the post-modern corporatist society. Many NGOs are, for example, being transformed from independent actors to service providers under contract to fill in gaps left by a receding state.[35] One can also view from this cautionary perspective the recommendation of the Commission on Global Governance for the convening of an annual Forum of Civil Society, to be attended by 300–600 'organs of global civil society.'[36] The Commission considered a People's Assembly to complement the UN General Assembly, but stipulated as a prerequisite to any move in this direction that the General Assembly first develop 'a revitalized role for itself.' It is worth noting that at the Fourth World Conference on Women in Beijing in September 1995 some 30,000 women, representing 2000 NGOs attended the parallel Women's Forum. Narrowing the representation at the proposed annual Forum of Civil Society, could well involve the exclusion of the more independently inclined of the NGOs. The Commission's disclaimers notwithstanding, limited access membership for a global NGO Forum could well serve as an impediment to broader democratization. Yet, like the 'price system,' the penetrative powers of deliberative democracy once unleashed may be unstoppable.

The globalization of civil society and, in particular, the recent manifestations of grass-roots expression relating to issues having global impact, reflects the changing frontiers of the limits to the involvement of the people of the world in global governance. While NGOs are still part of the sideshow, they occasionally steals the headlines. There are alternative summit meetings when the G-8 meets, there are electronic discussions prior to the G-8 meetings, NGOs are much in evidence when various international conferences are held, if not sharing center stage, then certainly present in force as an alternative conference—a kind of shadow cabinet or an unelected official opposition. The elaboration of numerous alternative treaties at the 1992 Rio Earth Summit of the International Forum of NGOs and Social Movements[37] is but one indication that the time may have arrived for the people of the world to take bolder action to wrest control of global processes from *les nouveaux maîtres du monde*. NGO representation at world summits has the potential to transform politics; to create a global politics where the people have voice to complement international fora where only states were heard.

The distinction between interested and disinterested participants made by John Ralston Saul is important to introduce in this context. Saul firmly believes that we live in an age of corporatism in which democracy is little more at best than a 'pressure valve release'—'a corporatist society with soft pretensions to democracy.'[38] In his view, legitimacy generally may reside today in either groups or individuals. Where legitimacy derives from the group, narrow interests predominate; where systems are centered on the involvement of citizens, one is more likely to encounter disinterested pursuit of the public good. Only where disinterest receives ample expression is the public interest preserved and advanced. There are, of course, NGOs which represent specific private interests; many others, however, labor passionately in the public interest. Saul recognizes the citizen as the basic unit of society, as the locus of disinterest. But individuals are not independent of the larger society and NGOs are one important agency for focusing and catalyzing individual disinterest and in fostering the reawakening of citizens. The NGO offers the paradox that a group that is created to pursue the public interest may be consumed by an ideology which is hostile to independent inquiry and criticism and may cease to admit dissenting perspectives. And yet, the pursuit of disinterest, even if relatively impervious to contrary evidence, still represents a helpful counterweight to corporatist propaganda. In that respect NGOs can serve as a framework for the planetary citizen insofar as they function as a consciousness raising alternative. We need such alternative voices to speak out on a regular basis to replace certainty with doubt and to replace solutions with process, where voice is an attribute of the many and not just the few. Interested disinterest may seem like a contradiction in terms, but individuals do not exist apart from society and to behave in a manner consistent with the hypothesis that the individual is (in Thorstein Veblen's words) 'an isolated, definitive human datum,'[39] is to cede political action to others.

Richard Falk speaks of our great hope as being 'the emergence of transnational social forces dedicated to a sustainable, equitable, and democratic human future.'[40] That development is occurring through the extensive networking of NGOs. If we can free ourselves from conditioning that puts a neutral focus on knowledge, then it may be possible to break through the neoliberal defaults that limit our perceptions.

Conclusion

My work on the global economy has brought me to cross the line from the technical to the political. Institutions intended to achieve global social justice must be embedded in a global political system where the peoples of the world can give expression to their will in a democratic context. The political awareness that is necessary to rescue the state (albeit with an altered scope) is the very same awareness that is necessary to construct political democracy at all levels of the hierarchy. What is needed is not a blind allegiance to the Father Land or the Mother Country, right or wrong, but an appreciation of the shifting limits of sovereignty and of the ever-shifting locus for action in distinct problem areas. More particularly we must recognize and embrace both our unity and our diversity.

Joseph Schumpeter directed our attention to the innovating entrepreneur, an individual with a vision of a possibility that could be advantageously developed.[41] The rescue and extension of meaningful democratic institutions requires institutional innovation, innovation by social entrepreneurs driven by disinterest; innovators working on behalf of inclusion and against prevalent forces of social exclusion.

Political awakening associated with a local issue may be the start of a long march toward support for global government, given the clear line of causation from supposed inevitabilities at the local level to power relationships extending to the global scale. To the extent that the fallout of neoliberal economic policy reawakens collective action, the next round may well feature a broadened focus, extending from the local to the global, in recognition of our interdependence and the common problems we confront around the world, whose resolution lays beyond local jurisdiction. That common perception is the current reality of the many NGO members who network regularly with counterparts in many countries of the world.

In the very first paper that I presented on global taxation in 1970, I closed with the following quote from Bertrand Russell: 'It is not by pacifist sentiment, but by worldwide economic organization, that civilized mankind is to be saved from collective suicide.'[42] Today, it is clear to me that Russell specified a necessary condition, but not a sufficient one for avoiding collective suicide. For E.B. White, the sufficient condition was unambiguous: 'Peace is the by-product of responsible government.'[43] That ideal must be our continuing objective as educators and citizens.

Individual action directed through groups is the galvanizing element. While outcomes do matter, process is of crucial importance. Deliberative processes are at the heart of solidarity, inclusion, personal growth, and the shaping of better, more lasting outcomes. As Albert Hirschman pointed out in his *Getting Ahead Collectively*: it is not the cumulative direct macroeconomic effects of grass-roots activity that matters, but rather the transformational effects of working together or sharing.[44] It is not the sum total of what these projects come to. They may not be representative of the larger society, but they are part of the *prise de conscience* that can ultimately displace the reigning dominator discourse. The effects are to be judged from the micro, macro, and global political levels as people act on their own and on the collective behalf; that is, the individual and the group using their governments in the manner in which noble rhetoric proclaimed they were originally designed. The state is us! And building a humane global state is the project that awaits our attention for our very lives depend on it.

The extension of solidarity beyond the face-to-face is required for the construction of what Benedict Anderson calls 'imagined communities.'[45] Building national communities required ingenuity and sustained effort over lengthy periods. For those of you who have added a European identity to your basket of loyalties, the possibility of adding at least one more allegiance should appear to be a plausible project. For most of the rest of us, this is likely for the moment to seem a giant step. Nonetheless, imagining a world community and building world-scale democratic institutions, including a world currency, world public finance and a planet-wide citizen's income (PWCI), may be the only peaceful and sustainable way out of our increasingly strife-prone global race to the bottom. When the dust finally appears to have settled, we may realize that the attainment of substantive global democracy, peace, and justice was the cultural impact of the electronic process.

Notes

1. With the exception still of the US and Somalia.
2. Aase Lionaes, Presentation Speech, Nobel Peace Prize 1969, 10 December 1969, http://www.nobel.se/peace/laureates/1969/press.html.
3. Eric Hobsbawm, *The Age of Extremes: A History of the World, 1914–1991* (New York, Pantheon Books, 1994).
4. The notion of an 'anti-politics machine' is developed in James Ferguson, *The Anti-Politics Machine: Development, Depolitization, and Bureaucratic Power in Lesotho* (Cambridge: Cambridge University Press, 1990). See also John H. Bunzel, *Anti-Politics in America; Reflections on the Anti-Political Temper and Its Distortions of the Democratic Process* (New York: Knopf, 1967).
5. Vandana Shiva, 'Monocultures of the Mind: Understanding the Threats to Biological and Cultural Diversity', University of Guelph: Inaugural Hopper Lecture, 21 September 1993.
6. E.B. White, *The Wild Flag: Editorials from The New Yorker on Federal World Government and Other Matters* (Boston: Houghton Mifflin, 1946), pp. 185–86.
7. 'In practice, there are no development institutions managing the new integrated global economy—much less doing so democratically in the interests of the world's people.' United Nations Development Programme, *Human Development Report 1992* (New York: Oxford University Press, 1992), p. 78.
8. Cox's idea of the *nébuleuse* is invoked by André Drainville, 'Of Social Spaces, Citizenship and the Nature of Power in the World Economy', *Alternatives*, 20 (1995), p. 53.
9. 'Les nouveaux maîtres du monde', *Manière de voir*, no. 28 (Nov. 1995).
10. Peter B. Kenen, *The Use of IMF Credit*, Princeton Reprints in International Finance 26 (December 1989).
11. Robert Gilpin, *The Political Economy of International Economic Relations* (Princeton: Princeton University Press, 1987), pp. 60–64.
12. Drainville, p. 60.
13. In its original usage the phrase referred to a pact between civil authorities and the military to establish limited democracy. Guillermo O'Donnell and Philippe C. Schmitter, *Transitions from Authoritarian Rule: Tentative Conclusions about Uncertain Democracies* (Baltimore: Johns Hopkins University Press, 1986), p. 41.
14. Susan Strange has observed that differences between policies of government and opposition parties disappear, as 'society, economy and authority are no longer bound by the frontiers of the territorial state.' Susan Strange, 'The Limits of Politics', *Government and Opposition*, 30 (Summer 1995), pp. 291, 310.
15. The phrase is that used by Robert Kagan, 'Power and Weakness', *Policy Review Online*, 113 (2002), http://www.policyreview.org/JUN02/kagan.html.
16. Daniel Mitrany, *A Working Peace System: An Argument for the Functional Development of International Organization* (London: Royal Institute of International Affairs, 1943).
17. See Sylvester C.W. Eijffinger and Jakob de Haan, *The Political Economy of Central-Bank Independence*, Princeton Special Papers in International Economics 19, May 1996.
18. Immanuel Kant, *Perpetual Peace* (1796), http://www.mtholyoke.edu/acad/intrel/kant/kantl.htm. John Hobson, *Towards International Government* (New York: Macmillan, 1915), Leonard Woolf, *International Government: Two Reports Prepared*

for the Fabian Research Department (London: Allen, 1916), Harold Laski, *The Foundations of Sovereignty and Other Essays* (New York, Harcourt Brace, 1921). See also Joseph P. Baratta, *Strengthening the United Nations: A Bibliography on U.N. Reform and World Federalism* (New York: Greenwood Press, 1987).

19. Cited in David Long, 'International Functionalism and the Politics of Forgetting', *International Journal*, 48 (Spring 1993), p. 365.
20. *New York Times*, 17 October 1945, p. 1.
21. See Dieter Heinrich, *The Case for a United Nations Parliamentary Assembly* (New York and Amsterdam: World Federalist Movement, 1992).
22. Andrew L. Strauss, 'Overcoming the Dysfunction of the Bifurcated Global System: The Promise of a Peoples Assembly', Richard Falk, Lester Edwin. J. Ruiz, and R.B.J. Walker, eds, *Reframing the International: Law, Culture, Politics* (New York: Routledge, 2002), p. 97.
23. Ibid., p. 94.
24. Franklin (1992), p. 51.
25. Jane Jacobs, *The Economy of Cities* (New York: Random House, 1969).
26. Drainville, p. 70.
27. Ibid.
28. Mitrany, in Long, p. 371.
29. Robert Putnam, *Bowling Alone: The Collapse and Revival of American Community* (New York: Simon & Schuster, 2000).
30. H.G. Wells, *The Work, Wealth and Happiness of Mankind* (London: William Heinemann, 1932), p. 650.
31. Commission on Global Governance, *Our Global Neighborhood* (New York: Oxford University Press, 1995), p. xvi.
32. Elise Boulding, *Building A Global Civic Culture: Education for an Interdependent World* (New York: Columbia University, Teachers College Press, 1988).
33. John Dryzek, 'Ecology and Discursive Democracy: Beyond Liberal Capitalism and the Administrative State', Martin O'Connor, ed., *Is Capitalism Sustainable? Political Economy and the Politics of Ecology* (New York: The Guilford Press, 1994).
34. The relentless assault by many within the US on the UN has effectively served to establish the fabled inefficiency of the UN as a default setting for our thought about the institution. For one recent reaffirmation of this view, see Francis Fukuyama, Book review of *Democracy and the Global Order: From the Modern State to Cosmopolitan Governance, Foreign Affairs*, 75 (July/Aug. 1996), p. 136.
35. See Michael Edwards and David Hulme, 'Too Close for Comfort? The Impact of Official Aid on Non-governmental Organizations', *World Development*, 24 (June 1996), pp. 961–74.
36. Commission on Global Governance, pp. 238–39.
37. Foro Internacional de ONGs y Movimientos Sociales, *Construyendo el Futuro: Tratados Alternativos de Rio 92* (Montevideo: Pacto Acción Ecológica de América Latina, 1993).
38. John Ralston Saul, *The Unconscious Civilization* (Concord, Ontario: Anansi, 1995), pp. 32, 34.
39. Thorstein Veblen, 'Why is Economics Not an Evolutionary Science?', *Quarterly Journal of Economics*, 12 (July 1898), p. 389.
40. Richard Falk, Book review of *Governance without Government: Order and Change in World Politics, American Political Science Review*, 87 (1993), p. 545.

41. Joseph Schumpeter, *The Theory of Economic Development* (Cambridge, MA: Harvard University Press, 1934).
42. Bertrand Russell, *Freedom and Organization 1814–1914* (London: George Allen & Unwin, 1934), p. 510. Cited in Frankman, 'Foreign Aid, World Government, and the Multi-National Corporation', a paper presented at the June 1970 annual meetings of the Canadian Economics Association, Winnipeg, Manitoba.
43. White, p. 41.
44. Albert O. Hirschman, *Getting Ahead Collectively: Grassroots Experiences in Latin America* (New York: Pergamon Press, 1984).
45. Benedict Anderson, *Imagined Communities: Reflections on the Origin and Spread of Nationalism* (London: Verso, 1983).

Bibliography

Aaron, Henry J., 'Distinguished Lecture on Economics in Government', *Journal of Economic Perspectives*, 8 (1994), pp. 3–21.

Anderson, Benedict, *Imagined Communities: Reflections on the Origin and Spread of Nationalism* (London: Verso, 1983).

Arnold, Matthew, *Mixed Essays* (London: Murray, 1903).

Arnold, Thurman, *The Folklore of Capitalism* (New Haven: Yale University Press, 1962).

Atlantic Charter (1941), http://www.yale.edu/lawweb/avalon/wwii/atlantic.htm.

ATTAC International, http://attac.org/indexfla.htm.

Baer, Werner, *The Development of the Brazilian Steel Industry* (Nashville, Tenn.: Vanderbilt University Press, 1969).

Bainbridge, Timothy, *The Penguin Companion to European Union*, 3rd edn (London: Penguin, 2002).

Bank for International Settlements The Triennial Central Bank Survey of Foreign Exchange and Derivatives Market Activity (2002), http://www.bis.org/publ/rpfx b02t.pdf.

Balogh, Thomas, 'The International Aspects of Full Employment', in *The Economics of Full Employment: Six Studies in Applied Economics Prepared at the Oxford University Institute of Statistics* (Oxford: Basil Blackwell, 1945), pp. 126–80.

Baratta, Joseph P., *Strengthening the United Nations: A Bibliography on U.N. Reform and World Federalism* (New York: Greenwood Press, 1987).

Barnet, Richard J. and Ronald E. Müller, *Global Reach: The Power of the Multinational Corporations* (New York: Simon and Schuster, 1974).

Baer, Werner and Larry Samuelson, 'Toward a Service-Oriented Growth Strategy', *World Development*, 9 (1981), pp. 499–514

Beatty, Jack, 'Who Speaks for the Middle Class?', *The Atlantic Monthly*, 273 (May 1994), pp. 65–78.

Berg, Andrew and Eduardo Borensztein, 'Full Dollarization: The Pros and Cons', *Economics Issues*, 24 (Washington: IMF, 2000).

Berle, Beatrice Bishop and Travis Beal Jacobs, eds, *Navigating the Rapids, 1918–1971; from the Papers of Adolf A. Berle* (New York: Harcourt Brace, 1973).

Berry, Albert, 'A Positive Interpretation of the Expansion of Urban Services in Latin America, with some Colombian Evidence', *Journal of Development Studies*, 14 (1978), pp. 210–31.

Bertram, Geoffrey and Rosemary Thorp. *Peru 1890–1977: Growth and Policy in an Open Economy* (New York Columbia University Press, 1978).

Bhagwati, Jagdish, 'The Capital Myth: The Difference Between Trade in Widgets and Dollars', *Foreign Affairs*, 77 (May/June 1998), pp. 7–12.

——ed., *Economics and World Order; From the 1970's to the 1990's* (New York: Macmillan, 1972).

Blaise, Clark, *Lord of Time* (Toronto: Knopf Canada, 2000).

Boorstin, Daniel J., *The Discoverers* (New York: Random House, 1983).

Boshara, Ray, 'The $6,000 Solution', *The Atlantic Online* (Jan./Feb. 2003), http://www.theatlantic.com/issues/2003/01/boshara.htm.

Boughton, James M., 'Harry Dexter White and the International Monetary Fund', *Finance and Development*, 35 (Sept. 1998), pp. 39–41.

Boulding, Elise, *Building A Global Civic Culture: Education for an Interdependent World* (New York: Columbia University, Teachers College Press, 1988).

Breton, Albert and Anthony Scott, *The Economic Constitution of Federal States* (Toronto: University of Toronto Press, 1978).

Bunzel, John H., *Anti-Politics in America: Reflections on the Anti-Political Temper and Its Distortions of the Democratic Process* (New York: Knopf, 1967).

Bureau, Dominique and Paul Champsaur, 'Fiscal Federalism and European Economic Unification', *American Economic Review Papers and Proceedings*, 82 (May 1992), pp. 88–92.

Calvin, William H., 'The Great Climate Flip-Flop', *The Atlantic Monthly*, 281 (Jan. 1998), pp. 47–64.

Carnegie, Andrew, 'The Gospel of Wealth' (1899), http://xroads.virginia.edu/~DRBR/wealth.html.

Carson, Rachel, *Silent Spring* (Boston Houghton Mifflin, 1962).

Chang, Ha-Joon, 'Kicking Away the Ladder: An Unofficial History of Capitalism, Especially in Britain and the United States', *Challenge*, 45 (Sept./Oct. 2002), pp. 63–97.

Clark, Grenville and Louis B. Sohn, *World Peace Through World Law* (Cambridge, MA.: Harvard University Press, 1958).

Cline, Howard F., *Mexico: Revolution to Evolution 1940–1960* (London: Oxford University Press, 1962).

Cline, William R., *Resource Transfers to the Developing Countries: Issues and Trend. Policy Alternatives for a New International Order: An Economic Analysis* (New York: Praeger Publishers, 1979).

——'Can the East Asian Model of Development be Generalized', *World Development*, 10 (1982), pp. 81–90.

Clinton, Bill, 'First Inaugural Address' (21 January 1993), http://www.bartleby.com/124/pres64.html.

Cockroft, James and Dale L. Johnson, eds, *The Chilean Road to Socialism* (Garden City: Anchor Press, 1973).

Cohen, Benjamin, 'Life at the Top: International Currencies in the Twenty-First Century', *Princeton Essays in International Economics*, 221 (Dec. 2000).

Cole, William E., *Steel and Economic Growth in Mexico* (Austin: University of Texas Press, 1967).

Collet, John, 'Participation-Personal, Organizational and Service User Perspectives', Paper presented to conference 'From Vancouver to Vladivostok: University Voluntarism for a Participative Society', organized by Helsinki-España Network, Santander, Spain, 28 June 2001, http://www.humandimension.com/foros/correo/John%20Collet%20(Manchest).doc.

Combined Mexican Working Party, *The Economic Development of Mexico* (Baltimore: The Johns Hopkins Press, 1953).

Commission on Global Governance, *Our Global Neighborhood* (New York: Oxford University Press, 1995).

Commission to Study the Organization of Peace, *Strengthening the United Nations* (New York: Harper & Brothers,1957).

Conway, Patrick, 'Currency Proliferation: The Monetary Legacy of the Soviet Union', *Essays in International Finance*, 197 (June 1995).

Cooper, Richard, 'A Monetary System for the Future', *Foreign Affairs*, 63 (Fall 1984), pp. 166–84.

Cox, Harvey, 'The Market as God', *The Atlantic Monthly*, 283 (Mar. 1999), http://www.theatlantic.com/issues/99mar/marketgod.htm.

Culpeper, Roy, 'Systemic Reform at a Standstill: A Flock of 'G's' in Search of Global Financial Stability' (Ottawa: North–South Institute, 2000) (June), http:// www.nsi-ins.ca/download/Gs_eng.pdf.

Darman, Richard, 'Riverboat Gambling With Government', *New York Times Magazine* (1 December 1996).

De Long, Bradford, Book review of Robert Skiddelsky's *John Maynard Keynes, Volumes I and II*, http://econ161.berkeley.edu/Econ_Articles/Reviews/skidelsky12.html.

Dernburg, Thomas, *Global Macroeconomics* (New York: Harper & Row, 1989).

Diamond, Sigmund, *Compromised Campus: The Collaboration of Universities with the Intelligence Community, 1945–1955* (New York: Oxford University Press, 1992).

Dosser, Douglas, 'Towards a Theory of International Public Finance', *Kyklos*, 16 (fasc. 1, 1963), pp. 62–82.

Dryzek, John, 'Ecology and Discursive Democracy: Beyond Liberal Capitalism and the Administrative State', Martin O'Connor, ed., *Is Capitalism Sustainable? Political Economy and the Politics of Ecology* (New York: The Guilford Press, 1994).

Diebold, William, 'The End of the I.T.O.', *Essays in International Finance*, 16 (Oct. 1952).

Dornbusch, Rudiger, *Open Economy Macroeconomics* (New York: Basic Books, 1980).

——'Fewer Monies, Better Monies' (Dec. 2000), http://econ-www.mit.edu/faculty/dornbusch/papers.htm.

Drainville, André, 'Of Social Spaces, Citizenship and the Nature of Power in the World Economy', *Alternatives*, 20 (1995), pp. 51–79.

Drèze, Jean and Amartya Sen, *Hunger and Public Action* (New York: Oxford University Press, 1992).

Edwards, Corwin D., 'Brazil's Economy in the War and After', in Seymour Harris, ed., *Economic Problems of Latin America* (N.Y.: McGraw-Hill, 1944).

Edwards, Michael and David Hulme, 'Too Close for Comfort? The Impact of Official Aid on Non-governmental Organizations', *World Development*, 24 (1996), pp. 961–74.

Eichengreen, Barry J., *International Monetary Arrangements for the 21st Century* (Washington, DC: Brookings Institution, 1994).

Eijffinger, Sylvester C.W. and Jakob de Haan, 'The Political Economy of Central-Bank Independence', *Princeton Special Papers in International Economics*, 19 (May 1996).

Eisler, Riane, *The Chalice and the Blade: Our History, Our Future* (San Francisco: HarperCollins, 1987).

Eisler, Riane and David Loye, 'Chaos and Transformation: Implications of Nonequilibrium Theory for Social Science and Society', *Behavioral Science*, 32 (1987), pp. 53–65

Fajnzylber, Fernando, 'Some Reflections on South-East Asian Export Industrialization', *CEPAL Review*, 15 (Dec. 1981), pp. 111–32.

Falk, Richard, Book review of *Governance without Government: Order and Change in World Politics, American Political Science Review*, 87 (June 1993), pp. 544–45.

Ferguson, James, *The Anti-Politics Machine: Development, Depolitization, and Bureaucratic Power in Lesotho* (Cambridge: Cambridge University Press,1990).

Ffrench, Ricardo-Davis and Manuel Agosín, *Managing Capital Flows in Latin America*, UNDP Office of Development Studies, Discussion Paper No. 8 (1995).

Final Act of the United Nations Conference on Trade and Employment Havana Charter for an International Trade Organization (1948), http://www.worldtrade law. net/misc/havana.pdf.

Forder, James, 'Central Bank Independence: Reassessing the Measurements', *Journal of Economic Issues*, 33 (1999), pp. 23–40.

Foro Internacional de ONGs y Movimientos Sociales, *Construyendo el Futuro: Tratados Alternativos de Rio 92* (Montevideo: Pacto Acción Ecológica de América Latina, 1993).

Frank, André G., *Capitalism and Underdevelopment in Latin America* (New York: Monthly Review Press, 1967).

Frank, Robert H. and Philip J. Cook, *The Winner-Take-All Society: How More and More Americans Compete for Ever Fewer and Bigger Prizes, Encouraging Economic Waste, Income Inequality, and an Impoverished Cultural Life* (New York: Free Press, 1995).

Franklin, Ursula, *The Real World of Technology* (Toronto: CBC Enterprises, 1990).

Frankman, Myron J., 'Foreign Aid, World Government, and the Multi-National Corporation'. Winnipeg, Paper presented at the Annual Meetings of the Canadian Economics Association (1970).

——'North American Economic Cooperation: The Wartime Experience', *Canadian Journal of Latin American and Caribbean Studies*, 16:2 (1991), pp. 35–57.

——'International Taxation: The Trajectory of an Idea from Lorimer to Brandt', *World Development*, 24 (1996), pp. 807–20.

——'Global Taxation: A Search for Generalizable Precedents', *Journal of Economic Issues*, 31 (1997), pp. 641–48.

——'Beyond the Tobin Tax: Global Democracy and a Global Currency', *Annals of the American Academy of Political and Social Sciences*, 581 (May 2002), pp. 62–73.

Frankman, Myron J. and Edwin Charlé, 'Employment in the Service Sector in Sub-Saharan Africa', *Journal of Modern African Studies*, 11 (1973), pp. 201–10.

Freeman, Richard B., 'Are Your Wages Set in Beijing', *Journal of Economic Perspectives*, 9 (1995), pp. 15–32.

Friedman, Milton, *Capitalism and Freedom* (Chicago: University of Chicago Press 1962).

Friedman, Thomas L., *The Lexus and the Olive Tree* (New York: Anchor Books, 2000).

Fukuyama, Francis, Book review of *Democracy and the Global Order: From the Modern State to Cosmopolitan Governance*, *Foreign Affairs*, 75 (July/Aug. 1996), p. 136.

Fuller, R. Buckminster, *Operating Manual for Spaceship Earth* (New York: Simon & Schuster, 1969).

Fundação Instituto Brasileiro de Geografia e Estatística, *Anuário Estatístico do Brasil*1978 (Rio de Janeiro: 1978).

Furniss, Edgar S., *The Position of the Laborer in a System of Nationalism: A Study in the Labor Theories of the Later English Mercantilists* (New York: Kelley & Millman, 1957).

Galbraith, John Kenneth, *American Capitalism: The Concept of Countervailing Power* (Boston: Houghton Mifflin, 1952).

Gardner, Lloyd, *Economic Aspects of New Deal Diplomacy* (Madison: University of Wisconsin Press, 1964).

Gardner, Richard N., *Sterling–Dollar Diplomacy: The Origins and the Prospects of Our International Economic Order* (New York: McGraw-Hill, 1969).

Gilderhus, Mark J., 'An Emerging Synthesis? U.S.–Latin American Relations since the Second World War', M.J. Hogan ed., *America in the World: The Historiography of American Foreign Relations since 1941* (Cambridge: Cambridge University Press, 1995), pp. 424–61.

Gills, Barry K., 'American Power, Neoliberal Globalization, and Low Intensity Democracy: An Unstable Trinity', in Michael Cox, G. John Ikenberry and Takashi Inoguchi, eds, *American Democracy Promotion: Impulses, Strategies, and Impacts* (New York: Oxford University Press, 2000), pp. 326–44.

Gilpin, Robert, *The Political Economy of International Relations* (Princeton: Princeton University Press, 1987).

Gleick, J., *Chaos: Making a New Science* (New York: Viking, 1987).

Goldsmith, Scott, 'The Alaska Permanent Fund: A Basic Income in Action', Paper presented at 9th Biennial Congress of the Basic Income European Network (BIEN), Geneva (12–14 September 2002), http://www.bien.be/Archive/Congress/Geneva2002.htm.

Goldstein, Morris, *Safeguarding Prosperity in a Global Financial System: The Future International Financial Architecture. Report of an Independent Task Force* (Washington: Institute for International Economics, 1999).

Gopnik, Alison, Andrew N. Meltzoff, and Patricia K. Kuhl, *The Scientist in the Crib: Minds, Brains and How Children Learn* (New York: William Morrow, 1999).

Green, David, *The Containment of Latin America: A History of the Myths and Realities of the Good Neighbor Policy* (Chicago: Quadrangle Books, 1971).

Grubel, Herbert G., *World Monetary Reform, Plans and Issues* (Stanford, CA: Stanford University Press, 1963).

Hacker, Louis, *The Course of American Growth and Development* (New York: John Wiley & Sons, 1970).

Hamada, Koichi, 'Taxing the Brain Drain: A Global Point of View', in Jagdish Bhagwati, ed., *The New International Economic Order: The North–South Debate* (Cambridge, MA: The MIT Press, 1977), pp. 125–55.

Hampton, Mark P. and John Cristensen, 'Offshore Pariahs? Small Island Economies, Tax Havens, and the Reconfiguration of Global Finance', *World Development*, 30 (2002), pp. 1657–73.

Haq, Mahbub ul, *The Poverty Curtain: Choices for the Third World* (New York: Columbia University Press, 1956).

Hayek, Friedrich, *The Road to Serfdom* (Chicago: University of Chicago Press, 1944).

Heilbroner, Robert and Aaron Singer, *The Economic Transformation of America: 1600 to the Present*, 2nd edn (San Diego: Harcourt Brace Jovanovich, 1984).

Heinrich, Dieter, *The Case for a United Nations Parliamentary Assembly* (New York and Amsterdam: World Federalist Movement, 1992).

Helleiner, Gerald K., *International Trade & Economic Development* (Harmondsworth: Penguin, 1972).

Henderson, William O., *The Zollverein* (Cambridge: Cambridge University Press, 1939).

Herman, Edward S. and Noam Chomsky, *Manufacturing Consent: The Political Economy of the Mass Media* (New York: Pantheon Books, 1988).

Heterodox Economics Portal, http://www.hetecon.com/.
Higgins, Benjamin H., *Economic Development: Principles, Problems, and Policies* (New York: Norton, 1959).
Hirsch, Fred, Michael Doyle, and Edward L. Morse, *Alternatives to Monetary Disorder* (New York: McGraw-Hill, 1977).
Hirschman, Albert O., *The Strategy of Economic Development* (New Haven: Yale University Press, 1958).
——'Obstacles to Development: A Classification and a Quasi-Vanishing Act', *Economic Development and Cultural Change*, 13 (1965), pp. 385–93.
——*Development Projects Observed* (Washington: Brookings Institution, 1967).
——*Journeys Towards Progress: Studies of Economic Policy-Making in Latin America* (New York: Greenwood Press, 1968).
——*Getting Ahead Collectively: Grassroots Experiences in Latin America* (New York: Pergamon Press, 1984)
Hirschman, Albert O. and Richard Bird, 'Foreign Aid—A Critique and a Proposal', *Essays in International Finance*, 69 (July 1968).
Hobsbawm, Eric, *The Age of Extremes: A History of the World, 1914–1991* (New York: Pantheon Books, 1994).
Hobson, John, *Towards International Government* (New York: Macmillan, 1915).
Hodges, Michael and William Wallace, eds, *Economic Divergence in the European Community* (London: George Allen & Unwin, 1981).
Hume, David, 'Of Refinement in the Arts' (1752), http://www.econlib.org/library/Hume/HumeEssArts.html.
Hull, Cordell, *The Memoirs of Cordell Hull*, prepared with the assistance of Andrew Berding (New York: Macmillan, 1948).
Hunter, Justine, 'US Dollar Could Lift Our Economy 37%', *National Post* (19 May 2001).
Huntington, Samuel, 'The Clash of Civilizations?', *Foreign Affairs*, 72 (Summer 1993), pp. 22–49.
Ickes, Harold L., *Fightin' Oil* (New York: Knopf, 1943).
Independent Commission on International Development Issues, *North–South: A Program for Survival* (Cambridge, MA: The MIT Press, 1980).
Innis, Harold, 'The Penetrative Powers of the Price System', *The Canadian Journal of Economics and Political Science*, 4 (1938), pp. 299–319.
International Financial Institution Advisory Commission. *Report* ('The Meltzer Report') (Washington, DC, March 2000), http://www.house.gov/jec/imf/meltzer.htm.
International Monetary Fund, *Government Finance Statistics Yearbook*, various issues.
International Monetary Fund, *International Financial Statistics Yearbook*, various issues.
International Monetary Fund, 'Report of the Acting Managing Director to the International Monetary and Financial Committee on Progress in Reforming the IMF and Strengthening the Architecture of the International Financial System' (12 April 2000), http://www.imf.org.external/np/omd/2000/report.htm.
International Monetary Fund, OECD, United Nations, and World Bank Group 2000, *A Better World for All*, http://www.paris21.org/betterworld/.
Jacobs, Jane, *The Economy of Cities* (New York: Random House, 1969).
——*The Question of Separatism: Quebec and the Struggle over Sovereignty* (New York: Random House, 1980).

Jenks, C. Wilfred, 'The Significance Today of Lorimer's Ultimate Problem of International Jurisprudence', *Transactions of the Grotius Society*, 26 (1940), pp. 35–65.

——'Some Legal Aspects of the Financing of International Institutions', *Transactions of the Grotius Society*, 28 (1942), pp. 87–132.

Jones, Charles, *Global Justice: Defending Cosmopolitanism* (New York: Oxford University Press, 1999).

Kagan, R., 'Power and Weakness', *Policy Review Online* (113) (2002), http://www.policyreview.org/JUN02/kagan.html.

Kaldor, Nicholas, 'Will Underdeveloped Countries Learn to Tax?', *Foreign Affairs*, 41 (Jan. 1963), pp. 410–19.

Kanbur, Ravi, Todd Sandler, and Kevin Morrison, 'The Future of Development Assistance: Common Pools and International Public Goods', Overseas Development Council Policy Essay No. 25 (Baltimore: Johns Hopkins University Press, 1999).

Kant, Immanuel, *Perpetual Peace* (1796), http://www.mtholyoke.edu/acad/intrel/kant/kant1.htm.

Kaul, Inge, Isabel Grunberg, and Mark A. Stern, eds, *Global Public Goods: International Cooperation in the 21st Century* (New York: Oxford University Press, 1999).

Kenen, Peter B., 'The Use of IMF Credit', *Princeton Reprints in International Finance*, 26 (Dec. 1989).

Keylor, William R., *The Twentieth-Century World: An International History* (New York: Oxford University Press, 1984).

Keynes, John Maynard, *The General Theory of Employment, Interest and Money* (London: Macmillan, 1936).

——'The International Control of Raw Materials', *Journal of International Economics*, 4 (1974), pp. 299–315.

——*The Collected Writings of John Maynard Keynes. Volume XXV Activities: 1940–1944, Shaping the Post-War World: The Clearing Union* (London: Macmillan, 1980).

——*The Collected Writings of John Maynard Keynes. Volume XXVII. Activities: 1940–1946, Shaping the Post-War World: Employment and Commodities* (London: Macmillan, 1980).

Kimball, Warren F., *The Juggler: Franklin Roosevelt as Wartime Statesman* (Princeton, Princeton University Press, 1991).

Kindleberger, Charles P., *The World in Depression 1929–1939* (Berkeley: University of California Press, 1973).

——'Government and International Trade', *Essays in International Finance*, 129 (July 1978).

——'International Public Goods without International Government', *American Economic Review*, 76 (1986), pp. 1–13.

King, David, *Fiscal Tiers: The Economics of Multi-Level Government* (London: George Allen & Unwin, 1984).

Kingwell, Mark, *The World We Want: Virtue, Vice and the Good Citizen* (Toronto: Viking, 2000).

Koestler, Arthur, *The Ghost in the Machine* (New York: Macmillan, 1968).

Kornai, Janos, *Anti-Equilibrium: On Economic Systems Theory and the Tasks of Research* (Amsterdam: North-Holland Publishing, 1971).

Korten, David, *When Corporations Rule the World*, 2nd edn (San Francisco: Berrett-Koehler Publishers; Bloomfield, Conn.: Kumarian Press, 2001, co-publishers).

Krugman, Paul, 'Competitiveness: A Dangerous Obsession', *Foreign Affairs*, 73 (Mar./Apr. 1994), pp. 28–44.

Krugman, Paul and Maurice Obstfeld, *International Economics: Theory and Policy* (Glenview, IL: Scott, Foresman, 1988).

Kuhn, Thomas S., *The Structure of Scientific Revolutions* (Chicago: University of Chicago Press, 1962).

Ladd, William, *An Essay on a Congress of Nations for the Adjustment of International Disputes Without Resort to Arms, 1840* (New York: Oxford University Press, 1916).

Laski, Harold, *The Foundations of Sovereignty and Other Essays* (New York, Harcourt Brace, 1921).

Lattimore, Owen, *Ordeal by Slander* (Boston: Little, Brown and Co., 1950).

Layton, Christopher, 'One Europe: One World; A First Exploration of Europe's Potential Contribution to World Order', *Journal of World Trade Law*, Special Supplement No. 4, 20 (1986), pp. 32–33.

Lerner, Max, *Ideas for the Ice Age: Studies in a Revolutionary Era* (New York: Viking, 1941).

'Les nouveaux maîtres du monde', *Manière de voir*, n. 28 (Nov. 1995).

Lionaes, Aase, Presentation Speech, Nobel Peace Prize 1969 (10 December 1969), http://www.nobel.se/peace/laureates/1969/press.html.

Long, David, 'International Functionalism and the Politics of Forgetting', *International Journal*, 48 (Spring 1993), pp. 355–78.

Lorimer, James, 'Book V. The Ultimate Problem of International Jurisprudence', *The Institutes of the Law of Nations: A Treatise of the Jural Relations of Separate Political Communities*, II (London: William Blackwood and Sons, 1884).

Lovelock, J.E., *Gaia: A New Look at Life on Earth* (Oxford: Oxford University Press, 1979).

Luxembourg Income Study, 'Income Inequality Measures', http://lisproject.org/keyfigures/ineqtable.htm.

Maddison, Angus, 'Economic Growth and Structural Change in the Advanced Countries', I. Leveson and J. Wheeler, eds, *Western Economies in Transition: Structural Change and Adjustment Policies in Industrial Countries* (Boulder, CO: Westview Press, 1980), pp. 41–60.

Marchak, Patricia, *The Integrated Circus: The New Right and the Restructuring of Global Markets* (Montreal: McGill-Queen's Press, 1991).

McNamara, Robert S., 'Foreword', World Bank, *World Development Report* (New York: Oxford University Press, 1978).

Marx, Karl, *On the Question of Free Trade* (1848), http://csf.Colorado.edu/psn/marx/Archive/1848-FT/.

Marx, Karl and Frioedrich Engels, *The Manifesto of the Communist Party* (1848), http://csf.colorado.edu/psn/marx/Archive/1848-CM/.

Maturana, Humberto, *La democracia es una obra de arte* (Bogotá: Cooperativa Editorial Magisterio, 1995).

Mauss, Marcel, *The Gift: Forms and Functions of Exchange in Archaic Societies* (New York: Norton, 1967).

Marshall, Alfred, *Principles of Economics: An Introductory Volume*, 8th edn, 1920 (London : Macmillan, 1949).

McChesney, Robert W., *Rich Media, Poor Democracy: Communication Politics in Dubious Times* (Urbana: University of Illinois Press, 1999).

McCloskey, Deirdre N., *The Vices of Economists, the Virtues of the Bourgeoisie* (Amsterdam: Amsterdam University Press, 1996).

McKinnon, Ronald, 'Optimum Currency Areas', *American Economic Review*, 53 (Sept. 1963), pp. 717–25.

McKinnon, Ronald, *An International Standard for Monetary Stabilization* (Washington, DC: Institute for International Economics, 1984).

Meade, James E., *The Economic Basis of a Durable Peace* (New York: Oxford University Press, 1940).

——*A Geometry of International Trade* (London: Allen and Unwin, 1952).

Mendez, Ruben P., *International Public Finance: A New Perspective on Global Relations* (New York: Oxford University Press, 1992).

——'The Provision and Financing of Universal Public Goods', M. Desai and P. Redfern, eds, *Global Governance: Ethics and Economics of the World Order* (London: Pinter, 1995), pp. 39–59.

——'Peace as a Global Public Good', I. Kaul, I. Grunberg, and M.A. Stern, eds, *Global Public Goods: International Cooperation in the 21st Century* (New York, Oxford University Press, 1999), pp. 382–416.

——'Global Taxation: The Rise, Decline and Future of an Idea at the United Nations' (Paris: Institut pour le développement durables et relations internationale, 2002), http://iddri.org/iddri/telecharge/fiscalite/mendez.pdf.

Milanovic, Branko, 'True World Income Distribution, 1988 and 1993: First Calculations Based on Household Surveys Alone', *The Economic Journal*, 112 (2002), pp. 51–92.

Mill, John. S., *Principles of Political Economy*, 5th London edn (New York: D Appleton and Co., 1865).

Mills, C. Wright, *The Sociological Imagination* (New York: Oxford University Press, 1959).

Milward, Alan S. and S.B. Saul, *The Economic Development of Continental Europe, 1780–1870* (London: George Allen & Unwin, 1973).

Mitrany, Daniel, *A Working Peace System: An Argument for the Functional Development of International Organization* (London: Royal Institute of International Affairs, 1943).

Moellendorf, Darrel, *Cosmopolitan Justice* (Boulder, CO: Westview Press, 2002).

Moggridge, Donald, *Maynard Keynes: An Economist's Biography* (London and New York: Routledge, 1992).

Morison, Samuel Eliot, *The Oxford History of the American People* (New York: Oxford University Press, 1965).

Mosk, Sanford, *Industrial Revolution in Mexico* (Berkeley: University of California Press, 1954).

Mouffe, Chantal, ed., *Dimensions of Radical Democracy: Pluralism, Citizenship, Community* (London: Verso, 1992).

Mundell, Robert, 'A Theory of Optimum Currency Areas', *American Economic Review*, 51 (Sept. 1961), pp. 657–65.

Mussa, Michael, Morris Goldstein, Peter B. Clark, Donald J. Mathieson, and Tamim Bayoumi, 'Improving the International Monetary System: Constraints and Possibilities', IMF Occasional Paper No. 116 (Jan. 1995).

Musgrave, Richard A., 'Theories of Fiscal Federalism', *Public Finance*, 24 (1969), pp. 521–32.

Mun, Thomas, *England's treasure by forraign trade*, 1st edn 1664 (London: Blackwell, 1965).

Myrdal, Gunnar, *An International Economy: Problems and Prospects* (New York: Harper & Brothers Publishers, 1956).

——*The Challenge of World Poverty: A World Anti-Poverty Program in Outline* (New York: Vintage Books, 1970).

Nacional Financiera, S.A., *Statistics on the Mexican Economy* (Mexico: 1966).

Neruda, Pablo, *Confieso que he vivido: memorias* (Barcelona: Editorial Seix Barral, 1974).

North, Douglass C. and Robert Paul Thomas, *The Rise of the Western World: A New Economic History* (Cambridge: Cambridge University Press, 1973).

O'Donnell, Guillermo and Philippe C. Schmitter, *Transitions from Authoritarian Rule: Tentative Conclusions about Uncertain Democracies* (Baltimore: Johns Hopkins University Press, 1986).

Orwell, G., 'Politics and the English Language', *The Collected Essays, Journalism and Letters of George Orwell Volume 4: In Front of Your Nose: 1945–1950* (New York: Penguin Books, 1970), pp. 156–70.

Osborn, Fairfield, *Our Plundered Planet* (Boston: Little, Brown, 1948).

Owens, Jeffrey, 'Taxation in a Global Environment', *OECD Observer* (1 March 2002), http://www.oecdobserver.org.

Paine, Thomas, 'The Rights of Man', Mark Philp, ed., *Thomas Paine: Rights of Man; Common sense; and Other Writings* (Oxford: Oxford University Press, 1995).

Padoa-Schioppa, Tommaso, *Efficiency, Stability, and Equity: A Strategy for the Evolution of the European Community* (Oxford: Oxford University Press, 1987).

Pearson, Harry, 'The Economy Has No Surplus', Karl Polanyi, Conrad M. Arensberg, and Harry W. Pearson, eds, *Trade and Market in Early Empires; Economies in History and Theory* (New York: Free Press, 1957), pp. 320–41.

Peden, G.C., *Keynes, The Treasury and British Economic Policy* (London: Macmillan Education,1988).

Pinder, John, 'Integrating Divergent Economies: The Extranational Method', Michael Hodges and William Wallace, eds, *Economic Divergence in the European Community* (London: George Allen & Unwin, 1981), pp. 192–204.

——*European Community: The Building of a Union,* 2nd edn (Oxford: Oxford University Press, 1995).

Plumptre, A.F.W., *Three Decades of Decision: Canada and the World Monetary System, 1944–75* (Toronto: McClelland and Stewart, 1977).

Phillips, Kevin, 'Too Much Wealth, Too Little Democracy', *Challenge*, 45 (Sept.–Oct. 2002), pp. 6–20.

Polanyi, Karl, *The Great Transformation: The Political and Economic Origins of Our Time*, 1st edn 1944 (Boston: Beacon Press, 1957).

Post-Autistic Economics Network, http://www.paecon.net.

Pritchett, Lant, 'Divergence, Big Time', *Journal of Economic Perspectives*, 11(1997), pp. 3–17.

Putnam, Robert, *Bowling Alone: The Collapse and Revival of American Community* (New York: Simon & Schuster, 2000).

Ramonet, Ignacio, 'An Empire has Vassals, not Allies', *Le Monde Diplomatique* (Feb. 2003), p. 2.

Reich, Robert B., 'The Challenge of Decent Work', *International Labour Review*, 141 (2002), pp. 115–22.

Richmond, Anthony H., *Global Apartheid: Refugees, Racism, and the New World Order* (Toronto: Oxford University Press, 1994).

Robinson, Joan, *Economic Philosophy* (Harmondsworth: Penguin, 1964).

Robinson, William I., *Promoting Polyarchy: Globalization, US Intervention, and Hegemony* (Cambridge: Cambridge University Press, 1996).

Russell, Bertrand, *In Praise of Idleness: And Other Essays by Bertrand Russell* (New York: Norton, 1935).

Roosevelt, Franklin Delano, *Franklin D. Roosevelt and Conservation, 1911–1945*, Edgar B. Nixon, ed. (Hyde Park, N.Y.: General Services Administration, National Archives and Records Service, Franklin D. Roosevelt Library, 1957).

Sachs, Jeffrey, 'Weapons of Mass Salvation', *The Economist* (26 October 2002), p. 82.

Said, Edward W., *Representations of the Intellectual* (New York: Vintage Books, 1994).

Sagasti, Francisco and Keith Bezanson, 'Financing and Providing Global Public Goods: Expectations and Prospects' (Swedish Ministry of Foreign Affairs and the Institute of Development Studies, Sussex, 2001), http://www.udse/prefak/Document.jsp?Document ID = 43161.

Sakakibara, Eisuke, 'The End of Progressivism: A Search for New Goals', *Foreign Affairs*, 74 (Sept./Oct. 1995), pp. 8–14.

Samuelson, Paul, 'International Factor-Price Equalisation Once Again', *Economic Journal*, 59 (1949), pp. 181–97.

Sanchez-Albornoz, Nicholas, *The Population of Latin America: A History*, translated by W.A.R. Richardson (Berkeley: University of California Press, 1974).

Saul, John Ralston, *The Unconscious Civilization* (Concord, Ontario: Anansi, 1995).

Schatz, Sayre, 'Socializing Adaptation: A Perspective on World Capitalism', *World Development*, 11 (1983), pp. 1–10.

Schrecker, Ellen W., *No Ivory Tower: McCarthyism and the Universities* (Oxford: Oxford University Press, 1986).

Schumpeter, Joseph, *The Theory of Economic Development* (Cambridge, MA: Harvard University Press, 1934).

Scremmer, D.E., 'Taxation and Public Finance: Britain, France, and Germany', in Peter Mathias and Sidney Pollard, eds, *The Cambridge Economic History of Europe. VIII. The Industrial Economies: The Development of Economic and Social Policies* (Cambridge: Cambridge University Press, 1989). pp. 315–49.

Sen, Amartya, *Poverty and Famines: An Essay on Entitlement and Deprivation* (New York: Oxford University Press, 1981).

Sennett, Richard, *The Uses of Disorder: Personal Identity and City Life* (New York: Knopf, 1970).

Shackleton, Michael, *Financing the European Community* (London: Pinter Publishers, 1990).

Shiva, Vandana, 'Monocultures of the Mind: Understanding the Threats to Biological and Cultural Diversity', University of Guelph: Inaugural Hopper Lecture, 21 September 1993.

——*Water Wars: Privatization, Pollution and Profit* (Toronto: Between the Lines, 2001).

Shute, Nevil, *On the Beach* (New York: W. Morrow, 1957).

Simon, Herbert, 'UBI and the Flat Tax', *Boston Review* (Oct./Nov. 2000), http://bostonreview.mit.edu/BR25.5/simon.html.

Singer, Hans W., 'The Terms of Trade Controversy and the Evolution of Soft Financing: Early Years in the U.N.', Gerald M. Meier and Dudley Seers, eds, *Pioneers in Development* (New York: Oxford University Press, 1984), pp. 275–303.

Smith, Adam, *An Inquiry into the Nature and Causes of the Wealth of Nations* (1776), http://www.econlib.org/library/Smith/smWN.html.

Smith, Gaddis, *American Diplomacy During the Second World War 1941–1945* (New York: John Wiley & Sons, 1965).

Smith, Warren, 'Are There Enough Policy Tools?', *American Economic Review*, 55 (1965), pp. 208–20.

Snider, Delbert, 'Optimum Adjustment Processes and Currency Areas', *Essays in International Finance*, 62 (Oct. 1962).

Spahn, Paul Bernd, 'The Tobin Tax and Exchange Rate Stability', *Finance and Development*, 33 (June 1996), pp. 24–27.

Standing, Guy, 'About Time: Basic Income Security as a Right', paper presented at 9th Biennial Congress of the Basic Income European Network (BIEN), Geneva 12–14 September 2002, http://www.bien.be./Archive/Congress/Geneva2002.htm.

Steinberg, Eleanor and Joseph A. Yager, with Gerard M. Brannon, *New Means of Financing International Needs* (Washington, DC: The Brookings Institution, 1978).

Steinem, Gloria. *Revolution from Within: A Book of Self-Esteem* (Boston, Little Brown and Co. 1992).

Stewart, Watt, *Chinese Bondage in Peru* (Durham: Duke University Press, 1971).

Stiglitz, Joseph, *Globalization and Its Discontents* (New York: Norton, 2002).

Stoessinger, John and Associates, *Financing the United Nations System* (Washington: The Brookings Institution, 1964).

Stone, I.F., *The Truman Era: 1945–1952* (New York: Random House, 1972).

Stone, I.F., *The War Years: 1939–1945* (Boston: Little, Brown and Company,1988).

Stotsky, Janet, 'Why a Two-Tier Tobin Tax Won't Work', *Finance and Development* (June 1996), pp. 28–29.

Strange, Susan, 'The Limits of Politics', *Government and Opposition*, 30 (Summer 1995), pp. 291–311.

Strauss, Andrew L., 'Overcoming the Dysfunction of the Bifurcated Global System: The Promise of a Peoples Assembly', Richard Falk, Lester Edwin. J. Ruiz, and R.B.J. Walker, eds, *Reframing the International: Law, Culture, Politics* (New York: Routledge, 2002). pp. 83–106.

Streeten, Paul, 'A New Look at Foreign Aid', *Frontiers of Development Studies* (New York: John Wiley & Sons,1972) pp. 223–38.

Sumberg, Theodore A., 'Financing International Institutions', *Social Research*, 13 (1946), pp. 276–306.

Suplicy, Eduardo Matarazzo, *Renda de Cidadania: A Saída é Pela Porta* (São Paulo: Cortez: Fundação Perseu Abramo, 2002).

Sunshine, Russell B. and Javade Chaudhri, 'Global Development Taxes: A Promising New Source of International Finance for Developing Countries', *Columbia Journal of Transnational Law*, 19 (1981), pp. 407–53.

Theobald, Robert, *The Guaranteed Income: Next Step in Economic Evolution?* (Garden City, N.Y.: Doubleday, 1996).

Thomas, William L. Jr, *Man's Role in Changing the Face of the Earth* (Chicago: University of Chicago Press, 1956).

Tinbergen, Jan, *International Economic Co-operation* (Amsterdam: Elsevier, 1945).

——*International Economic Integration* (Amsterdam: Elsevier, 1954).

——'International Co-ordination of Stabilization and Development Policies', *Kyklos*, 12 (fasc. 3, 1959), pp. 283–89.

——coordinator, *Reshaping the International Order: A Report to the Club of Rome* (New York: E.P. Dutton, 1976).

Tobin, James, *The New Economics, One Decade Older* (Princeton: Princeton University Press, 1974).

——'A Proposal for International Monetary Reform', *Eastern Economic Journal*, 4 (1978), pp. 153–59.

——'On the Efficiency of the Financial System', *Lloyds Bank Review* (July 1984), pp. 1–15.

Tsoukalis, Loukas, *The New European Economy: The Politics and Economics of Integration*, 2nd edn (Oxford: Oxford University Press, 1993).

United Nations, 'Towards a New International Financial Architecture', *Report of the Task Force of the Executive Committee on Economic and Social Affairs of the United Nations* (New York, 21 January 1999), http://attac.org.uk/attac/html/view-document.vm?documentID = 53.

United Nations Development Programme, *Human Development Report 1999* (New York: Oxford University Press, 1999).

UNDP, *Human Development Report 2002* (New York: Oxford University Press, 2002).

US Agency for International Development, *US Foreign Assistance and Assistance from International Organizations: Obligations and Loan Authorizations, July 1, 1945–June 30, 1961* (1962).

United States Basic Income Guarantee Network (USBIG), *USBIG Newsletter*, 3: 18 (2002), http://www.usbig.net.

US Department of Commerce, Bureau of the Census, *Historical Statistics of the United States: Colonial Times to 1957* (Washington: 1960).

US Department of State, *Foreign Relations of the United States: Diplomatic Papers* (Washington, 1941), various issues.

Van Parijs, Phillipe, *Real Freedom for All: What (If Anything) Can Justify Capitalism?* (Oxford, Clarendon Press, 1995).

——'Does Basic Income Make Sense as a Worldwide Project?', Documents de travail de la Chaire Hoover No. 93 (2002), http://www.etes.ucl.ac.be/Publications/dochs.htm.

——'A Short History of Basic Income' (2003), http://www.bien.be/BI/HistoryBI.htm.

Veblen, Thorstein, 'Why Is Economics Not an Evolutionary Science?', *Quarterly Journal of Economics*, 12 (July 1898).

——*The Theory of Business Enterprise* (New York: Scribner's, 1904).

——*Imperial Germany and the Industrial Revolution* (London: Macmillan, 1915).

——*The Vested Interests and the Common Man* (New York: B.W. Huebsch, 1919).

——'Salesmanship and the Churches', Max Lerner, ed., *The Portable Veblen* (New York: Viking Press, 1948).

Videlier, Philippe, 'Immigration et conscience citoyenne: L'honneur de désobéir', *Le Monde Diplomatique* (May 1997), p. 17.

Von Hagen, Jurgen and Barry Eichengreen, 'Federalism, Fiscal Restraints, and European Monetary Union', *American Economic Review Papers and Proceedings*, 86 (May 1996), pp. 134–38.

Wade, Robert H., 'Capital and Revenge: The IMF and Ethiopia', *Challenge*, 44 (Sept./Oct. 2001), pp. 67–75.

Wallich, Henry, *Monetary Problems of an Export Economy: The Cuban Experience 1914 –1947* (Cambridge, MA: Harvard University Press, 1950).

Walsh, Mary Williams, 'I.R.S. to Ask Working Poor for Proof on Tax Credits', *New York Times*, 25 April 2003.

Wells, H.G., *The Work, Wealth and Happiness of Mankind* (London: William Heinemann, 1932).

Welles, Sumner, *The Time for Decision* (New York: Harper & Brothers, 1944).

White, E.B., *The Wild Flag: Editorials from The New Yorker on Federal World Government and Other Matters* (Boston: Houghton Mifflin, 1946).

Widerquist, Karl, 'A Failure to Communicate: The Labour Market Findings of the Negative Income Tax Experiments and Their Effects on Policy and Public Opinion', Basic Income European Network 9th International Conference, Geneva (12–14 September 2002), http://www.bien.be/Archive/Congress/Geneva2002.htm.

Wilde, Oscar, 'The Soul of Man Under Socialism' (1890), http://wilde.thefreelibrary.com/Soul-of-Man-under-Socialism.

Wilder, Thornton, *The Skin of our Teeth: A Play in Three Acts* (New York: Harper, 1942).

Williamson, John, 'The Crawling Peg', *Essays in International Finance*, 50 (Dec. 1965).

Williamson, John, 'Democracy and the Washington Consensus', *World Development*, 21 (1993), pp. 1329–36.

Williamson, John, *The Crawling Band as an Exchange-Rate Regime: Lessons from Chile, Colombia, and Israel* (Washington, DC: Institute for International Economics, 1996).

Wilson, Woodrow, 'Fourteen Points' (8 January 1918), http://www.yale.edu/lawweb/avalon/wilson14.htm.

Winchester, Simon, *Krakatoa: The Day the World Exploded, August 27, 1883* (New York: HarperCollins, 2003).

Wogart, J.P., *Industralization in Colombia: Policies, Patterns, Perspectives* (Tubingen: JCB Mohr, 1978).

Woolf, Leonard, *International Government; Two Reports Prepared for the Fabian Research Department, with an Introduction by Bernard Shaw* (London: Allen, 1916).

World Bank, *World Development Indicators On Disk 2001*.

World Bank, *World Development Report* (New York: Oxford University Press), various issues.

Zuleta, Estanislao, *Educación y democracia: un campo de combate* (Bogotá: Fundación Estanislao Zuleta: and Corporación Tercer Milenio 1995).

Index